SEX IN ELIZABETHAN ENGLAND

In Loving Memory of my Parents
Eve and William Haynes

SEX IN ELIZABETHAN ENGLAND

Alan Haynes

WRENS PARK

A Sutton Publishing Book

This edition published in 1999 by Wrens Park Publishing, an imprint of
W.J. Williams & Son Ltd

First published in 1997 by
Sutton Publishing Limited · Phoenix Mill · Thrupp · Stroud · Gloucestershire

Copyright © Alan Haynes, 1997

All rights reserved. No part of this publication may be reproduced, stored in a retrieval
system, or transmitted, in any form, or by any means, electronic, mechanical,
photocopying, recording or otherwise, without the prior permission of the publisher
and copyright holder.

A catalogue record for this book is available from the British Library

ISBN 0 905 778 359

Typeset in 11/14pt Bembo.
Typesetting and origination by
Sutton Publishing Limited.
Printed in Great Britain by
Redwood Books Limited,
Trowbridge, Wiltshire.

CONTENTS

LIST OF ILLUSTRATIONS

PREFACE

In any Elizabethan household, whether furnished by a prince, playwright or yeoman, the most important item of furniture was the bed, with its bedding. Each new born Elizabethan came into the hubbub of the world in a domestic bed (if lucky), attended by a woman of the truly oldest profession, that of midwifery. So we have the birth bed, the marriage bed, the sick bed, the bed for sleep and the death bed. In *The Flower of Friendshippe* by Edmund Tilney there was an insistence on the merry bed, which meant the setting aside of the day's upsets before repose. Given the emphasis by many male writers over generations on the sweet-tempered docility and silence of the best kind of wife, it is not so surprising to find Iago in Shakespeare's tragedy *Othello* objecting that his wife Emilia will not let him sleep when they retire to bed but regards it as a space for a privileged torrent of conversation. In *A Curtaine Lecture* Thomas Heywood has talkative wives endlessly regaling tired husbands with many whispered 'private lectures' – whispered because the bedchamber might often be shared with other adults and children. Putting up with curtain lectures and bed-requests was one of the fifteen joys of marriage noted by Antoine de la Sale. Scarcely anyone slept alone in Elizabethan England; exceptionally, of course, the queen did and always had done presumably, even if a female attendant slept in the same room – a gentlewoman of the Bedchamber.

Elizabeth's grandfather, Henry VII, had slept in a four-post bed in the Painted Chamber of the Palace of Westminster. This was the highly decorated bedroom of his medieval predecessor Henry III, where the king was long expected to sleep with his crown placed on a bedside cushion. Henry VII's bed required ten attendants to make it ready. The first action of the Groom of the Bedchamber was to summon in turn four yeomen of the wardrobe carrying sheets and blankets, four yeomen of the bedchamber and a gentleman usher to direct the octet. On entering the chamber the groom stood at the foot of the bed holding a flaming torch, with the yeomen in fours on each side. One of them, using a dagger as a probe, searched the straw for any suspect item. The straw was then covered with a length of canvas to depress it and on top of that went the feather bed on which one man flailed about to disperse any clusters. Sheets and blankets were laid in a time-honoured ritual, each lowered by eight pairs of hands to reach the bed corners simultaneously. Pillows were beaten and according to the royal preference placed high or low. On top of the blankets went a sleek ermine coverlet, and then came the complicated tucking. each yeomen then made a sign of the cross upon the spot where his hands had touched the bed, and he kissed the same. The

The original verse with this reads:

> *This wife a wondrous racket means to keep,*
> *While th'Husband seems to sleep but does not sleep:*
> *But she might as well her Lecture smother,*
> *For ent'ring one ear, it goes out at t'other*

This was designated the Queen's Bedroom at Loseley House, near Guildford, Surrey – the home of Sir William More and then Sir George More, whose daughter Ann, aged fifteen years, secretly married the poet John Donne.

usher drew the heavy curtains and left a page to watch the bed, while the bed-making party departed ensemble for a nightcap of the liquid variety.

The daughter of Henry VIII and Anne Boleyn lived an oppressive childhood. Princess Elizabeth had no opportunities to dive into the warmth of a parental bed. Her mother, liberal and intelligent, was brought to the block for execution on spurious charges. Elizabeth went on sleeping alone, whatever the ill-founded rumours much later that she was as sexually promiscuous as her mother. Certainly when queen she favoured rich hangings and bedding for this most intimate space where the future of the nation was decided in silence rather than chat. In 1581 a wardrobe account noted an order from the queen of a bedstead of walnut wood, richly carved, painted and gilded. The selour, tester and valance were cloth of silver figured with velvet, lined with changeable taffeta and heavily fringed with Venice gold, silver and silk threads. The bed curtains were to be of tapestry, with the seams and borders trimmed with gold and silver lace caught up with long loops and buttons fashioned from precious metal. The head-piece was of Bruges crimson satin, edged with crimson silk and decorated with plumes – these were ostrich feathers variously colour dipped and dusted with gold spangles.[1] All remarkably ostentatious and majestic, but with no indication of size, so perhaps it was no wider or taller than the bed in the room designated the Queen's Bedroom at Loseley House, near Guildford, Surrey; the home of Sir William More was visited by the queen on progress in August 1569.

From rustic and unyielding beginnings the bed had developed in size, comfort and ostentation, with the woollen blanket being introduced from France in the fourteenth century. For the next few centuries, in homes and lodgings of all kinds it was common for friends and for strangers to share a bed. In small manor houses visitors often had to sleep in the same room as the master and mistress, but as a desire for greater privacy grew so did the number of bedrooms. Still, the truckle (or trundle) bed remained in use, rolled out from under the larger bed when required. In his will made in the early 1580s Robert Southern, an Evesham farmer and inn keeper, had his property inventoried and in the 'parlour next the street', converted into a bedroom, was a bedstead with featherbed, coverlet, bolster and pillow and a red blanket (value £4). There was also a truckle bedstead with featherbed, coverlet, bolster and pillow valued at 30s. Over the parlour was the only upstairs chamber where the bed and bedding were valued at £6, and a minor second bed with bedding and mat was judged worth 20s. Some thirty years and less miles away from Evesham a very successful playwright and gentleman made his will and allocated the household beds: the double bed (the matrimonial) went to his daughter Susanna and her husband, Dr John Hall, the smaller or 'next-best' to his wife Anne. There was nothing mean or illogical as far as we can tell in Shakespeare so doing; it was just utilitarian and quite forward looking. Anne Shakespeare (née Hathaway) was his senior by some eight years, and her husband correctly anticipated she would not remarry, although she lived on until 1625.

Familiar objects like beds became authentic family objects, but Shakespeare's perhaps unspoken hope that his family would also prosper and burgeon did not come about. Susanna and John Hall had only one daughter, Elizabeth, born in 1608. In 1613 the child's mother was accused of having a sexual liaison with Rafe Smith, a married neighbour, a claim defended in Worcester Cathedral by the accused. Elizabeth, like her grandfather, married at eighteen and when her husband, the lawyer Thomas Nash, died she married Sir John Barnard of Abington (Northants.) When she died there he had the 'old goods and lumber' in the house disposed of, or burned. Did the double bed of William Shakespeare that day go up in flames? A bed from Crackenthorpe Hall, Appleby (West.) has survived and is now part of the Victoria and Albert Museum loan collection, but we may suspect that curators would themselves set fire to it if they could have that of William Shakespeare. Perhaps not, for the headboard of this museum piece bears the strong carved inscription DREDE GOD LOVE GOD PRAYES GOD. It has too a series of carved shields with the initials HF and on the footrail three inverted Js, which suggest that it was commissioned by a merchant whose armigerous

This headboard for a four-post bed is of carved and painted oak with acanthus-decorated frieze brackets in walnut; it dates from about 1590.

bearing consisted of bale hooks. This was a bed for navigating through the hazards of life; it was not a bawdy and burlesque item like the notorious, outsize bed of Ware (Herts.) This colossus became a tourist attraction; capable of occupation by six couples, it exercised the libidinous imaginations of many. By it was a large horn from which visitors would drink to enhance ribald conviviality. In Thomas Dekker's collaboration with John Webster on the play *Northward Ho!* the curtain line at the end of the farcical comedy refers to the bed and the epic possibilities of partner swapping and simultaneous couplings within the confines of the bed. As a prodigious item of more colourful days the bed is now chastely museumed at the V&A. And it is not clear now if anybody did get sexual diversion or even sleep in a bed which seems more fanciful than real.

'Nothing is more protean or more susceptible to cultural pressure', according to Germaine Greer in a recent article, 'than human sexuality'. This observation suggests that she has at some time been Foucaulted, for Michel Foucault, historian, social commentator and homosexual bandit, argued at inordinate length, developing Freud's culturally inscribed sexual categories, that sexuality is a construct of the human

The notorious bed of Ware, a four-post bed on a huge scale, showing the fashion for elaborate decoration, with ornamental caryatids and inlay; some of this may well have been the work of Flemish immigrants.

imagination. It changes from time to time, like preferences for styles in food preparation, literature and clothes. If this seems unlikely consider when last you ate roast swan, wrote a villanelle (to your lover or anyone) or employed the discourse of courtly love. Sexuality is as much a matter of images today as it was four hundred years ago. 'When we talk about sex, we talk mostly in metaphors'. And the affectional consequences of biology and bio-chemistry are the area with which literature best deals.

ACKNOWLEDGEMENTS

While working on this book I moved to live in part of a Jacobean house in Worcestershire, beguiled by the architecture, local accent and clean air. Though remote from academic libraries it has proved inspirational and I offer my thanks to the late John Hanford (d. 1616) for the work he did on the building he inherited.

The most particular and direct contribution to sourcing the book has been that of Dr Mark Nicholls, Department of Manuscripts and University Archives, Cambridge University. In a busy professional and private life he has still managed to respond with cordiality and generosity whenever I have sought his help. Moreover, he has read this book in typescript so my debt remains incalculable and spectacular.

With the book before them I hope my family, friends and neighbours will think their kindness and tolerance has brought forth something worthwhile – maybe 'something understood'. Completing it on a tiny budget has been made possible by my sister and brother-in-law, Hilary and Tony Keen, who have a warm house, a sofa-bed and a willingness to pour drinks for the exhausted researcher.

A Note on the Text

Dates in this book conform to the modern style with the year beginning on 1 January, and not on 25 March.

To assist the reader I have modernized the spellings in quotations from late sixteenth- and early seventeenth-century texts. Titles remain in their original form, though the longest have been trimmed. The original £ s d currency has been retained. A rule of thumb devised by Charles Nicholl to calculate rough modern values is to multiply by a factor of 500:

1 penny (1d) = £2
6 pennies (6d) = £12
1 shilling (1s) = £25
1 angel (10s) = £250

CHAPTER ONE
VESTIGIAL VIRTUE

Before the Church Council of Florence held over fifteen years (1431–46), the outsize blemish on marriage had been its correlation with sexual activity. The late medieval idealization of celibacy took a knock when marriage was officially recognized as a sacrament. Until then celibacy had been appropriate for nuns and priests, with the hope that the whole community would regard this as ideal behaviour. After the Reformation this ideal, with its profound distrust of sexual desire, 'continued to haunt the Renaissance imagination of the moral and spiritual life well into the seventeenth century'.[1] An attitude of mild unease with the only available option then for humans was recorded by the Norwich doctor, Sir Thomas Browne (1605–82): 'I could be content that we might procreate like trees, without conjunction . . .' Many edgy churchmen would have agreed that sex was 'an odd and unworthy piece of folly': John Donne's late advancement in the church gave him time to form a different view, and to write erotic poetry.

Trees had no governable inheritance and could do without 'this trivial and worldly way of union'. For the upper classes with blood lines to transmit as securely as possible, and for the enhancement of family property, marriage was of critical importance. Moreover, it was a mode of controlling fornication, an otherwise unruly and irregular form of sexuality. For those with such concerns the greatest life disappointment was infertility after procreation. Sexuality can be free and radical; opinions, attitudes and behaviour would collide and overlap. Out of the disturbances and changing sensibilities emerged slowly the view of affectionate marriage as the foundation of an ordered society, and also a willingness to view sex as a game or sport expressing conviviality and harmless pleasure. 'Those who clung too firmly to the image of sermons, household manuals and social theory had nothing but disappointment awaiting them.'[2] Aristocratic marriages by the end of the sixteenth century were in great number afflicted by failure, with a third of older peers estranged or separated.[3] If nothing else this wrecked the possibility of any marital sex and it hints at a dwindling of marriage as morally neutral for the participants. Marriage had been politicized, and politics is contestatory. Also the law made marriage an assortment of tribulations for the unwary. Matrimonial suits came into the courts because of 'confusion, conditions by one party or parental pressure.'[4] Even a civil lawyer could be blithely ignorant of ecclesiastical law, and the matter of the secret marriage of the Attorney-General Edward Coke to Lady Elizabeth Hatton, led to his appearance before a church court to refute the charge of irregular marriage. To obtain a dispensation even he had to plead ignorance.

Sir Thomas Browne, physician and essayist, evidently found human sexual reproduction a source of some awkwardness, lacking formal control and any shred of dignity.

The propositions of 'household order' defined by men might hold for some, but for many quotidian behaviour caused a slide of such things into desuetude. To illustrate this a specimen from 1624, when eighteen-year-old Henry Scrope entered the household of Sir Edward Plumpton for service, and within days had clandestinely married Anne Plumpton. Neither her father nor her mother were present at the night nuptial, and there was no certainty that the man who had taken the ceremony was a priest of any sort. Moreover, Henry had an impediment to his desire – he was already married – but living with his new bride he fathered several children before his past caught up with him. The case came before the Star Chamber in 1631 when he was charged with bigamy. Court cases, and sometimes thereafter plays and pamphlets projected into the public domain the collisions between competing public and private notions of what was appropriate and permissible. So in a play like John Marston's *The Dutch Courtesan*, the focus is on the 'domestication of sexual energies', and by giving voice through his characters to various opinions of marriage he wrote a morality play about a vexed institution still central to a unstable society. Re-evaluation could also be made in poetry and reflecting a different state of mind. In John Donne's poetry there is the junking of idealized love for an explicit collision of bodies – bodies are sex, that is the truth of experience – as he reminds his coterie readers in *The Extasie*. Prior to this love had been a single-minded ardour, 'idealized in solitary suffering'. In the English Renaissance, along with language which echoed the medieval, Petrarchan and neo-Platonic traditions of love discourse, the object of desire was frequently immobilized. 'Women's honesty was determined and judged by their sexual behaviour', so that of Mary Stewart, Queen of Scots, seemed a challenge not only to her cousin Elizabeth, but also to the men of England. For many Protestants she was both enchantress and whore; in the 1590 *Faerie Queene* Spenser was quite explicit: Duessa stands for deceit, the exiled queen and Catholicism. For a Puritan-inclined statesman like Sir Francis Walsingham, locking away Queen Mary in a remote castle or country house was a preliminary to permanently immobilizing her in death.

For Catholic gentlemen like Anthony Babington who sought freedom for the Queen of Scots, substituting treason for quiet fidelity to his wife and child did not seem hideously improbable. If Babington had read all the earlier literary defences of Mary's harmless virtue and purity, no doubt he was scandalized by the vituperation in Parliament of men like Peter Wentworth who called Mary 'the most notorious whore in all the world'. Babington's associates were other like-minded men and no case of treason in Elizabethan and Jacobean England ever involved a husband and wife in the way that *Macbeth* (*c.* 1606) does. The play was written in the gloomy aftermath of the greatest act of treason ever broached by an Englishman against the royal family and the great men of the government, aristocracy and Church. To advance himself and his progeny Macbeth fashions himself into a tyrannical mass-murderer in a play that trawls through many aspects of Robert Catesby's Gunpowder Plot. At the same time in the play a marriage is held up for critical inspection, with the thane of Glamis and his wife strikingly united in anxieties about gender and procreation. Moreover they are correct, as it turns out, to fear the worst: insanity and destruction. The play famously begins with bearded women, manlike images of feminine power whom the lady of Glamis would ape. She redefines her gender and purpose in life and by persuading her husband to undertake evil she swamps his promptings of pity. For the rest of the play the sterility of violence becomes achingly clear to the audience.

The instructors and pundits took the view that the principal duty of a wife as loyal subject was to obey her domestic monarch, and when this did not happen, so the aggrieved declared, the household fell into disarray and dispute. The husband's duty was to shape his wife's personality in such a way as to bring out the good in her, but he must also befriend her 'that she might walk jointly with him, under the conduct and government of her head.' This has been sardonically subverted by the end of *Macbeth*. The queen has gone off her head forcing her withdrawal from the action, and Macbeth has had his head hacked off by Macduff in symbolic retribution. Now it is Macbeth's blood that flows post-mortem rather than that of his wife who earlier had raged against her menstrual cycle. It was witches, held the view of the time, who could turn a woman into a man. In the infamous *Malleus Maleficarum*, a Renaissance study of witches, it is noted that 'witchcraft comes from carnal lust', and in respect of the latter women are insatiable, capable of endless coupling with sexual partners. In many of the tragedies of the period sexual obsession vents itself in savage declamations against incest, adultery, promiscuity, fornication, prostitution and perversities, as well as against love and marriage, against men and women, most often against women as such and in the mass.

Until *Macbeth* begins with the unspecific sexuality of the witches, it seems that the thane of Glamis and his lady have lived the companionate marriage. The speed with which this disintegrates may be satirically inflected. Having annexed marriage for intense scrutiny, and then broadened the matter to gender relations, Protestant reformers looked again at sexual relations and at least two attitudes emerged towards sex in marriage. In one the ethical idea of moderation holds sway; in the other there is the dominating attitude that the body rules, not out of elementary lust but a more meaningful conjunction of mind and body. According to William Whately the two strands can be harmoniously united: 'To sanctify the marriage bed, and use it reverently, with prayer and thanksgiving, will make it moderate.' This is the so-called canonization of heterosexuality; the Catholic ideal of celibacy derived from the saints was in full retreat. 'Poor greenheads' was the Puritan phrase for those who having married purely for 'love' forfeited society's strained goodwill when the first fissures appeared. When young aristocrats, like Lucius Cary, made a marriage entirely based on his feelings for his impoverished bride, it could lead to acute family disharmony and a flow of angry retorts from father to son Yet this was at least a quarter of a century after the beginning of the liberation of affectional feeling among the young in the 1590s. In the early comedies of Shakespeare there is a triumphant surge towards marriage as the ultimate good, but as has been recently noted it is also a dangerous option when the older generation are finessed by the young with blood pounding in their veins. Indeed, when Romeo and Juliet 'chill out' they do so permanently which may not be the best option for young lovers, but they do achieve a fine gender equality in death.

'All the fun is in the wooing.' The froth on the milk quickly curdles after marriage, and as Stephen Orgel has noted most families in Shakespeare have only one parent; where there are rarely two there is usually only one child, a situation exceedingly dangerous to the child.[5] It is noticeable that for the playwright's own wife and family he was an often absent husband and father; were they totally persuaded that he needed to be in London so frequently and for so long? Did Anne Shakespeare resist moving south, or was the question never asked? There is an open and trusting marriage in that of Brutus and Portia, but it is strikingly rare as are the sexually compatible husband and wife, Claudius and Gertrude. In a clutch of his early comedies Shakespeare tricks out the commonplace notion that the course of true love never did run true with festive larks. In *Hamlet* we have the most sinister reflection that true love is the province of a murderer and an adulteress; the court conspires to revel in this union, only Hamlet resists it on the promptings of a ghost claiming to be his late lamented father. By the end of Elizabeth's reign the fun has gone out of the wooing to be replaced by a singular harshness in expressing disgust with sex. The bitterness against women does not occur in Elizabethan tragedy until about 1600, by which time the country was awaiting her death while imbibing a morale-sapping cocktail of anxiety, irritation and even a guilty boredom. Satire on women and cynical utterances on love are, of course, not unfamiliar to Elizabethans who had seen John Lyly's comedies. In *Campaspe* (1584) what Diogenes most dislikes about women is their gender; some may even now regard this as a laudable frankness, but it does not come near in acrid expostulation the hard-bitten fury that Hamlet directs against his mother and Ophelia.

Is it possible to identify a particular event in the 1590s that resonates as the possible direct cause of this literary revolution in the treatment of sex? It seems unlikely that the shift from a comparatively carefree view of sex to one of ill-tempered revulsion should have happened to most Elizabethan poets simultaneously around 1595. Nor does it seem even remotely likely that prostitution, venereal disease, promiscuity, sodomy, perverse jealousy and adultery were conditions suddenly more rife after that date. Then the growing predisposition of writers, especially dramatists, to incorporate such things into their texts must be a collective whim. The unsavoury and the more acceptable exposures of sex were present simultaneously in late Elizabethan England, some glaringly, some sombrely. If we expose male anxiety of the period to more scrutiny then we may be approaching the subjective core of the matter. The mechanism for the action of the stage is often concerned with individual efforts by those who profess love for another to overcome all obstacles to union. As in life the lovers are young, passing ignorant of the world (and themselves), and the young men are especially excitable and callow. The girls often fare better from an indulgent author. This is certainly true of the main female character Margaret in Robert Greene's *Friar Bacon and Friar Bungay*; she is vital, gracious, witty and chaste in a play written for the popular theatre in 1589–90. The dominant love story gives a controlling shape to the play, and the struggle that goes on within it arises from the conflicting social, sexual and emotional needs of the three main characters. This collision provides the suspense that engaged the audience, with a resolution to suit them and the characters – all are married and happy. The hugely expectant and positive attitude to marriage for life, whatever the bumps and stumbles that might happen, chimed with this constant theme of Protestant (mainly Puritan) theologians of the sixteenth and early seventeenth centuries. In many thousands of sermons over decades nuptial propaganda was included, and in some cases these sermons became a form of theatre – a dramatic monologue delivered from the pulpit. Preaching undoubtedly influenced dramatists, just as Renaissance dramatists influenced preachers. Moreover, being a Puritan-minded person did not preclude a love of theatre.

Marriage in the deliberations of one writer was viewed as 'an high and blessed order ordained of God in Paradise' – which has a sublimely affirmative ring to it. As the old English proverb noted more earthily, 'there belongeth more to marriage than two pair of bare legs'. It must be a union of minds rather than just procreative bodies, since that is the only way to 'increase unto Christ'. Anthony Nixon found four reasons for marriage: first, that God instituted it; that it is a kind of ingratitude to deny to our posterity the life which has been granted us; we achieve immortality by means of our offspring and that by this institution comes a welcome increase in kinsfolk, friends and allies.[6] Not only has God ordained matrimony but history bears witness that mankind has long favoured it. According to Robert Cleaver and John Dod in their widely read courtesy book *A Godlie forme of householde Government* (1598), those who are most vociferous against marriage are the ones who offend most against it because of the unchaste lives they lead.

The bigamist in Renaissance England was nearly always a man. Adultery was far less gender specific, yet the law took little notice of it. Under the common law it could not be prosecuted because it was a spiritual matter governed by ecclesiastical courts and canon law. Adultery seized the public imagination (and hence that of playwrights) after 1595 or so because of the unshackled behaviour of one woman, an inspirational beauty of huge vitality and sexual allure, whose adultery became notorious. Whether there was ever any attempt to disguise it is difficult to say, but the poets who acclaimed Penelope Rich could not avoid knowing of her adultery with Charles Blount, Lord Mountjoy, and when they punned in open text on her married name, how could they avoid punning on his in secret. Indeed, new evidence is now emerging that Mountjoy, one of the best friends of Shakespeare's court patron the Earl of Southampton, was also an important connection of Shakespeare's at the court. Is this perhaps the reason that Shakespeare never treated the question whether an adulterous wife might be forgiven? It was a topic to be taken up and debated by others; for example, Chapman's *Bussy D'Ambois*; Beaumont and Fletcher's *Maid's Tragedy* and later Philip Massinger's *Fatal Dowry*. The law did not favour a husband whose wife had taken up with another man, and no dramatist found it compatible with 'honour' for a husband like Lord Rich to live with a wife guilty of adultery as Lady Penelope straightforwardly was. Some playwrights took the view that a husband could at least forgive, and some Puritan moralists seem in addition to have thought a husband could continue to live with a penitent adulterous wife. But not even Thomas Heywood chanced this view on stage, and although he allows for the rehabilitation of a fallen women, and the pardoning of an adulterous wife by her husband, the forgiven adulteresses all die. One particular irritant, a point of conflict between Catholics and Protestants, was the question as to whether marriage was really a contract or truly a sacrament. The latter, said Catholics, so all questions pertaining to it must be determined by ecclesiastical judges only. The Protestants argued for the contract – the marriage of Olivia and Sebastian in *Twelfth Night* is described as 'A contract of eternal bond of love' – so all matters germane, such as impediments and degrees of kindred, are social not sacral matters. As such they are the exclusive prerogative of the civil magistrates. There were two definite parts to marriage: the contract (or spousals/espousals), and the marriage itself which gives form to the contract. Enough time should elapse between the two for the minister to proclaim or publish the banns (announcements), by which time if the bride lived in rural Devon there was over a 30 per cent chance that she would be pregnant, whereas if she lived in Yorkshire this figure plunged to 13 per cent. There were two types of espousal: *in verbis de futuro* and *in verbis de praesenti*. If the ceremony includes the expression 'I shall take thee to my wife' or 'I will take thee' then this espousal expresses future intention (*de futuro*) and even in the presence of a priest it was not binding upon either party. Two young people, or parents acting for them, could make such a contract, but if the intention decayed and just cause for it shown then an unwilling party to the contract could withdraw. The exception to this was when the couple had slept together: 'where there hath been a carnal use of each others bodies, it is always presupposed, that a mutual consent, as touching marriage, hath gone before.' This was the view of William Perkins in his *Christian Oeconomie* (1609).

The espousal *de praesenti* was different because it contained the key words – 'I do take thee'. Perkins highlights the importance of this form of espousal when he states clearly that the marriage has begun, 'though not in regard of fact, yet in regard of right and interest'. Church and state both held such a union to be valid, so it is the contract that is crucial, projecting itself before the actual marriage service. It is often been observed as likely that the *de praesenti* espousal took place between young William

Shakespeare and Anne Hathaway when she was pregnant in the summer of 1582. So a *de praesenti* espousal such as happens in *Twelfth Night* is in effect an abbreviated form of marriage, squeezed into a few core items. As the Duchess says in John Webster's *The Duchess of Malfi*:

> I have heard lawyers say, a contract in a chamber
> Per verba de praesenti is absolute marriage

The Duchess is correct in respect of English law but it could be hard to prove and parents who were not party to the business would sometimes seek to sunder a couple so joined. A lengthy court action culminating in a judgement by the dean of the Court of Arches followed the secret and hasty wedding of Thomas Thynne and Maria Audley in 1594. The couple were the sixteen-year-old children of quite prominent rival west of England families, and within hours of being introduced at the Bell inn, Beaconsfield, they were married, so wrecking the plans of the Thynnes for their son who was currently rather an idle student at Oxford. Indeed, despite conciliatory efforts Thomas's parents remained unforgiving and conducted a lengthy effort through the courts which eventually in 1601 they lost. As has recently been noted, the approach to the matter and the comments made after its inception 'suggest tensions between public perceptions of a valid marriage and matrimonial law.[7] The senior Thynnes thought their lack of consent and the age of their son made the marriage invalid; but they were proven wrong. Although there was a general understanding in society that a couple should be older than the legal ages of twelve for girls and fourteen for boys, these teenagers were old enough to marry even without consent which was not required in law. Nor were witnesses necessary, although they might prove useful. There were no banns, the ceremony was not in a church at approved hours; it was not taken by a beneficed minister and there was no record of it in a parish register, nor probably in writing at all. Since it was for long kept secret it was virtually an invisible nuptial – but it was valid. England had quaintly retained medieval canon law on contract marriage despite its abolition in Catholic Europe by the Council of Trent.

The response of Elizabethans to young people wild at heart was infinitely varied and evidently worth testing on stage in *Romeo and Juliet*; the heroine in Shakespeare's tragic drama is fourteen, and the Thynnes who may have inspired the play were exceptionally young. They differed from Romeo and Juliet in one respect; there was no sexual consummation of the marriage. Thomas and Maria did lay on a bed that had been made up for them, but it was under scrutiny and they kept their clothes on as they kissed 'very lovingly'.[8] The first sexual encounter in a marriage in the view of many with an opinion should not take place until the couple had first knelt in prayer while alone in their chamber, commending themselves to God. Early marriage was widely regarded with some disquiet (and evidently still is when an English schoolgirl marries a

Turkish national), because of unease about childbirth at such an age. Most couples married in their mid to late twenties, and among the gentry the heirs averaged twenty-three years old, while the brides were usually one or two years younger. Curiosity about marriage and sex, the first visible, the second mostly invisible, was likely aroused before this, and it seems that the number of illegitimate births reached a peak between 1590 and 1610.[9] It would require individual testimony to decide if marriage was so obviously preferable to a paternity suit, and men wriggled mightily to avoid such things blemishing their lives.

> But womankind in mischief is ringleader of the rest,
> The instrument of wickedness enkindling first desire,
> Whose vile incestuous whoredom sets so many towns afire.

Cousin to anxiety is derision and this was heaped on the married man whose wife betrayed him sexually with other men. With the phenomenal growth of London, life in the noisy, crammed city was often a joltingly physical experience. Through the combination of energy, toiling and pressures of social upheaval the monied middle class became obsessed with 'the integrity of commodity and the seemingly inevitable hazards of ownership'.[10] A highly significant component of the marriage market was the dowry, which excited the attention of all classes. This highly visible aspect of investment in marriage was part of a process that increasingly made women into commodities in a transaction that might, if properly handled, increase financial profitability well after the ceremony and the conveyance of the dowry. Drama of the period shows a powerful tendency to become obsessed with loss and gain in commerce and sexuality; the accusation against Bassanio in *The Merchant of Venice* can be made that he is selfish and prodigal, since he frankly admits that he hopes to retrieve his lost fortunes by a rich marriage. From the end of the thirteenth century in England the common law held that marriage made the wife's chattels absolutely the property of her husband. A little slippage in the thinking and the wife too becomes a chattel; a little slippage in the language and commodity comes to mean the female pudendum. Marriage in theory presented a social and ethical barrier to the free male with piratical instincts, but husbands remained nervous of the light-fingered wanderer. His predations could ruin the reputation of a husband, the profits of marriage passing to an interloper. Struggle and predation are thematic sinews within the dramas of the day.

'Idle hopes' drove Edmund Spenser from the court one day to walk along the shore of one 'silver streaming Thames'. In the poem *Prothalamion* he emphasized a river of sweet meadow margins, but the river was more than a decorative channel to the sea. The vessels that took the tides up and down the Thames had, in Elizabeth's time, to sail past a celebrated spot on the Surrey shore some 3 miles east of St Paul's. It was known as Cuckold's Haven or Cuckold's point and there stood an eye-catching pole

Map of Shakespeare's London; his great contemporary Edmund Spenser wrote of 'the silver streaming Thames'.

topped with animal horns. This folkloric contrivance became an urban totem, alerting and deriding simultaneously, having first been noted at the beginning of Elizabeth's reign in the diary of Henry Machyn, a London merchant. According to the godfather/T.S. Eliot of Elizabethan literature, Nicholas Breton, in his pamphlet *Cornucopiae* (1612) the pole was raised to honour Lady fortune, the subversive spirit of marriage and cuckoldry. He remarks too that wealthy men were most often cuckolds; the trophy wife as a commodity slips from their grip and their sight. In dealing with a wife's infirmities, Edmund Tilney in 1568 counselled husbands to be wise and patient (even as their 'investment' is seized by freebooters). The husband must always abstain from 'brawling, lowring and grudging'. As to the wife – she 'puts back', said Tilney 'the serving mans putting forward, with a frown'.

That may be the properly demure behaviour of a conduct book, but it is evident that reality could be very different. The lady and gentleman of a household had to deal with male and female servants who had a substantial age range; some would be single and some married. Employment and duties were gender based – maid and manservant served wife and husband with little room for overlapping of tasks. While the same sex relationship of maid and mistress, master and manservant could lead to subtle shifts in the power structure within the house, the relationship between master and maid, wife and manservant needed to be negotiated with extreme care. How far was the 'trusty' servant to be trusted? With power over other servants? With money, or your life? Or your wife? 'There is no greater torment, than the vexation of a jealous mind.'

The commanding frown of the wife to a too forward serving-man was evidently never summoned by Mary Stawell, the daughter of Sir William Portman, and married in 1556 to a Somerset gentleman of means, Sir John Stawell. To many it would have seemed an enviable marriage but evidently it dwindled even as she allowed herself (and it seems was allowed) to become besotted with the servant John Stalling. She might have tried a little harder to disguise her feelings, and Sir John might have couched his rebukes to her less mildly: 'Wife, if you will not leave these light toys with my men, you shall not find me to be your husband.' By this statement he seems to signal his disinclination to become a wittol – that is, a complacent husband who meekly accepts his status as cuckold. Yet Sir John did not drive Stalling from his employment and we remain uncertain about the nebulous 'boundaries of power and propriety between master and servant'. Did Sir John make access to his wife difficult for Stalling? Evidently not. Perhaps Sir John was after all 'an accessory to the stealing of his own goods' because Mary Stawell had a dominating sexual appetite. Living at Cothelstone she was bedded by Stalling, a matter known by other servants and used to their own advantage. Instead of being paid solely by Sir John they were able to squeeze bribes from his surrogate. Elizabeth Goore obtained black satin sleeves from Stalling, ruffs, gloves, pins and a cloak. On one occasion Arthur Guntrey was given 3s (perhaps £75 in today's values), and on another a pair of sarsenet lined fine black hose.

Not only did the adulterous couple sleep in the marriage bed, but on one occasion they were found in bed in Stalling's house near the manor. Even within her husband's house Mary took extravagant risks, quitting her bed early to move to Stalling's room in the house. He had become a man feared and yet admired – the eroticized servant – who appears often in the satirical texts of the 1590s, preparing for the satiric comedies of Jonson and Chapman. *The Gentleman Usher* by Chapman makes the threat of the unruly and sexually unscrupulous servant very clear. Bassiolo ultimately claims authority over both lovers – his social superiors:

Ah, I do domineer and rule the roast (5.1.ii.)

The eponymous gentleman usher has become the 'friend' of Prince Vincentio, whom he calls with cheerful insolence 'Vince', or 'sweet' or 'dear'. The inversion of status guides the playgoer to a further shock: the probable sexual component in such a relationship. Cuckolds like Sir John and wives like Mary had something further to fear: a pregnancy carried to term and the threat of contaminated bloodlines for inheritances. To prevent this disaster it seems likely that the lovers used anal intercourse as a form of birth control. In early modern England the practice was known and alluded to, generally with a smirk or a shudder. But then Mary did become pregnant in her husband's absence and was artful enough to conceal it prior to a drug induced abortion. It was not an uncommon method, albeit risky, and not always condemned by public voices because of the widely held view that the soul only entered the foetus when movement could be felt – usually the fifth month.[11] Only when her infatuation faltered and Mary began to bait any male servant did Sir John decide to act to defend himself against dishonour and derision.

The delay in seeking to rectify is intriguing and not a little puzzling. It may have been that he wanted to protect his own new partner, the sister of the poet and courtier Sir Edward Dyer, an intimate of the Sidney circle. Or Sir John may have recoiled from the compelling sex drive of his wife, and hence allowed Stalling privileged access to her. Perhaps he could abide a single affair but not serial adultery, neither of which could have enhanced his parochial reputation. Or his vanity was such that what seemed to others a torrent of evidence against the adulterers was to him but a weak trickle. Or even that there was some complicity between the husband and the lover based on the premise that 'he that kisses my wife is my friend'. Until, that is, the matter becomes an affront, and a barrier to the husband's gratification. At last Sir John made a presentation to Gilbert Berkeley, Bishop of Bath and Wells from 1560 to his death in 1581. Berkeley gave him a sympathetic hearing, and wrote to Archbishop Parker commending Stawell's request that he should be allowed to remarry despite having a wife who was very much alive. Disentangling himself from the wreckage of this first marriage actually proved far from easy and the effort had to be sustained over years.

The suit was first bought in the Wells consistory court of the bishop, and it was opposed by Mary Stawell and her friends. Then the suit was lain before the Court of Delegates of the Archbishop of Canterbury. What was allowed was a judicial separation – not a divorce *ad vinculo*. By 1572 Stawell was growing ruffled at the delay, for as Berkeley pointed out to Parker he was a landowner without an heir given that his daughter's parentage was so problematical after such flagrant adultery by her mother.

In April 1572 Stawell did receive a licence to marry from Parker, but in November Mary Stawell sued her husband for restitution in the Court of Arches. Simultaneously (and no doubt to his chagrin) he was charged in the Court of Audience of the Archbishop with 'the public offence given by him to the country where he dwelleth for cohabiting with a gentlewoman as his wife, his former wife being alive'. Writing to Burghley, the archbishop noted Stawell's anger and that he 'careth not what to spend so as he may have his fair lady'. Several members of the archbishop's household had been offered bribes of £100 and £200 to influence Parker, and when the briber refused to confirm or deny that he had remarried (fearing to prejudice his case), the archbishop had him imprisoned. This bestirred both Lord Burghley and the Earl of Leicester who wrote in protest to Parker; the agent for this was surely Dyer. Parker himself was perturbed by the whole domestic coil and upset that a Protestant gentleman had to be imprisoned 'to avoid further example'. Very soon after Dyer helpfully made a double covenant with Stawell and Mary Stawell's brother against any suit being pursued in the church courts. The sum of £600 was put up as a means of halting any further challenges to the marriage of Stawell and Frances Dyer; in effect it was a bribe and it worked handsomely. The couple lived together unchallenged and had a son and heir. Mary Stawell, formerly so active, was now hemmed in by male embargoes, but she bided her time and when the heir died in 1604 very shortly after his father, leaving a child of three as a ward of court, she submitted with alacrity a petition for the recognition of her marriage nearly fifty years before and her right in old age to dower payments. Remarkably she won on both counts, but Sir John had late got the measure of her greed and had protected his estates and their inheritance by his descendants. To fend off any charges of illegitimacy he had resettled them so that they went to his heir and so on by purchase and not descent. In a case fought pertinaciously by both sides Sir John won a technical knockout.[12]

CHAPTER TWO

THE UNHOLY
ROYAL FAMILY

As royal daughters and rulers of England, Queen Mary and her half-sister Queen Elizabeth had stirring personal, even spiritual, reasons for marrying. For the former it was the piercing hope of tethering England to Rome once again; for the latter, marriage offered the hope of extending the line of Tudor rulers. For both, the friction between private inclination and the perception of national well-being was acutely discomforting. A Protestant minister wrote some years later that the obedience of a wife to a husband must be 'the ornament of his government'. Could a curb like this be placed on a queen? In the most strictly personal and private realm of marriage a queen *regnant* would indeed be subordinate to her husband, 'but as a magistrate she would be dominant and could command and even punish her husband if he broke the law'.[1] When Mary married Prince Philip of Spain and Burgundy the marriage treaty made plain enough where the power lay – and it was not with the prince. Mary resisted the possibility of his being made an integral part of the government – her government – by denying him a personal landholding and so squeezing out any chance of him achieving an independent starting point for patronage. However, Philip was campaigning in wars abroad so service in his armies had drawing power even for the remaining Dudleys who had suffered in the early part of Mary's reign. Yet Philip was subservient to her and the matter was neatly symbolized in court ritual; he ate from silver plate, she from gold; he had a throne smaller than hers.[2] Even the great cost of his considerable entourage was his as Mary declined to make any publicly acknowledged payments. The benefit to her of the marriage in 1554 nestled in Philip's codpiece, but it was not a union of enticing qualities and pious Mary, better suited for a nunnery than a nursery, remained barren. This timely gynaecological defect made possible the accession of the third Tudor virgin after Henry VIII.

Elizabeth came to the throne in 1558 when already twenty-five years old. This in itself did not absolutely preclude marriage but it signalled her novel status. She was an unmarried princess (now a queen) without pressing parents trawling Europe for a suitable husband. In other realms princes would pause to consider her: one rarity of fairness and wit who had emerged from childhood and youth unencumbered by a dynastic marriage. This was an unusual advantage for the daughter of a king in the sixteenth century and had been arrived at despite occasional flurries of nuptial diplomacy. It was, of course, actually her father who markedly devalued her prospects

Queen Elizabeth I (c. 1570), a strong, iconic image of the atramentous eyes, pale visage and golden hair of a Boleyn daughter by a Tudor father.

when his marriage to her mother Anne Boleyn was annulled, Elizabeth declared illegitimate by a new Succession Act, and debarred from 'any inheritance as lawful heir'. Once done not easily forgotten, least of all in the palaces of Europe where this action toppled her value. Only the Scots were more amenable and she might have been married off to the heir of the Earl of Arran, but the larger plan collapsed, and on Henry VIII's death her prospects were dulled almost to extinction. Male domination of the court of Edward VI was unchallenged, and the Duke of Northumberland's initiative in dynastic politics excluded Elizabeth.

However, she was not without women of some influence about her. Not Mary to be sure, with whom she appears to have had few and then only cool contacts, but her temporary stepmothers and a constant companion, Blanche Parry (ap Harry). Of those who may be deemed to have influenced the royal princess when a child and young adult, Mistress Parry is perhaps unrivalled because of her length of service and unswerving loyalty. She was born in about 1508 at Newcourt, the family mansion of Bacton, Herefordshire, a county house of some age and parochial importance, surrounded by a deer park. She had several brothers and sisters and since girls at that time were given little formal education it is reasonable to assume she was taught at home. Her father died when she was about sixteen as did Elizabeth's; Alice Parry, her mother, remarried.[3] When Blanche left the family home is not known, but later she recorded having seen Princess Elizabeth rocked in her cradle, and she was an official lady-in-waiting to the remarkably precocious three-year-old. So Blanche was about the court of Henry VIII when quite young, and the likeliest agent for this was her own aunt Blanche, her mother's sister who had married twice. Her first husband was Sir Robert Whitney and her second Sir William Herbert, an illegitimate son of the Earl of Pembroke. There was no severe social embarrassment in being born a bastard since aristocratic fathers generally made provision for them, and the blood of parents counted for much more than the social blemish in law. Lady Herbert of Troy (or Lady Troy as she became known) was herself a woman of some influence at the Henrician court. Having carried the hem of the train of Elizabeth at the christening of Prince Edward, she became chief lady of the female child's household in 1536, the year Blanche Parry was taken on as a lady in attendance. If the princess, busily and unusually immersed in Greek and Latin, also had a knowledge of Welsh, Mistress Parry was the likeliest source. In her home land the Stradlings, her cousins, were important gentry and the marriage of her elder sister and two of her nieces into the Vaughan family still further extended her solid connections; Frances Vaughan, a cousin of Blanche, became a maid of honour in the 1570s.[4]

Blanche Parry was always on hand to assist her young royal charge in frequent and likely wearisome changes of residence. It may have been in the early 1540s that she became responsible for jewellery, a care she did not relinquish until 1573. When the Elizabethan entourage come to Cheshunt in Hertfordshire, there was the additional pleasure that a Parry cousin was a page in the household, a favourite pupil of Roger Ascham when the latter first came from Cambridge to tutor the princess. At John Whitney's sudden death the 'whole household was filled with lamentations'. For the vividly imaginative Elizabeth, the association of tender feelings (not necessarily her own) with death and grief now openly expressed was reinforced. Devotion to daily routines helped in the assimilation of sorrow and given the remarkable, taxing teaching regime organized by Ascham, Elizabeth's intellect must have been constantly engaged so the cerebral ruled the emotional aspect of her life. The earliest part of the day 'was always devoted by her to the New Testament in Greek, after which she read select orations of Isocrates and the tragedies of Sophocles, which I judged best adapted to supply her tongue with the purest diction, *her mind with the most excellent precepts,*★ and her exalted station with a defence against the utmost power of fortune'. So wrote Ascham, solemnly and dutifully, to Johann Sturmius† rector of an academy and meeting place for other reformed theologians in Strasburg. So how did the child feel when she read *Antigone* by Sophocles? There was an ancient drama of a woman caught between a pious duty to a family harbouring sexual transgression, while feeling within herself a vehement reluctance to accept this.

Renaissance culture was obsessively taken up with the kaleidoscopic aspects of transgressive sexuality, most particularly the insistent pull of family relationships and the counterweight of desire. It was a subject frequently explored in drama, poetry and prose fiction. So Spenser allegorized the most extreme form of sexual incontinence imaginable at that time with the twin giants Ollyphant and Argante, born of incest between a Titaness and her own son, doubling the incest of their genesis by a unifying sexual act in the womb. In their reading of Sir Thomas Malory's version of the Arthurian legends, the Elizabethans were jolted by King Arthur's begetting of a bastard son Mordred by his sister, and Mordred compounds this shock later by seeking an adulterous relationship with his stepmother Guenevere. It was especially perturbing since 'Elizabeth was metaphorically and commonly seen as the living Arthur.'[5] In the play *The Misfortunes of Arthur* (1588) by Thomas Hughes the material is rejigged in the style of a Senecan tragedy, shortly after the original plays of Seneca were collected into a translated version by Thomas Newton. Of the ten, seven involve incest directly or as a background. Seneca was steeped in the topic, just as were so many classical writers read by young Elizabethans in their bare, cold classrooms during the long hours of formal teaching. The favourite was Ovid, who in his *Heroides* (XI), took up the myth of the children of Aeolus, five pairs of incestuous brothers and sisters, reminding many

---

★ My italics.
† Sturmius later acted as an agent for the Privy Council.

Elizabethans of their own numerous siblings and hinting at erotic possibilities. *Metamorphoses* offers even more myths on the topic such as Myrrha's passion for her father which produces Adonis, and Phaedra's desire for her stepson Hippolytus, with its deadly consequences.

The concept of carnal contagion – *contagio carnalis* – was a familiar doctrine to educated people at this time.[6] Within generational memory it had been used to claim that Henry VIII's marriages with both his first two wives, Catherine of Aragon and Anne Boleyn, were incestuous. If Prince Arthur (the late brother of Henry) had slept with his bride Catherine, so the argument went, then she was kin to Henry and his marriage to her null and void. The child of such a union (Princess Mary) would be illegitimate, as would her half-sister Elizabeth if the King had indeed seduced Mary Boleyn, sister of the new queen. This may appear to be a quaint time-worn doctrine, but the notion of carnal contagion has yet a new resonance for the Elizabethans of the late twentieth century. The view of the medieval theologian Rabanus Maurus can be summarized in a way that chimes with current counselling for sexual health. 'If one sleeps with a woman who sleeps with another man who sleeps with another woman who sleeps with me, then whether I will it or not my flesh is inextricably bound up with the flesh of that first man.' The consequences of fornication are venereal disease, illegitimacy and incest; also leading to incest through the contagion of flesh lurks clandestine kinship. Compress the arguments on contagion to arrive at the brusque contention of Jonas of Orleans that any immoral carnal relations are incestuous.[7] Even the approved institution of marriage cannot escape the carnal contagion of incest 'which undermines and transcends the ordinary notion of kinship'. Henry VIII's 'extraordinarily incestuous marital career' produced some complex legislation and so reduced the number of prohibited relationships to those close relations noted in Leviticus – abandoning spiritual prohibitions 'but not those established by carnal knowledge'. Catholic polemical writing in the 1580s alleged that Elizabeth was the child of an incestuous, monstrous carnal union, 'and therefore an insatiable sexual deviant herself'.[8] How often and how deeply did the pale, strained-looking young princess reflect on the calumnies heaped on her mother and father? The answer may be for us to consider in a fact that has been widely heeded – her indifference to the memory of her parents and, above all, the generations before them.

In Shakespeare's *Richard III*, Elizabeth of York's hand is sought by her uncle Richard to defuse possible opposition to his rule. But it was Henry Tudor who married her, this unifying the red rose with the white, a unifying symbolism harped on by the playwright who scampers over the fact that the new king and queen descended in different branches from Catherine Swynford, the third wife of John of Gaunt. Shakespeare also glides purposefully over the fact that special permission had to be obtained from the pope to legalize the union. Their son made a disastrous personal conundrum for himself by his marriage of his brother's widow Catherine – still a virgin at the time of her Levirate marriage. And he followed this with a second symbolic incest by his affair with Mary Boleyn whose sister Queen Anne was later charged with sleeping with their brother, Lord Rochford. By his third marriage Henry was breaching the affinity principle and so required Archbishop Cranmer to supply the dispensation. Then of course Henry's approach to Jane Seymour was actually made through her brother Sir Edward, who acted as co-participant in the wooing. After her death he considered but rejected a marriage to Mary of Guise, already betrothed to James V of Scotland, Henry's nephew. The royal psycho-sexual problems were chaotic but the chief of them seems to have been that he wanted to marry a woman who was simultaneously sexually experienced yet withal chaste. When he was dead it was safer for Elizabeth to test the role for herself as it were, becoming nubile and skittish with an attractive adult man, but determined to remain chaste.

When Henry VIII died in 1547 Elizabeth was under the general care of her fourth stepmother, the esteemed Catherine Parr, who remarried with an almost indecent alacrity even at a time when such things were less remarked. Her new husband was Lord Thomas Seymour, who had previously given regard to the idea of wooing Princess Mary. This had led to a serious rift with his own brother, Edward, Earl of Hertford, soon to be elevated to the Dukedom of Somerset, which marked his political ascendancy early in the reign of Edward VI. If the new Lord Admiral Thomas Seymour had expected that his new wife Catherine, with a household that was a centre of reformist thinking, would have a say in government, the will of Henry must have produced a prior pang of disappointment. It specifically excluded her and Princess Mary from any participation in the government of the young king which was dominated by Somerset. Baron Thomas Seymour of Sudeley was aflame with the desire for power and position and willing to take sundry risks for self-gratification. As the younger uncle of the king his attitude to his privileged older brother was soon tainted by a nagging jealousy, while his coup in snatching up the widowed queen was further enhanced as it seemed by free access to the young Princess Elizabeth, her future as yet unformed. Stepfather and uncle, a surprisingly flimsy double shackle on a man who knew an erotic challenge when he saw one in this slender, bookish girl. With his new wife swiftly made pregnant Seymour looked about for a surrogate and the nearest and freshest was undoubtedly Elizabeth. His approach was distinctly unsubtle; he took to entering her bedchamber early in the morning and tickling her in bed, an eroticized substitute for penetrative sex, an attempt to subordinate her to his will. Whatever stirred in her body and emotions at this sly activity, Elizabeth was not completely naive about Seymour's intentions and she took to dressing early for the sake of propriety. Yet however innocent she took herself to be, when her stepmother discovered Seymour's libidinous behaviour, it was Princess Elizabeth who had to quit the household. Catherine Parr did not live long after Elizabeth's departure in July 1548; she died after childbirth and the incorrigible Seymour took up the idea of marrying Elizabeth after

Catherine Parr, briefly Queen of England until the death of Henry VIII, remarried with almost indecent haste the ragingly ambitious Thomas Seymour.

the preliminary 'rough wooing'. The lines of incest are strikingly evident even now and must have been so to her since she had a particular interest in the topic. The evidence for this is literary, a translation from French of a text by Queen Marguerite of Navarre – *Le Miroir de l'âme pécheresse* (*The Mirror/Glass of the Sinful Soul*) – a book written by an author 'known for her spiritual libertinism and love for her brother' (who was François I), and a text also given as seems likely to Anne Boleyn. There was even a link between Henry VIII and Marguerite (appraised as a possible wife) in that the king had sought to arrange a marriage for dynastic reasons between Elizabeth and the Duke of Angoulême, Marguerite's nephew.

In her New Year's letter to her stepmother to accompany the translation (1544), Elizabeth declared that the text showed how 'a woman for whom it was once sin to be related to a being as both his daughter and wife can become affined guiltlessly to another Being' in most female relationships.[9] In physical incest two blood related individuals behave as if untrammelled by this link, and Elizabeth's effort in the face of what society regards as an affront is to rehearse the way to progress beyond forbidden limits. It is a mode that in part derives from the French tradition of elevating kinship by alliance above blood kinship 'and which looks to universalist standards of kinship'. These define sexual intercourse between men and women as equally chaste, unchaste or incestuous. Ultimately it supposes the fusion of the libertine whore with the virginal mother, and this resembles strikingly how Elizabeth would appear across the religious divide in the nation for praise or blame. In another of her purposeful translations she would have come across the charitable view that all men are the children of God. How consoling to her would this compassionate view have been?* It is true that such a universalist view would swamp the allegation that she was illegitimate, but kinship on such a basis had woven into it a discordant thread. If kinship by blood has no profound meaning then the Tudor claim to the throne was no more compelling than any other. The paradox is that by replacing blood relationships as the standard for kinship so the idea of family and nation is tilted and amended.

The formative years for Princess Elizabeth chimed with incest as the pivotal aspect of the torrid politics of the day. The aversion that it aroused then was frequently cloaked by riddling, as in the ancient case of the Theban Sphinx whose riddle Oedipus must live but cannot pre-emptively solve. Elizabeth's translation of *The Mirror/Glass* makes it a kinship riddle, with herself cast as 'so naughty a sister that better it is for me to hide such a name'. The evidence is that the topic much absorbed her and its immediacy erupted into scandal as very soon her uncle/father was accused of 'handling' her. Such an accusation, with its lewd overtones, was very serious indeed. In 1549 the

---

* It was taken from *The Consolation of Philosophy* by Boethius.

Baron Seymour of Sudeley, Lord Admiral of England, wooed and married Catherine Parr before trying to seduce the thirteen-year-old Princess Elizabeth, his stepdaughter and stepniece.

protectorate of the Duke of Somerset faced a series of crises from which there was no recovery, and the rancour felt between him and his turbulent younger brother, now the Lord Admiral, made matters worse. The problem with Thomas Seymour was that his ambition was soaring out of control and it would require a violent reversal to halt this. One apparently frail presence in this turbulent affair was Elizabeth, whose behaviour came under scrutiny while those most intimately about her were subjected to examination by Sir Robert Tyrwhitt. Elizabeth herself wrote a shrill denial to the Protector when a rumour burst that she was pregnant by Thomas Seymour: 'My Lord, these are shameful slanders.' Kate Astley and Thomas Parry, cofferer to the princess, were both dismissed from her household for encouraging, a misdemeanour that got them a period of imprisonment in the Tower. It was Tyrwhitt who tried to obtain Blanche Parry's assistance in unearthing the facts in this delicate matter and to assist his efforts he even forged a letter purporting to come from a friend of Elizabeth. On showing it to her he hoped for some spontaneous outpouring (or confession), but his ruse failed and all he got was the manufacture of tears by an artful juvenile. Elizabeth understood the drift of matters; Seymour was brought to trial, judged by his peers and executed on 20 March 1549 on the order of his own brother. It was a judicial fratricide tending to reinforce the acutely wretched notion harboured by Elizabeth that a sexual transgression might hurl the transgressor to a violent end. An accusation did not have to be true to promote terror.

The dire physical decline of Edward VI led to his early death in July 1553. His legal successor was the Catholic Princess Mary whom the Dudley faction tried to exclude from the throne. The Duke of Northumberland (John Dudley) gave lukewarm support instead to Lady Jane Grey, married to the duke's son, Lord Guildford Dudley. Despite the tougher efforts of Lord Robert Dudley, who ended up in the Tower like his father and brothers, Mary rallied much of the nation to her since Northumberland's actions were nakedly self-serving. The half-Spanish virgin won the day, she became queen, and until she found a husband virile enough to get her with child, Elizabeth was her immediate Protestant heir. The new queen chose rather dismally a son of the Emperor Charles V, Prince Philip, a groom whose antecedents led to the rising of Sir Thomas Wyatt. Suspected of complicity in Wyatt's rebellion, Elizabeth was likewise incarcerated with a few of her favourite gentlewomen, amongst whom was probably Blanche Parry. When these troubled days had passed they were allowed to return to the old, red brick mansion of Hatfield (Herts.) after a brief sojourn at Woodstock. Philip's actual arrival for the marriage at Winchester stimulated interest and also hostility, and after the ceremony the court was variously at Greenwich, Richmond and Whitehall. Still the general atmosphere surrounding the newly weds was so strained that they took up residence at Hampton Court. This retreat along the Thames took the couple away from public scrutiny at a critical time. Unfortunately for the husband and wife of this dynastic union little could be discovered or done to enliven their time together.

Sexually they faltered; Philip was not enticed by the ageing queen and in fact he seems to have recoiled from her physically. In a few months he made a diplomatic excuse to quit the country that hated him. He would remarry for a third and then a fourth time, finally to his own niece, Anne of Austria. When he died some forty years later he did have an heir, but the key question after his departure was whether he had left one in England. After their departure Mary again prepared for childbirth, but it was a passionate wish that fathered this phantom baby. It seems that many of her ladies, more knowing in these matters than she, encouraged her in her delusional state long after the correct time for delivery, hoping for nursery posts. Mary was in fact only swollen with mortality; she died early in 1558, leaving the throne to Elizabeth. Her reproductive system was never tested and her course from now on was to consider marriage, beginning with the notorious platonic infatuation with Lord Robert Dudley.

The most gifted and handsome of the surviving Dudley sons, Robert, was soon made Master of the Horse, a ceremonial post that suited this expert horseman. He and Elizabeth had known each other for years, and she rewarded herself for having survived too by commanding his company. Despite his wife, Amy, living in the Oxfordshire countryside, Dudley did not stubbornly resist the queen since her tender regard for him offered the prospect of being able to rebuild the family fortune. Dudley swiftly became an ornament of the court, witty and bold, with a saving deference in his dealings with the queen. Although not an intellectual he had been broadly educated in the arts and sciences. Above all, for a young queen beset with problems of order and organization, he was polished in his manners and accomplishments. He was able to divert her in conversation and dancing, the most popular group entertainments for Elizabethan women. Dancing was thought to produce the desirable quality of grace in young ladies and thus enhance their marriage qualities. But in the view of some of the pamphleteers all forms of dancing, whether at court or in the country, were likely to disgrace the participants, 'serving as the bellows to inflame lust?' Galliards, brawls, caper, courants, canaries and lavoltas involved much energy and some risk. Philip Stubbes noted that some less accomplished dancers broke legs, and in the famous painting at Penshurst Place, the central male dancer (often identified as Lord Robert Dudley) is on tiptoe as he hoists the central female dancer high off the carpet (she is usually called Elizabeth).

Some of their countrymen (and women) may even then have felt some real unease that the queen danced so frequently, and with a married man whom society thought impudent and opportunistic. Dudley already had enemies as well as friends, and for the queen to single out such a man gave an inkling that marriage for her was not a priority. Had this been generally better understood, had the powerful men about Elizabeth not miscalculated, then there might have been a succession crisis early in the reign. In February 1559 she was petitioned by her first Parliament to marry, though in public and private pronouncements she made known her aversion to doing so.

Evidently the patriarchal expectation was that she would quickly jettison immature hesitations for the greater good. But Elizabeth was not a child, she had no parental pressures in the matter, and the last marriage within her immediate family had foundered. In her response to Parliament she endeavoured to set out her thinking on the matter, touching as it did the private and public, shifting the matter to divine guidance rather than temporal need, and declaring that it was sufficient for her to have lived and died a virgin. She had been untutored in that general expectation of marriage which swamped all girls, as stepmothers came and went. The most permanent woman in her life was undoubtedly Blanche Parry, who when she died in 1589 was buried with the honours of a baroness, while the words on her tomb described her as 'a maid in court, and never no man's wife'. Whether she had ever discussed at length the affirming aspects of being a spinster, her example and influence chimed well with Elizabeth's buried feelings. In theory the queen was long available for marriage and even motherhood; there were European princes sliding between indifference and eagerness ready to negotiate, and there was Lord Robert Dudley, free to marry when his wife died young.[11] Yet over many years as it happened these marriage negotiations became a public form of dynastic foreplay, executed as much for the satisfaction of her male councillors as anybody. Availability was certainly politic, but Elizabeth's secret was no particular secret at all – she would never give herself to one man unless he was beloved of all.

CHAPTER THREE

LOVE BITES

While Elizabeth considered her state – and she declared several times that she was only tolerating the idea of marriage to please her subjects – it was essential for subjects close to her to exercise great caution before being wed. She maintained a high interest and sturdy legal leverage over kinship marriages. Wardships and lineal proximity to her quite often did collide with the boisterous erotic urges of young men and women, those around the court being often close to amatory insurrection, and showing little more decorum then their lower class contemporaries. Between 1553 and 1603 it has been estimated that some four hundred women were at court; each was the personal choice of the queen, and all were drawn from social groupings traditionally active in politics.[1] Whenever any infatuation/love match sprang up at court or beyond, those involved had always to reckon with Elizabeth's unconstrained personal feelings and sometimes her acute displeasure. For them to elevate, as it seemed to her, personal gratification above duty was a shameless failing.

From the time of Henry VIII a law had established that it was a penal offence to marry any woman standing in the first degree of relationship to Crown, without first notifying the sovereign. The rigour with which the younger sisters of the executed Lady Jane Grey were treated after their clandestine marriages, showed early in her reign Elizabeth's intentional severity with such errant behaviour. Their defiance proved to be bruising because the royal rebuke was so unexpected. After all, the mother of the Grey sisters, the niece of Henry VIII, Frances Brandon, Duchess of Suffolk (d. 1559) had defied society to marry her secretary and Master of Horse, Adrian Stokes – her junior by sixteen years. Born in 1538, Lady Catherine Grey had been betrothed at fifteen to Henry Herbert, later 2nd Earl of Pembroke. A political marriage set in motion by the Duke of Northumberland, it had never been consummated and the couple likely divorced early in 1554 when Mary came to the throne. It was while living at court some six years later that Catherine Grey married Edward Seymour, Earl of Hertford; and his mother too (being the widow of the late Protector Somerset) had remarried without regard to her social position, selecting her steward, Francis Newdigate. Now, to jangle Elizabeth's nerves even more, two possible claimants to the throne were defiantly united in a ceremony conducted by a Catholic priest at Hertford House, Canon Row. No one knew this until August of the following year when her pregnancy could not be obscured and Catherine confided in Lord Robert Dudley. Not successfully as it turned out, for she and her husband, when he returned from France, fetched up in the Tower. While in custody they were questioned about every aspect of

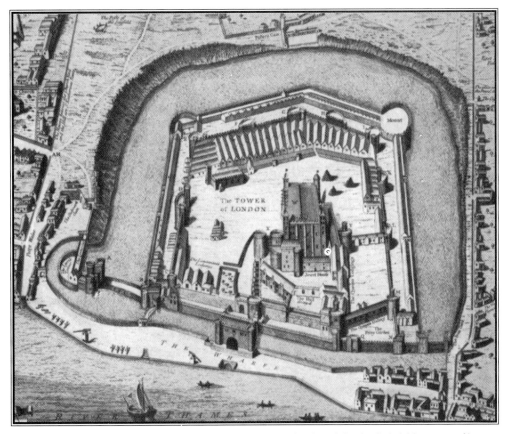

The Tower was the oldest, most secure building in Elizabethan London, but while Elizabeth did keep some of her clothes there in the Wardrobe, she could only rarely bring herself to revisit it after her two months in the Bell Tower in her half-sister Mary's reign.

their marriage, yet they claimed repeatedly to have forgotten the date. Examined by a commission headed by Archbishop Parker in February 1562, Lady Catherine declared that they had waited for Elizabeth to quit the capital for Eltham Palace.

There was a further wait of an hour or so for the hubbub to subside, before two ladies walked to Canon Row – Catherine was accompanied by Lady Jane Seymour, soon to be her sister-in-law. When a clutch of Hertford's servants were questioned none of them could remember the exact date of the wedding either; John Fortescue simply said it was 'in November'. Of course, the priest for the clandestine ceremony was not to be traced and Lady Jane died early in 1561, so it is only by consulting the account of the Cofferer of the Household that the marriage date has been settled for 27 November.[2] Given its particularities it is not surprising to find it declared invalid so that the baby boy, Edward Seymour, born in September 1561, became illegitimate, and his father was fined £15,000 in Star Chamber for 'seducing a virgin of the blood royal'. Even so, the wrath of the queen did not yet keep them apart, nor did it teach them discretion. Despite the staggering fine (almost certainly never paid in full), Hertford found means to bribe jailers within the Tower to allow him procreative time with his wife. In February 1563 Thomas Seymour, their second boy, was born to scandalize the queen who chose to construe it as some sort of dynastic plot. Typically the greatest opprobrium was heaped on the mother who remained in prison – albeit not too uncomfortable, her bed had damask, the walls tapestries and she was allowed toy dogs and monkeys. There were even occasional country excursions to avoid the plague, but then these were curtailed when Elizabeth heard a whisper of a conspiracy to legitimize the marriage. It seemed to confirm her corrective ill-treatment of the Seymours, leaving the boys as bastards, while their mother was reduced to periodic excursions to the lieutenant of the Tower's house at Cockfield Hall. When Lady Catherine died in 1568 a much relieved Elizabeth paraded her phoney sorrow by paying £74 for a superior funeral at Salisbury Cathedral. Hertford was at length allowed out of the Tower to reappear at court and 'sink his roots in Wiltshire'. Meanwhile, his boys seem to have spent some time in the formal, protective household of Burghley, being only a little older than his second son, Robert Cecil.[3]

In 1582 Hertford married one of the famous Howard sisters. Frances Howard and Douglass Howard (later Lady Sheffield) had vied for the roving sexual attentions of the Earl of Leicester during the 1570s, as his courtship game with Elizabeth reached its zenith with the Kenilworth Festivities. Douglass won and lost since her union with him was never proven and the son born (also Robert Dudley) was never legitimized despite lengthy legal submissions. The union of Frances with Hertford was also secret and remained so for a decade, Lady Hertford continuing to serve as a gentlewoman of the Privy Chamber. Fretting about his sons, Hertford in 1595 unwisely sought to have his current marriage set aside so as to clear their claim to the throne. For this gratuitous insult to his wife and his queen he was again arrested. Frances died in 1598 and after a brief period Hertford sought to marry Lady Anne Herbert, daughter of the Earl of Pembroke. Early in 1600 a settlement satisfactory to both sides was indeed negotiated, but the bride-to-be herself was not persuaded and despite Hertford's final and costly endeavours the agreement was sundered. To console himself, within two months he was just as ardently wooing Mrs Prannell, widow of the wealthy vintner Henry Prannell, who was missing declared dead.

Remarkably (some would say eerily) Mrs Prannell had been born Frances Howard, the daughter of Thomas, Viscount Howard of Bindon, and his third wife Mabel Burton. Both parents were soon dead and little Frances was orphaned before her fourth birthday. At least part of her childhood was spent as a ward of her cousin Lord Howard of Walden (later Earl of Suffolk), who helped to confuse historians by naming a daughter Frances, after he had married off the thirteen-year-old to Prannell. This spoilt Burghley's plans to arrange a match under the queen's authority for one of her kinswomen. Remarkably, Prannell was

Marriage by Lady Catherine Grey might affect the English succession, so her secret marriage to Edward Seymour, Earl of Hertford, enraged Elizabeth. The child seen here is Edward, born in the Tower.

Frances Howard; well connected through the huge Howard clan, she married first a rich vintner, then a richer earl and finally a duke.

not punished directly (possibly because he supplied wines to the royal cellar), and he was absent when she became smitten with the Earl of Southampton – a matter of the heart that led her to consult the London astrologer and medicine man, Simon Forman. She hoped for a tender reciprocation, but Southampton was much too preoccupied by his affair with Elizabeth Vernon, and so eventually Mrs Prannell looked about for another superior marriage. By November 1600 she had narrowed the candidates to two – Sir William Evers and Hertford; even though the latter was over sixty years and very small he was consolingly rich. In May 1601 after many consultations with Forman she married Hertford in his Canon Row house, in secret, so as to trump Elizabeth again.[4]

Given the luckless experience of her sister Lady Catherine Seymour (née Grey), it was probably generally expected that Lady Mary Grey well understood the cost of defiance. Yet remarkably she too went through with a clandestine marriage ceremony to burly Thomas Keys, the giant serjeant porter at court. Subjected to the same sort of examination as her sister about the event, she proved slightly less vague, recalling that it had coincided with the public marriage of Henry Knollys to Margaret Cave. The groom was the eldest son of Sir Francis Knollys and Catherine (née Carey), whose own father William Carey had married Mary Boleyn. To affirm her benign approval of this marriage Elizabeth arrived at Durham Place on the evening of 16 July 1565, for supper, dancing, a tourney and two masques. Meanwhile, Lady Mary married Keys at about 9 p.m. by candlelight in his chamber at the palace of Westminster, a ceremony carried out by the inevitable unknown priest – 'old, fat and of low stature'. The bride was at this time a maid of honour (see Chapter Four) with a claim to the succession, and Elizabeth soon became aware of it. As it coincided with the impetuous marriage of Mary Stewart, Queen of Scots, to Henry Stewart, Lord Darnley, it is not surprising that this double snub served to infuriate Elizabeth. Keys was sent to the Fleet prison, having forfeited the trust placed in his absolute loyalty. For three years he rued his marriage and hoped for reinstatement. Although his offer of service in Ireland (a measure of his desperation) was ignored, eventually he was freed to live alone in Lewisham, south-east of central London, and there he died in 1571. His wife, meanwhile, lived at Chequers in Buckinghamshire under the custody of William Hawtrey, before permission was granted to move to Greenwich. 'Mary Keys', as she continued to sign herself, died in 1578 and was buried in St Botolph-without-Aldergate. In her will she bequeathed a small covered gilt bowl to Blanche Parry.

Lawyers have been infamous over many generations for their subtle ability to contort language. Elizabeth was also adept at this, relying on metaphor 'to avoid the necessity of irrevocable action'. With a teasing flourish she justified her single life by claiming the kingdom as her spouse, so 'every one of you, and as many as are English, are my children, and kinsfolk'.[5] Compensating for the emptiness of her womb her mouth was pregnant with dutiful phrases, claims that either Mary, Queen of Scots, or Lady Catherine Grey was needfully her 'child'. The Spanish ambassador recorded that Elizabeth had talked about formally adopting Catherine Grey. Mary's representative in London, the Bishop of Ross, John Leslie, made use of the phrase 'children of the crown'. In the House of Commons, the Speaker, John Puckering, would use the same language, a residue as it seems of his time at Lincoln's Inn. Two masques for the Inn, written by Thomas Pound, establish the tone adopted. The queen missed the first, a fictional embassy of the Gods to the wedding of Henry Wriothesley, 2nd Earl of Southampton, to Mary Brown, probably because both were avowed Catholics. A decade or so later Southampton was accusing his wife of adultery with a servant, and early in 1580 he had her locked away for it. However, Elizabeth was present at the second masque given at the wedding of Frances Radcliffe, a sister of the Earl of Sussex, and Thomas Mildmay, when the goddess Juno chides Pound for being a bachelor and he in turn presents her frank advice to Elizabeth.[6]

George Gascoigne, soldier and poet, who sought and received some patronage from the Earl of Leicester, thought a prologue necessary to such works to alert the audience to covert meanings. The queen, as Marie Axton has pointed out, had only herself to blame if misliking 'what was shadowed in the mirror' she indulged even so metaphorical equivocation in high places. Not everyone at court did actually catch the drift.

Gascoigne's translated production *Jocasta** was a tragedy that Elizabeth's maids of honour had in a manuscript prepared especially for them. In the two printed editions of Gascoigne's works (1575 and 1587) uncommon words were glossed at the request of a gentlewoman who evidently faltered when she came across unfamiliar terms or references such as that to the Gorgon Medusa. The literature of the Inns of Court was freighted with contemporary political and social commentary, sometimes obvious and at other times veiled. Another example is the tragic poem *Romeus & Juliet* by Arthur Broke of the Inner Temple, a translation printed in November 1562 at a time when many were agog at the offence of Lady Catherine Grey and Hertford. The preface to Broke's poem, which was handy for Shakespeare, also alludes to a recent stage version of their story. Or there was the play *Horestes* (usually ascribed to John Puckering), which concealed reflections on the issues surrounding the murder of Lord Darnley, King of Scotland, who managed to father a son, James, in June 1566, before his abrupt murder at the hands of his wife, Mary, and her lover, the Earl of Bothwell. For ill-judged marriages of the period few could rival that of Mary to Bothwell, leading as it did to civil strife renewed in Scotland, the failure of Marian resistance and her profitless flight into England in 1568.

When this royal maverick was in the custody of George Talbot, Earl of Shrewsbury, he had just married as his second wife Elizabeth Stanley (Bess) of Hardwick. He was her fourth husband and by his predecessors she had accumulated a great fortune, so her attitude to marriage was practical and steeped in attitudes of accumulation and advancement. The marriage of heiresses meant an intense scrutiny of possibilities and much effort by families. To the Crown, troubled by the endless task of rewarding services, a profitable marriage could be a wonderful inducement. An interruption to royal projects, even the least tangible, could send Elizabeth spinning into a rage. Prison beckoned when she was out-manoeuvred and Bess of Hardwick contrived this by marrying Elizabeth Cavendish, her daughter, to the demonstrably frail Charles Stewart, Earl of Lennox. He was 'inclined to love with a few days acquaintance', and seems to have summoned all his energy to fathering a child, born just before he died. The solace for Elizabeth was that her namesake produced a daughter, albeit one with succession rights in England and Scotland – Lady Arabella Stewart (b. 1575), daughter of the uncle of the King of Scotland and the great-granddaughter of Margaret Tudor, sister of Henry VIII. She was doubly unfortunate in having two overbearing women control her from childhood to early middle age. To escape from this oppression, in her late twenties all Arabella could imagine was marriage and of course this was one of the most fraught of options.

Sir Walter Ralegh had certainly found this to be true in the early 1590s. In March 1592 there was a scandal connecting him to the maid of honour Elizabeth Throckmorton who was at least twenty-five years old; he was forty and frantically busy

---

* BL Add. Ms. 34063.

Lady Arabella Stuart, dogged by her royal parentage and good claim to the English throne, lived a constrained and very frustrating life.

Elizabeth (Bess) Throckmorton, ardent, sweet-tempered wife of Sir Walter Ralegh, who like her husband felt royal ire when they married: a period of reflection in the Tower was meted out to them.

with preparations for an expedition against Spanish shipping in which he risked all his financial resources. The fleet had barely sailed before the queen commanded him home, anxious for his safety and perhaps subtly prompted by her maid. His unexpected return led to their marriage, with Ralegh going about his normal business until the end of June. To keep such a marriage secret for very long was possible but not easy, especially when the queen was surrounded at court by people with bonds of kinship and friendship to the Earl of Essex who abominated the humbly born royal favourite. Marriage was what incensed her, although when Elizabeth was actually alerted is not clear and neither is the date when Ralegh fetched up in the Tower; presumably early rather than late July, when Sir Edward Stafford wrote to Anthony Bacon that Sir Walter and his wife would both be available at the Tower the following day – 31 July. Sir Walter remained there until mid-September, being released under the care of a Mr Blount (Sir Charles Blount?) to bring order to chaos in the disposal of the prize goods from the staggering haul of the captured *Madre de Deus* carrack. Ralegh's imprisonment officially ended in December and he retired from court to his Dorset home, Sherborne, to live with his wife for whom he sacrificed worldly preferment. Shortly after they had established their country residence Elizabeth Ralegh became pregnant and Walter jnr was born (presumably late in October 1593), being baptized at Lillington on 1 November.

CHAPTER FOUR

THE HONOUR OF
THE MAIDS

Queen Elizabeth held court over a bustling royal household of some seventeen hundred people. Of these, one thousand were 'below stairs'; five or six hundred had access to the public rooms 'above stairs'; and perhaps eighty to one hundred of the nobility, privy councillors and intimate servants routinely entered the privy apartments of the queen. Like a family ruled by a matriarch of uncertain temper there were frictions, exacerbated by the high Elizabethan temperament which was far from phlegmatic. Life at court was not always a pleasurable pageant, and many felt it choking their vitality. It was 'politically fluid and culturally polycentric'. One unblinking reporter wrote :'It is a world to be here, to see the humours of the time. Blessed are they that can be away and live contented.' Impossible, other then intermittently, for the most senior of the men and sometimes their wives too. The more senior ladies might be appointed to the Bedchamber – there were usually three or four of them. Of the gentlewomen or maids of the Privy Chamber there were usually a dozen and all went before the Lord Chamberlain to take an oath of service and loyalty.[1] This was not required of the young maids of honour, generally daughters of the aristocracy or gentry. Those about Queen Mary had all had a reputation for personal virtue, but those about Elizabeth over the years sometimes skipped and tumbled into disgrace. Even so, no mother of the maids was ever sacked.[2] At the beginning of the reign Katherine Astley (née Champernowne) supervised the six maids. Undoubtedly her death in 1565 was a blow to Elizabeth, who then appointed the Shropshire-born Mistress Eglionby, probably a protégée of the Earl of Shrewsbury. Her duty was to oversee the actions of Mary Radcliffe, a daughter of the Earl of Sussex; Mary Howard, daughter of the queen's great-uncle, Lord Howard of Effingham; Catherine Knyvett, placed by the Duke of Norfolk, as well as Anne Windsor, a protégée of Leicester, and Dorothy Brooke, from the Lord Warden's family.[3]

The maids of honour were required to be all-purpose companions to Elizabeth, cosseting her, sweetening her moods by bright conversation, singing popular ballads, playing a musical instrument, spinning silk, dealing hands of cards (knowing she hated to lose), and sewing. It was no disgrace to excel at needlework, one of the few genteel occupations for women of the day that allowed excellence to flourish. Elizabeth and her maids are credited with the needlework for two low, but ornately carved chairs once at Loseley House, near Guildford, the home of Sir William More. The girls were

These elaborately carved low chairs – maids of honour – may have had cushion covers embroidered by Elizabeth and her ladies.

also kept busy daily by the lengthy ceremonials surrounding royal mealtimes. Food in quantities was carried from the lowly kitchens, and though hot when prepared was likely cold when eaten. The dishes were set down on a table in the Withdrawing Room before being set before the queen at her table in the Privy Chamber. To lay the former table took some thirty minutes, and when done a lady-in-waiting and maid of honour would enter to rub the trenchers with bread and salt. The ceremonial routine went on with the queen's meat carved by the Carver, one of the trusted women of the Privy Chamber, Katherine Carey, later married to Lord William Howard. With the queen and any guests seated, a lady-in-waiting with a tasting knife would give a morsel of the dish he had carried in to each yeoman of the guard who carried dishes to the Privy Chamber for royal choice. On ordinary days Elizabeth ate by herself, though the stately presentation was apparently maintained. Maids were assigned a table in the Great Chamber, and shared between six the table allowance of a lone duchess.

Flushed from their efforts to be dignified under scrutiny and generally to please, the young maids naturally caught the eyes of the men about the court – the great men like Leicester, whose good looks attracted women other than the queen, or the less mighty politically and socially but withal handsome, athletic and improvident Sir John

The sedentary practice of needlework was then regarded as a thoroughly good diversion for women of all classes; it was useful in that something was made and it was likely to abate all manner of female discontents.

Pakington – 'Lusty Pakington' as the queen cheerfully called him. If a young man about the court, while actively scattering the family hoard, came across a maid of honour with whom he became infatuated and she responded ardently, then he was confronted by a very intricate problem, of risk – what could be called an Elizabethan love-knot. If he declared himself to a patron like Leicester he could not guarantee the latter's mode of presentation to the queen would actually advance his interest. Leicester might have an entirely different view on the matter, and very likely so would the difficult female supremacist who held the reins of power. If she bridled against the proposed match then he could not claim ignorance of the royal will. But if he presumed on her indulgence by failing to seek her permission then he might not see the sky or the seasons change for years to come. Or if the maid herself, so taken with him, sought permission and was refused, like Mary Arundell, what then to do? One

Royal kitchens were actually so remote from the royal table that it is doubtful if Elizabeth ever had a truly hot dish set before her.

possibility was to wed under parental guidance but without the queen's nod of approval. It was still risky, but not as openly defiant as elopement. That was the resolution adopted by Lady Bridget Manners, who, in 1589, aged about sixteen years, became a maid. In August 1594 she was married at Belvoir, the home of her mother the dowager Countess of Rutland, who over many years made trouble for Lord Burghley. Many of the Manners family knew that the marriage of Bridget to Robert Tyrwhitt was imminent and it was suggested that she should feign having measles in order to separate herself from her duties. A month's absence when Elizabeth was no longer sighting her daily would create a space for supplication. But the ruse collapsed and its failure may be that of her mother, who died early in 1595. By then the couple had been separated by royal order, but her brother Roger, Earl of Rutland, was still willing to pay £1,300 of the £2,500 marriage portion.[4] Robert Tyrwhitt spent some time in prison and his new wife was sent to lodge with Lady Bedford.

By suppressing their feelings and holding back on marriage, increasingly an aspect of personal autonomy, the maids could look forward to observing the direction of the nation. They brushed up against the great men and when Elizabeth went on her summer progress they saw something of their country. Despite her prickly disinclinations to accept change the queen knew that most of these girls wanted to marry; probably the key to the problem was age. As Elizabeth aged, hating to advance beyond her prime which she seems to have set arbitrarily at thirty-five, the maids seemed to reverse time without any benefit to her. They were ever younger and fresher, and rhetorical flourishes from supplicants had no ability to smooth wrinkles, reduce liver spots or bring the gold of youth back to her naturally greying hair. Every aspect of ageing exasperated her, indeed made her a termagant, so a maid like pretty, saucy Mary Shelton, felt her hand – 'blows and evil words'. And on rare occasions worse might happen. Luce Morgan, close to Elizabeth in the late 1570s and early 1580s was suddenly ejected from the court, leaving us to speculate whether the cause might have been an accusation of theft. Luce Morgan became Lucy Negro in London's demimonde, a bawd in a brothel in St John's Street, Clerkenwell. In 1600 she bumped into Bridewell to beat hemp, the usual corrective for immorality.

On another occasion Elizabeth ordered two maids to quit the Coffer Chamber where they lived, and they had to take refuge with Lady Dorothy Stafford, long an intimate of the queen. Even so, these rumpuses did not usually persist, and an incident at court was rarely enough to smother youthful high spirits within the little sorority. When Sir William Knollys was Treasurer of the Household he had a court lodging located next to a room where 'some of the ladies and maids of honour used to frisk and hey about' so keeping him awake to all hours despite his admonitions. One night, exasperated beyond all acceptance he discarded his night attire and wearing only his spectacles marched in next door carrying a copy of a text by Aretino. The Italian writer had a reputation as a pornographer and Knollys paraded about, possibly reading aloud some of the filthier passages marked up for the occasion. We do not know how such an hour effected the maids, but frustrated Knollys, as we shall see, presented a lively libido into old age.

The modesty of the maids, their virginity, as they attended the queen, had a fairly obvious consequence. The heterosexually active men of the court saw them as quarry, rare specimens to be courted, bedded and even wedded, Elizabeth Throckmorton was swept off her feet by Ralegh, whose disregard of the rules cost him dear. The energy and passion of court dancers was a vertical representation and substitution for sexual activity. The hand used to hoist a female partner in a leap on the dance floor might become investigative; neither the court nor society at large was 'organised towards a rigorous control of social relations between the sexes'. The queen was actually fighting a losing battle, probable divined this and became angry with her own failure to persuade and coerce when she was 'in loco parentis'. But even intimidating parents might fail and it is by no means certain that all the maids were indeed virgins when they arrived at court. Suspicion hangs over Anne Vavasour, herself illegitimate, an equine-faced young lady of the broad Howard clan. In 1580, aged fifteen, she came to court under the tutelage of her Knyvett relatives, especially her aunt, the widow of

Lord Henry Paget (d. 1568). During that summer Anne was wooed by the Earl of Oxford, and Ralegh gallantly observed and advised in an elegant little poem ascribed to him, 'Many desire, but few or none deserve'. Perhaps he considered himself the first of the few. In that he was outflanked by Oxford, and by late summer she was pregnant.

The earl was a singular representative of the old nobility; lofty and quick to take offence as well as fickle in his domestic and public life. His marriage to Burghley's daughter, Anne Cecil, he regarded as a fix and suitable for disdain, so he may well have thought of fleeing abroad with Anne for a bigamous marriage. With his political and private relationship with Burghley so soured Oxford turned to Leicester, who at this time was straining to wreck the marriage negotiations of Elizabeth and the Catholic Duke of Anjou. Oxford's former associates were arrested and so briefly was he, but in March 1581 when he became a father he was out of gaol. Anne failed to find discreet premises for her labour and gave birth to a son 'in the maidens' chamber'. Directly the babe was delivered she was sent to the Tower, and she was followed by Oxford, whom rumour had preparing to flee abroad after settling property on his son and £2,000 on Anne. Released on 8 June, he was still confined to his house a year later, and for two years was excluded from the court despite his holding the great office of hereditary Lord Great Chamberlain. He had also to face the wrath of the Knyvetts, and the matter of tit-for-tat bloodshed came close to being a vendetta. Even as late as 1585 Burghley filed among his papers a written challenge to a duel from Thomas Vavasour, Anne's brother, to Oxford. The former was going to fight in Leicester's motley army campaigning for the Dutch against the Spanish. Another ally of Leicester was Sir Henry Lee, whose mistress Anne Vavasour became by pushing aside his wife – also Anne (née Paget). By the time she died in 1590 Anne Vavasour was herself married to a Mr John Finch, who in 1605 received an annuity of £20 from Lee himself.

Given the rapid decay in the circumstances of Anne Vavasour, her sister, Frances, might have been more sharply tutored by her family in respect of dealings with men, especially ardent men. Clearly there was a headstrong streak in the Yorkshire Vavasours, because in November 1590, Sir John Stanhope, the vice-chamberlain, remarked in a letter that 'Our new maid Mistress Vavasour, flourisheth like the lily and the rose', almost certainly a sexual simile. Also flourishing at court at this time was the illegitimate son of Leicester (d. 1588) from his liaison with Lady Douglass Sheffield (but now Stafford). Robert Dudley had not only inherited substantially from his father's estate, but he also possessed in great measure the Dudley energy, charm and good looks. Frances Vavasour became his mistress before he married and early in 1591 they made a formal contract to marry, having it seems the grudging consent of Elizabeth, who held that they should wait until Robert was a little older. Frances chose not to comply, as if she already suspected that his declared feelings for her were transient. Instead, later in the year she married Thomas, son of Sir Thomas Shirley, in another secret ceremony. There followed the inevitable banishment from court, and

Anne Vavasour (born c. 1565) was a maid of honour who gave birth to an illegitimate son by the Earl of Oxford, before becoming the mistress of Sir Henry Lee. The lady and her lover were godparents to Henry Gheeraerts, son of the painter Marcus Gheeraerts (II).

Robert Dudley (born 1574), the handsome, illegitimate son of Robert Dudley, Earl of Leicester, and Lady Douglass Sheffield. As whimsical a husband as his own father, the younger Robert deserted his wife and fled abroad with his mistress.

her husband spent months in the Marshalsea prison. Frances may have intuitively understood Dudley, for he paid little heed to her. Instead he wooed another maid, Margaret Cavendish, cousin of the renowned sea captain Thomas Cavendish. The fact that his marriage to her only secured him a temporary exclusion from court suggests that Elizabeth was this time milder because of his likeness to Leicester. The young man was not a favourite but he was favoured, for it felt comforting to have such enthusiasts at court. She allowed him to immerse himself in sea-faring matters for which he had found an extraordinary enthusiasm.[5]

In the Cadiz expedition (1596) under the overall command of Essex, Dudley's gallantry was rewarded with a knighthood, one of a heavy number which led to a certain amount of national derision. That same year he married the daughter of Sir Thomas Leigh, a wealthy merchant and former lord mayor of London, now established in a country residence near Kenilworth. Alice Leigh brought Dudley 'a fair portion' (dowry) and they were married at Kenilworth Castle, which Sir Thomas and other local gentry had been instrumental in securing for the groom when it had been avidly sought by Leicester's widow, Lady Lettice, mother of the Earl of Essex and Lady Penelope Devereux (Rich). By this time Essex was the most audacious and worldly figure at the late Elizabethan court. Not only was his wife Frances (née Walsingham; formerly Sidney) pregnant, but he was having affairs with four maids of honour simultaneously. One of them, Elizabeth Southwell, half-sister to the mariner Sir Robert Southwell, was also pregnant and gave birth to a boy, who was taken into the Essex clan. At about the same time her niece, also Elizabeth, the goddaughter of the queen and Robert Dudley's cousin once removed, arrived at court as yet another adolescent maid. There she was greeted by her erring aunt and namesake, who had already been forgiven. Although sharply devalued on the marriage market at a dangerous age, she was not yet without suitors. One of them was the startlingly unsightly Sir Barrington Mollins who was keen to marry, but a repulsive nasal condition seemed to have wrecked his chances. In March 1598 he consulted Simon Forman to learn if his engagement to the older Elizabeth Southwell would hold. He had obtained a licence for marriage but no bride immediately and in January 1600 she had three competing suitors – which makes it rather hard to figure why then, even with time running out at thirty, she married Mollins.[6] Two years later she gave extra cheer to her husband by giving him an heir.

Sir Clement Heigham, another Forman client, was greatly taken with the younger Elizabeth Southwell (b. 1586), but the maid of honour now to Queen Anne, wife of James I and VI, continued in the wayward tradition of Elizabethan maids by a scandalous elopement. In 1605, just at the time Robert Catesby's anti-government conspiracy, the Gunpowder Plot, was bowling towards its November climax, Sir Robert Dudley, a recent convert to Catholicism, fled abroad with Elizabeth, leaving behind his wife, Alice, and daughters. It was a dash made possible by Elizabeth disguising herself as a male page, borrowing from drama or poetry. There was Lorenzo's flight with Jessica from Shylock's residence in *The Merchant of Venice*, or the travelling lovers in Donne's *Elegy (16)*. Reports of this scornful rebuff to the new dynasty in England soon reached most capitals in Europe. 'The fact', wrote Ottaviano Lotti to Grand Duke Ferdinand of Tuscany, 'has created great scandal.' The runaways meanwhile found a haven in Lyons and despite his bigamy a papal dispensation to marry was conjured up. From there the lovers moved to Florence, a city-state where other Englishmen had served the Medici family, including Sir Thomas Shirley. There Dudley's naval and ship-building expertise won him distinctions and wealth; he built himself a palace and was given a country villa by Duke Ferdinand II as a mark of distinction.

The see-sawing career of one more maid of honour will suffice to illustrate the risks (if nothing else) of sending a daughter to a privileged but exposed position. Mary Fitton (1578–1647) was the daughter of a Cheshire gentleman of old family, Sir Edward Fitton, granted part of the Desmond estates in Ireland for the services there of Sir Edward and his father. Daughter Anne had not been groomed for the honour of being a maid, instead at thirteen she had been married to a boy of sixteen, John Newdigate, whose family home was Arbury in Warwickshire. It is true to say that Sir Edward and his wife Alice (née Halcroft), also parents of two sons, were reluctant to allow Mary to depart for London with its metropolitan debaucheries – traps for the foolish virgin. He tried to protect his daughter form the over-familiar attentions of courtiers, but his choice of Sir William Knollys, the uncle of Lady Penelope Rich, for benign protector of his precious daughter proved to be misguided. Knollys was married to Dorothy Braye, widow of Edmund Brydges, Lord Chandos, but was her junior in years and they remained childless. Now as an old friend of the Fittons and Newdigates he had placed before him for benign attention a seventeen-year-old woman, young enough to be his daughter and sexually desirable too; brown hair; grey eyes, long nose, again a rather equine visage. In this case the horse comparison is rather fitting because Mary Fitton was allowed the privilege of riding one of the queen's horses that came to be called Bay Fitton. No doubt coarse jokes were muttered in certain quarters about how well she could ride. From court Knollys wrote to Sir Edward, to state forcefully, 'I will be as careful of her well doing as if I were her true father'. But this benign intention became warped and Knollys was soon wishing his wife dead; his passion for Mary swamped everything. He wrote to Anne Newdigate of his heart's unease, and when she invited him to be godfather to her unnamed baby Knollys called her Mary and acknowledged his desire for fatherhood. His infatuation was the cause of much court laughter, and the derision was seized upon by Shakespeare for use in *Twelfth Night*. The Comptroller of the Royal Household was puritanically inclined, but the interest he had in Mary was a late expression of desire. No doubt it was John Florio, the great dictionary compiler, who gave Shakespeare 'Malavoglia' (meaning evil concupiscence) which slides into 'Malvoglio' – 'I want Mal/I will have

Mary Fitton, bold and vivacious as a maid of honour, failed in her ardent pursuit of the young William Herbert, later 3rd Earl of Pembroke.

Mal', and so to Malvolio of the yellow cross garters, a mode of dressing that pokes fun at the Comptroller's passion for dressing up. Knollys was also derided as 'Party Beard' since his facial adornment registered three colours: white at the roots; yellow mid-way and black at the ends. This conspicuous vanity had him fixed in song:

> Party beard, party beard . . .
> . . . the white hind was crossed:
> Brave Pembroke struck her down
> And took her from the clown.[7]

We have seen how the maids were much sought after, like pre-war débutantes. They made a delightful substitute in royal courtship merriment which even to the most self-abasing seemed creaky and rather bogus when directed at the queen. But serving a sometimes abusive old woman, who broke a finger of Jane Scudamore to make a point, was not always conducive to a personal sense of well-being. Mal Fitton became ill in 1599 and had to quit the court to recover from a diagnosis of having what the Elizabethans called 'the mother'. This was a disease of women of child-bearing age, not of adolescents. 'Suffocation of the mother' was believed then to be caused by retention of fluids that needed to be vented from the body. It has recently been pointed out that this flexible diagnostic account represented ailments of the mind and body.[8] The first published treatment of it came in 1603 from a Fellow of the College of Physicians, Edward Jordan, who went beyond the classical notion of hysteria as a disease of the uterus. While he accepted amenorrhoea and sexual abstinence as significant causes, he held that 'perturbations of the mind are oftentimes to blame'. Treatments varied, though many doctors assigned their usual remedies for menstrual problems and just about everything else – purging and vomiting.[9] Whatever the causes of Mary's mental and physical ailments, by the time she returned to court she had boldly decided to refuse Knollys, whose woe at her absence had been profound. So, much as he desired her she declined to give herself and thought to find someone else, having been at court on and off for five years.

In recovery Mal had an example to make her all the more steely and purposeful. It was the society wedding of Lady Anne Russell, a maid of honour like her sister, to the son of the Earl of Worcester; an event recorded with sumptuous detail by the painter Robert Peake. The bride's mother had her home in Blackfriars, an exclusive residential district on the Thames of some 5 acres, and the wedding supper was held at Lord Cobham's residence in the same district. After food and wine Mary Fitton had a perfect opportunity to reinstate herself as the cynosure of the court. Led by her the maids performed an allegorical dance of new invention and eye-catching oddity and when they had done they sought substitutes among the watchers. With characteristic boldness Mary advanced to the old queen, who asked whom she represented. Mary replied: 'Affection' – to which the vinegary old monarch replied: 'Affection? [it meant then passionate love]; Affection's false.' Then, as the French ambassador de Boissise noted, 'Elle danse gayement et de belle disposition'.

Watching all this was William Herbert, the son of the Earl and Countess of Pembroke, therefore eligible, his father having already broken off one projected match in 1595. William had been having secret meetings at Wilton with Elizabeth Carey, the only daughter and heir general of George, Lord Hunsdon.[10] With this projected match in ruins Elizabeth hied off to marry immediately Sir Thomas Berkeley, the only surviving son and heir of an improvident father. Over the next fourteen years, before he died at thirty-seven, Thomas Berkeley proved equally profligate. William Herbert's father did negotiate for a marriage between his son and Burghley's granddaughter, Bridget Vere, but this failed because having been offered £3,000 and an annuity to begin at Burghley's death, Pembroke greedily wanted immediate payment of the annuity. Bridget Vere eventually married an aristocrat who became an earl. William Herbert remained unassigned, a civilized young man formerly tutored by the poet Samuel Daniel and after that a student at New College, Oxford. When the career of Essex began to falter there was some talk of Herbert substituting for him but he lacked the internalized imperatives that wrung Essex's nerves. Still, in May 1600, accompanied by Sir Charles Danvers, Herbert did venture down the Thames almost as far as Gravesend to visit Lady Penelope Rich and Lady Southampton.[11] Such an outing was comparatively rare because he was distinctly bookish, preferring to keep to his study with heavy pipe-smoking to keep his so-called 'migraines' at bay. They may have been the head pains which often accompanied syphilitic infections, but whatever – Mary Fitton set her sights on marrying him, despite her lack of crafty family supporters at court.

It was, inevitably, a clandestine romance and one in which standard gender roles were reversed as Mary boldly took control. The young man was twenty, she a couple of years older and willing to risk quitting the court in an unfamiliar guise – without a head-dress, with her skirts tucked up and covered by a capacious cloak. The London home of the Herberts was Baynard's Castle, near Puddle Dock, but given the size of the household and the speedily sexual aspect of their assignations they probably took an inn room nearby. Mal's intention seems to have been to become pregnant as quickly as possible, but this brazenness on her part may have made him obdurate after he had succeeded in doing this. By the end of 1600 when her weight and carriage began to betray her he did nothing further. Early in 1601, following his father's death, William became Earl of Pembroke and he must now have anticipated the distress of his mother and the rage of the queen. She was indeed infuriated and when Pembroke admitted paternity he was sent to the Fleet prison, while Mary for her confinement was placed with Lady Margaret Hawkins, the widow of Sir John Hawkins. In March 1601 a baby boy was born but died immediately, perhaps because Pembroke had given her syphilis

William Herbert, 3rd Earl of Pembroke, felt more at ease with a pipe of tobacco in his study than at court among the factions swirling about the old queen. He married eventually a dwarfish heiress and they remained childless.

too, a very common cause then of stillbirths. He remained phlegmatic while imprisoned, writing verse and refusing to marry his mistress. Naturally he petitioned Sir Robert Cecil, as the queen's right-hand man and Secretary of State. Eventually he was released but being barred from court quite cheerfully took himself off to Wilton. His marriage, when it came, was to Lady Mary Talbot, co-heiress of the vast holdings of the Earl of Shrewsbury. Unlike the stately Mal she was dwarfish and deformed and the marriage remained childless so that some judged Pembroke to have totally misjudged where his advantage lay.

Mary Fitton's bold play for a great marriage was in ruins, but her spirits held and she showed a purposeful resilience. Her father was far more abashed by the business, which he considered to be social ruin. Still, he took his daughter home in some secrecy, while the old Comptroller pined for what he had lost. He tried to woo her at a distance but Mal was adamant, and when in 1605 his wife died he was two months a widower before marrying his new wife of nineteen years. He had a long life, becoming Viscount Wallingford and then Earl of Banbury, so if Mary hankered after a title she miscalculated. Others would have settled for Knollys while covertly taking a younger lover; she could have emerged from her rural retreat as a countess. However, the manly, protective embrace that was offered her by Vice-Admiral Sir Richard Leveson was accepted. When he was seventeen he had married Margaret Howard, daughter of the lord admiral, and as husband and wife they had been plagued by the ungovernable behaviour of Leveson's father, the piratical Sir Walter. He died in prison but not before an accusation that he had tried to kill the couple. After the death of her premature baby, Margaret was stricken by incurable depression and Leveson looked for a lover who understood his situation. When he died prematurely in 1605 he left Mary £100, and his unfortunate wife had to be committed to the care of her own father.

In Leveson's fleet there was a pinnace called *Lion's Whelp*, under the command of Captain William Polwhele from an old Cornish family. The modestly placed mariner replaced his senior officer and Mary gave birth to another son who was evidently his. This personal decision to reject convention completely distressed her widowed mother, whose response to a letter from Anne Newdigate spoke of 'such shame as never had Cheshire woman, worse now than ever. Write no more to me of her.' Nor did a regularizing of Mary's situation reconcile her mother; even after the marriage he remained 'a very knave'. It is to be hoped they were briefly happy for in 1610 Polwhele died leaving Mary with a young son and daughter. Through all her tribulations her sister, Anne, offered affectionate support and on the death of John Newdigate, Mary in turn supported Anne's admirer, Francis Beaumont, for a companionable remarriage. She did it herself, joining up with a Pembrokeshire captain called Lougher. When he died in 1636 she lived on and bequeathed the little Welsh property to her daughter, who married and had children herself before Mal died in 1647 and was buried in Gawsworth.[12]

CHAPTER FIVE

'A PROUD SPIRIT'

Mary Fitton had hitched up her skirt to allow some extra freedom of movement as she raced through London streets to her lover. This behaviour was in itself indecorous and may have shocked Herbert somewhat while stimulating his sexual appetite. Women who seized hold of their own lives and prospects, propelling themselves forward without hesitation did not win universal male approbation. Nicholas Breton thought an unquiet woman 'the misery of man', and in writings of all kinds there is the recurring image of the disorderly woman, one who compels attention from the unwilling male. According to the risky caricature of Breton, 'she looks at no law and thinks of no lord, admits no command and keeps no good order'. This from a man ruled by a woman, who sought the patronage of another, the Countess of Pembroke. Of the latter, Mary Sidney, sister of Philip and mother of William Herbert, John Aubrey was specific in his goatish gossip perhaps because she lived while her brother died young. His scandalous allegations about her 'may well form his response to a reputation that was already soiled by literary activities'.[1] Since an intelligent woman could not be trusted to behave with decorum, according to Aubrey, her father-in-law supposedly feared she would cuckold his son, so she remained at Wilton rather than being free to move in society. But even this quaint speculation is not enough, so Aubrey turns her into a voyeur, not as one might have expected, of her servants, but even more bizarrely of horses. He has her squinting through a peep-hole as the mares in season are covered by the stallions. To satisfy her own lusts Aubrey has her sleeping with her own brother and even the widower Sir Robert Cecil, the hunch-back Secretary of State; freakish, misogynistic stuff bordering on the deranged. Despite these lurid attempts to scribble over a public reputation Aubrey could not erase the fact that it was Sir Philip Sidney's name which provided a protective rampart for those in his family who aspired to write, like his sister, his niece and his daughter. Quite by chance he also empowered Lady Penelope Devereux in an unexpected and personally enriching way for her.

The ripple of repetitions about the maids of honour, the inability of the queen or anyone about her to much alter things, makes the status of maid of honour appear almost robotic. Young, pretty and sexually innocent, they are lodged with the great virgin, and seemingly to protect her they falter and are swept aside into marriages where the power lies with husbands. Occasionally a maid elects for a different route and she is socially ostracized like Mary Fitton. Uniquely, one maid shredded all the rules; she had high birth, beauty and intelligence, along with a controlling wit. She

Mary Sidney Herbert, Countess of Pembroke, holds her own translation of the Psalms of David, *hinting perhaps at Protestant politics as well as personal piety.*

was not Elizabeth (surely *sui generis*) but Penelope Devereux, queen of the little court that gathered about the Earl of Essex, her equally gifted brother. During the 1590s these two became the most fiercely controversial figures at court and beyond. Their father, Walter Devereux, Earl of Essex, was campaigning in Ireland when he died of dysentery aged thirty-six. Having employed him Elizabeth might have been expected to condole his widow, Letitia (Lettice Knollys), whose grandmother Mary Boleyn had been the sister of Queen Anne Boleyn, but Elizabeth was only ever petulant in her dealings with the woman who embodied the unspeakable past. When Lettice married the Earl of Leicester in 1578 it was kept secret for a time because more than any other action it bespoke the beautiful Lettice's indifference to the queen. It suggested too that Elizabeth had been a fool not to marry Leicester herself in the early 1560s. So Lettice had the husband Elizabeth might have dared to have had if her nerve had not failed her; she had four children, all healthy and spirited and with beauty to boot, unspoilt by disease. Elizabeth had her revenges over the years but it was never enough and always pained her.

Second in rank to Essex, earl marshall in Ireland, was Sir Henry Sidney, lord deputy or Viceroy during three terms of service, and although the two men were sceptical of each other there had been talk of Philip Sidney – then heir presumptive of his childless uncles, the Earls of Leicester and Warwick – marrying Penelope Devereux (then aged

Letitia (Lettice) Knollys, Countess of Essex and Leicester, the high-born beauty who wisely chose to absent herself from the court of a close relative who loathed her. The revenge of the countess was not only to raise four healthy children, but also to live to a great old age.

thirteen). One particular problem for both fathers was that service in Ireland had been shockingly expensive as they subsidized the queen. Sir Henry's conduct in regard to the marriages of his children was perfectly consistent with the practical considerations of the time. When Mary Sidney was sixteen she was married to Henry Herbert, Earl of Pembroke, then in his early forties and already twice married. According to a Shakespeare lyric, 'Crabbed age and youth cannot live together'; the coarse-grained Aubrey evidently thought the same. At the time of talk of his marriage to Penelope, Philip Sidney was twenty-two, but nothing happened to advance the matter and after her father's death Penelope's future was marked out not by her mother, but by her guardian, the puritan Earl of Huntingdon, the brother-in-law of Leicester whom Lettice had married. The Countess of Huntingdon was Philip's aunt and he was at court to welcome her arrival with Penelope late in 1580. The new girl was as memorable in appearance as her mother, with the striking sun-gold hair and atramentous eyes of her Boleyn forebears. She was soon courted and the Master of the Court of Wards, Burghley, and Huntingdon agreed to a match with the wealthy and orphaned Lord Rich. Despite her protestations everyone else approved and so the marriage took place on 1 November 1581. Then Philip Sidney fell in love with her. He had perhaps reason enough to be indignant with others for bringing this about, but principally his anger was directed at himself; the wound was self-inflicted – a wound 'that while I live will bleed' – a line of almost prophetic horror given the manner in which he died.

There was nothing striking or even especially agreeable about Lord Rich. There was only the quirky conjunction of his personal wealth and his surname, a circumstance that Elizabethan poets frequently alluded to in rhymes. With his social inferiors Rich was a bully, and there is every indication that he was a surly, dull man; one who could hardly believe his luck at his marriage to a woman who possessed not only beauty, but also amiability and social skills. Rich had been a student at Cambridge without much self-improvement; Penelope played the lute and was fluent in both Spanish and Italian. Probably like so many dullards Rich thought that anything in her manner that did not chime with his low puritanism could be smothered by contempt. He failed and Penelope was to prove as bold, resourceful and optimistic as her mother. Penelope was married but remained the most enchanting woman in the Essex circle which constituted a loose cluster of his relatives, friends (like the Bacon brothers), servants (like Henry Cuffe) and allies at court. The central core of this grouping met together to share their mutual enjoyment of music and literature. The French court lutenist Charles Tessier dedicated his *Premier livre de chansons & airs de court* to Lady Rich. The curiosity of her marriage is not that it took place given their temperamental differences, or that she had to give way, but that after the ceremony she cheerfully excised much of normal marriage from her life, save for fairly regular child-bearing. It seems as if Rich was given an opportunity for sex as a reward for good conduct and allowing her to lead her own life. His licensed occasions seem to have been at about eighteen month intervals. Presumably to fill the gaps he found alternative women lured by his wealth.

The Countess of Pembroke found fulfilment in her country house academy and in writing and translating. There she remained visible to the few, the largeness of the estate protecting her from discord, but not the obscene trivializing of Aubrey. The civility of Wilton is underlined by the poetic reading and inclinations of the family's doctor, Thomas Moffett, who drew on Virgil for the first Virgilian georgic written in English, *Silkewormes and Their Flies* (1599).[2] Such civility was also found in Essex House where, in the benign company of her brother and the loyal males who clustered round him to give service, Penelope found more freedom than constraint. Still, before this shift in her life she had for a time to live at court as a maid of honour, and then periodically with her husband. Her first child was Letitia, named after her own mother, who only recently had hazarded her life in late childbirth. The boy born to Lettice and Robert Dudley was the much longed-for male heir to the title Earl of Leicester and the land holdings. Unfortunately 'the little imp' Lord Denbigh was a sickly infant and died young, before both his parents. As for the thriving Penelope, she had several houses belonging to her husband to choose from. Among the properties he had inherited was the Priory of St Bartholomew, dominating the Smithfield area of London, but it is doubtful if Penelope ever lived there on any sustained basis. Out of London was Leighs Priory in Essex, and both indicate earlier secularizing of ecclesiastical property: protestant profit passed to a puritan.

Another marriage proposal for Sidney was temporarily raised as he was wrestling with the emotional discovery of his life set out in *Astrophel and Stella,* his song and sonnet sequence. The new idea focused on Penelope's younger sister, Dorothy, for whom Leicester was marking out marriage plans. Neither of the two young people were remotely interested and Dorothy had been able to gauge for herself the distress caused by economic motives bearing down on young women. With suitable Devereux pluck she had arranged matters for herself having arrived at court at seventeen, and with the solid support of her sister. The chosen suitor was Thomas Perrott, son of Sir John Perrott, holder of the same office in Ireland as her father, a Lord Deputy with land holdings in Pembrokeshire, near Lamphey, where the Devereux children had summered. Thomas Perrott wrote to Penelope seeking her support and blessing which he considered he had through her silence, interpreted as benign. So in mid-July 1583, when the couple took out a marriage licence there was no interference despite a certain improvisatory haste. Dorothy had been staying at Broxbourne (Herts.), and a clergyman who was retained by the Perrotts agreed to conduct the marriage if his identity was disguised. When asked for the keys of the local church the incumbent refused to give them up, and so the wedding party broke in for the rapid ceremony while two armed guards held the doors against a late family attempt to snatch Dorothy. None came so the

The splendid double portrait of the Devereux sisters, Dorothy and Penelope, the two beautiful daughters of Lettice, then Countess of Essex.

remainder of the story is obvious: royal rage, the Fleet prison for Thomas and a coaxing campaign that eventually got him out in 1583.

This was a year freighted with significance for Penelope. It saw the arrival at court, as a spectator for the queen dining, of Charles Blount (b. 1563), a younger brother of an impoverished Dorset family with the Mountjoy title but little else. After Oxford and the Inns of Court he had to make his own way in the world. Fortunately he was not only educated but tall, with brown curly hair and 'of a sweet face, and of a most neat composure'. To record this after his gallant service in Leicester's army in the Netherlands, Blount, freshly knighted in 1587, was the sitter that year for a portrait miniature by a disciple of the techniques of Holbein, the limner Nicholas Hilliard: '*Amor amoris premium*' is the inscription. Hilliard showed a fine mastery of the technical difficulties of painting in miniature and so won the patronage of the most powerful family cluster in the court. The last three of the seven surviving Hilliard children were Lettice, Penelope (baptized in October 1586) and Robert.[3] Even so, Essex in the period after Leicester's death (1588) showed a prickly exasperation with Charles Blount, whose financial footing was steadied in 1589 when the queen made the scholar-soldier one of her Gentlemen Pensioners. By then Essex himself was struggling with financial problems, yet he married Frances Sidney, widow of Sir Philip, and took on her five-year-old daughter. It was of course kept secret for a time before the inevitable – Frances, Lady Essex was denied access to the court, but not it seems her husband. Like her sister-in-law she saw nothing pleasing in court or in its effortless transmission of rumours and lies. She remained in company with her mother, Ursula, either in their home in Seething Lane or in their out-of-town residence Barn Elms, near Mortlake. Lady Walsingham had means and could probably better provide for her daughter than could Essex, unless he borrowed money at usurious rates.

In the early 1580s when the Privy Council and, in particular, Sir Francis Walsingham wanted access to all mail going in and out of the household in the country of Mary, Queen of Scots, they chose to move her to Chartley. Essex had at first resisted this because it looked like a naked attempt to make life difficult for his mother, Lettice, who lived there. Eventually, despite the absence of a malt house, it was used by Walsingham in his furious campaign to bring the Scottish queen to the block. Then it was returned to more mundane private use, although when Leicester died his wife settled at the manor of Drayton Bassett, near Chartley. For nearly twenty years its ownership had been disputed by the Robinson family and Richard Paramore, a London merchant and land speculator, before Leicester went to Staffordshire in 1581 to acquire it for Lettice. With the earl dead, John Robinson seized the estate by force, and Essex had to intervene to protect Lettice's interest. Naturally it did not escape her that if others preyed on her weakness, especially the venomous ill-feeling of Elizabeth, then ruin was indeed a possibility. She needed a man to protect her and she selected a kinsman of Charles Blount, very likely poised to become her daughter's lover – Christopher Blount. Essex could hardly maintain a feud against Charles Blount, who had wounded him in a duel in Marylebone fields; the high-spirited Penelope would not permit it having just become Blount's lover. A confirmation of this surely comes in George Peele's *Polyhymnia*: the Accession Day Tilts of 1590, the public performance of duty and chivalric values, showed a striking personal spin on this for despite his permanent leg wound Blount not only took part but announced his amour:

> Comes Sir Charles Blount, in or and azure dight:
> Rich in his colours, richer in his thoughts,
> Rich in his fortunes, honour, arms and art

Sporting the colours gold and azure replicates those of Pyrocles, lover of Princess Philoclea in Sidney's *Arcadia*, as he makes his first appearance in the text. The thumping pun on Rich needs no explication, but the section allows into the public domain, apparently without qualms, the latest personal sexual adventure at court. In his *Autobiography* the Jesuit priest Fr John Gerard made claim that he had almost convinced Penelope to become a Catholic but that the effort had been scattered by Blount in his role as champion of Protestantism. His passion on the subject proved overwhelming and included a threat of suicide, so that Penelope drew back. The passage in Gerard is undated but suggests these events took place in 1592. A further vagueness surrounds the fading out of Penelope's marriage and the permanent substitution of a lover: 'The story of sweet chastity's decay/The impious breach of holy wedlock vow' (*The Rape of Lucrece*, 1594). New work has recently suggested that Mountjoy was a well-placed connection of Shakespeare's at court.* *The Rape of Lucrece* was like *Venus and Adonis* dedicated to Southampton; was this a delicate substitution by a cautious poet who might otherwise have chosen Mountjoy? The decay of the Rich marriage would surely have begun in the late 1580s, while the neutral separation took place in about 1593. This imperfect sketch of the privileged matrimonial trio stems from their own lack of interest in accurate dating, although it had repercussions for the many children. When Mountjoy, then Earl of Devonshire, died, the oldest child mentioned in his will (truly a labour of love) was Penelope, and it seems very likely that she married Sir Gervase Clifton. She died on 26 October 1613, aged twenty-three years, and so was born in 1590 – but was she ever sure of her father? Probably neither Rich nor Blount (Mountjoy) knew with total certainty either, although later genealogies placed her among the children of the former: Robert, Henry and Charles, Lettice, Penelope, Essex and Isabel Rich. In addition there was another child, who died in infancy, a daughter born in 1588 and the subject of two sonnets by Henry Constable. He wrote a sonnet published in 1594 expressly addressed to Lady Rich, and obviously inspired by Sidney's sonnet 13.

Where is eight followed by six? In, of course, the reproductive life of Lady Rich, who by her audaciously constructed sexual freedom made her husband into that peculiarly Elizabethan and Jacobean figure of derision and laughter – the cuckold; unkind rhymesters named Lord Rich, Cornu Copia. Gossip dogged the children too as they became marriageable; because unassignable to fathers, they violated decorum and the strict inheritance rules. Was Isabel a Rich or a Blount? Marrying in haste in 1618 she was called Rich, and the earliest date for her birth seems to be 1592; 1594 at the latest. This places her in the waning period of the Rich marriage, or the primary

* Work done by Professor Richard Abrams at the University of South Maine.

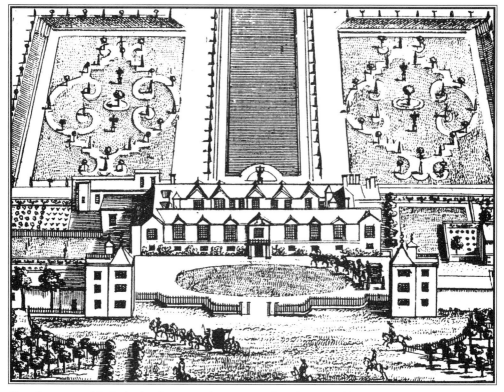

Once the property of Sir Richard Rich, Wanstead House, east of London, was sold to the Earl of Leicester before passing to his stepson, Robert Devereux, Earl of Essex, who sold it to Lord Mountjoy, so that it became a retreat for him and his married lover, Lady Penelope Devereux Rich.

period between the lovers. The wealthy household steward of Essex, Sir Gelly Meyrick, organized a great supper party at Essex House in their honour and they sat among friends until the small hours watching two plays by candlelight. Given the degree of connection of Shakespeare with the Essex clan it seems quite possible that one at least was by him. The rift with Rich was not absolute, but Penelope would be absent for long periods, which meant that care for the children was a problem despite attendant ladies like Jeanne de Saint-Martin, wife of Jean Hotman. Given her tenderness for the children she probably chose to take them with her when she visited her mother, who had remarried after a brief widowhood and was back at Chartley, or when she retreated to Wanstead. It had been bought by Leicester from the heirs of Lord Chancellor Richard Rich, and was later sold by an impoverished Essex to Mountjoy. When the latter died his complex will made provision for Penelope (by then his wife) and six of her children, whom he held back from naming as his to reduce complications. They were Mountjoy, St John, Charles, Penelope and Isabel, and the unborn child Penelope (his wife) was carrying. Readers will note the two sons

Charles Blount, Lord Mountjoy and later Earl of Devonshire, is centred here on the right side of the picture which shows the negotiators at the 1604 Somerset House Conference. It led to the signing of the Treaty of London.

named Charles: Sir Charles Rich apparently died during the English attack on the Ile de Ré in 1627, while the so-called Charles Blount supposedly lived until 1645. As for the supposed two Penelopes and two Isabels – perhaps two was actually one in each case. If there was only one daughter of that name, Devonshire as he then was apparently did not hanker for (unlikely) definitive proof of parentage; perhaps he saw sufficient of himself in a daughter's face? Or it may have been enough for his purpose that Penelope gave birth to them from her super-charged womb.

The characteristic of the Devereux family in late Elizabethan England was defiance of custom. Convention was skirted with a nonchalance that was almost perverse, even though the house of Tudor had shrunk to one. Bravura performances are always risky and can end tearfully, as Essex himself discovered. 'Terminal embarrassment' brought him to the block in 1601, but not before he had tried to scatter blame for the absurd London rising on Penelope: a tragic farce played out in the streets. Visibility and haranguing the mass of Londoners who had hitherto sung his praises proved to be useless in the face of sullen self-absorption. To sever the head of Beauty personified in Penelope was ultimately unthinkable because she seemed to inhabit a singular category – 'the privileged wanton'. When Essex, Rutland, Southampton, Robert Dudley and Danvers were arrested and sent to the Tower, Penelope was merely placed in the custody of Henry Sackford, keeper of the Privy Purse. Having nursed her former husband very recently through a dangerous illness she felt able to demand from Rich her male cook, bedding and hangings for her chamber. He sent them and later she was released into his custody. Perhaps for the first time Penelope grappled with the notion of 'malicious tongues', and thought of divorce.

CHAPTER SIX

'LOVE'S NO LOVE'

The life of the maid of honour who became pregnant through ignorance, or as with Mary Fitton, purposeful inclination, could be bumpy. Yet the court if taken in the right mood could muster protection after the event, and the fecund young lady who had blundered in the eyes of the queen was not abandoned to her own sexual indiscretion. Abigail Heveningham was found out but made an easy hop to gentlewoman. The queen's mildness may have stemmed from a presentation by Leicester, because his friend Sir George Digby of Coleshill married Abigail. Even a woman about the court who was not a maid of honour and who became pregnant out of wedlock might be offered a redemptive union. An example can be found in Emilia Bassano (1569–1645), the mistress of the elderly Lord Hunsdon, who was found a husband among the court musicians. Alfonso Lanier came from a prolific family originating in Rouen. His new wife's forebears came from the equally prolific family of Bassano in Italy, with the English branch of the family founded by five immigrant brothers – Anthony, John, Alvise, Jasper and Baptista.[1] The latter was Emilia's father, whose career as a music-maker evidently tailed off, so he died not only young but poor, leaving a daughter to be raised by her mother, Margaret Johnson. In May 1597 Emilia went to consult Simon Forman, and made two follow-up visits in June. She wanted to know then if her husband being in service to Essex on the Islands Voyage (a military expedition to the Azores) would benefit by looting or payment. Forman noted how her maintenance from Hunsdon had been eagerly plundered by a spendthrift husband who left her very needy and hence vulnerable. He formed the view that to make some easy money she might be persuaded to sleep with him, which does suggest her physical allure since Forman as a rule declined to pay for sex. As it was she chose not to and though he felt pangs of disappointment the hope of a change meant he maintained the friendship.

Forman takes us directly to the thronging streets and alleys around Westminster where civic life and low life might collide at any moment to gratify somebody. When in October 1597 he went to watch the State Opening of Parliament he found himself in the press of people beside a woman whom he engaged in conversation. Evidently he charmed her enough for her to tell him (a total stranger) her name and probably where she lived. A few days after this encounter Forman sent a manservant there with a missive intended to encourage Joan Harington. She was, and so arrived at his home with alacrity and they had sex despite their breezy ignorance of each other. She was a gentlewoman, not a prostitute. The latter were often shrill in their denunciations of wives who daily quit their husbands for sexual encounters, a category of sexually active women frequently characterized by writers in Elizabethan England as 'loose'. The wives declared themselves not verbally but by assigning their bodies for diversion with equally reticent men. The acute irony is that in Renaissance England the silence of the wife betokened bodily purity.[2] The male misreading of silence has a wild consequence; silence does not equate with submission to his patriarchal intention, but allows a space for development of private ideas and fantasies. It is doubtful if Joan Harington spoke first to Forman; she probably said very little from her mouth but had what may be called 'speaking eyes' or she simply nodded at the suggestion from Forman she found most useful to her purpose of having uncomplicated sex with a man. Joan's purpose in going to watch all the male members of Parliament was not conversation; she wanted to find a male member for her private amusement.

The number of women who scrambled to eke out a fluctuating living for themselves, their children, dependent parents perhaps or a war-wounded husband through commercial sex, was colossal. There were many thousands of prostitutes in London, Norwich, Oxford, York, Exeter and so on. Just as today brothel districts can be sharply delineated so Elizabethan London had a good many such 'hot' spots in a city that was expanding feverishly. The most notorious brothels were densely clustered on the Southwark Bankside. These were the 'stews' – so named from the original meaning of a heated room used for hot air or vapour baths, and formerly controlled by the bishop of Winchester (hence 'Winchester goose', the Elizabethan slang for a diseased Southwark whore or an infected client). Even during Henry VIII's reign the bishop of Winchester (Stephen Gardiner) had himself not been above something akin to pimping for royal approbation. He was the ally of the Duke of Norfolk, whose seductive young niece Katherine Howard was a dainty dish set before the king at the bishop's own palace. As it was, by the end of the sixteenth century prostitutes could be found in many more locations: outside the east city walls in Petticoat Lane; Hog Lane and St Katherine's; in Smithfield; Shoreditch; Westminster; Clerkenwell (Turnbull Street) and in the liberties of Whitefriars, St Martin le Grand and Coldharbour, while others fetched up within city jurisdictions like Billingsgate, Queenhithe and Ave Maria Alley near St Paul's.[3] No modern English town today (even Birmingham) could have within its boundaries so many prostitutes, a class of enterprising poor for whom there was no other survival option. Hence their raucous fury, mimicked in plays, at women like Joan Harington.

For a thoroughly knowing and detailed trawl through the shadier spots of the London underworld, with much attention given to prostitutes, there remain Robert Greene's pamphlet writings such as *A Notable Discovery of Cozenage* (1592), which details the full-frontal trickery of the whores and their bawds – a procuress – the 'apple-squire' being the male equivalent. Greene's whores not only sell sex but they have acting skills which frequently allow them to part the gullible and their money.

These are middle-class Englishwomen, as their clothes and the original captions by the Flemish illustrator declare.

Money/coin is of course sexualized by the Elizabethans; to 'coin' a child was to engender one or create one as one mints a coin; 'market price' meant a prostitute's fee. Greene's attitude to whore and client is coolly realistic and he presents a moral lesson.[4]

The clients – the men keen to drop their breeches and part with their money for a fleeting moment of pleasure – 'are not always sympathetic figures' but often deserve their destiny. The women themselves are not pictured as victims but professionals with a pride in unsavoury skills, thus making them less sympathetic. They are women who know the score and they represent 'a considerable change from the idealized heroines of Greene's earlier romances'.[5] Unfortunately, even education is not a prophylactic when dealing with whores, as Greene's *Mourning Garment* outlines for the edification of scholars at both universities (and presumably those at the Inns of Court). This is because education engages the intelligent but allows a free-floating susceptibility to the more lurid ways of the world. The whores work in parallel and in close association with male con-artists, with the latter 'all either wedded to whores, or so addicted to whores, that what they get from honest men, they spend in bawdy houses among harlots, and consume it as vainly as they get it villainously'. So Greene's prostitutes are not naive fallen girls, but rapacious professionals full of tricks to cozen any male lustful enough or stupid enough to succumb to their performances.

Early in the sixteenth century serious attempts to close the brothels had begun – the first in 1506. According to John Stow, the whitewashed premises facing the Thames with their identifying signs – The Gun, The Castle, The Crane, The Cardinal's Hat, The Bell, The Swan and possible others less famous – were shut for a season and on reopening numbers had diminished. By then the women had scattered across London. Forty years later all the stews were closed by royal proclamation, although prostitution hardly faltered. It was effectively left to its own devices and made even more hazardous by the risk and increase in sexually transmitted diseases. Still, the economic conditions of the day gave it a tenacious hold, and for many a muddy whore a garret was better than a ditch. Since life was a lottery there was also the obstinate hope for the whore that one day a man might want a permanent liaison with her, perhaps leading to marriage. Evidently Greene knew men married to whores and so the notion was not so dim and perplexing. Part of Greene's realism may have been directed against Puritan social reformers; a number of critics have identified a satirical turn to his work. Among social reformers what was viewed as a threatening poison in the system had to be compressed by moral rigour. Philip Stubbes favoured branding and execution, forms of response so extreme that they failed utterly to seize the collective imagination. The problem had to be dealt with in a less vehement fashion and the core foundation for the extirpation of London vice already existed: the Bridewell had been granted its charter in 1553 'for to be a workhouse for the poor and idle persons of the city'. It was one of four institutions established to counter the inexorable rise of rootless country people thronging the streets. Their plight was increased by the absence of monastic charity, by inflation and 'demographic diarrhoea' such as is found today in Latin America and parts of Asia.

The citizens of London had already done something to help the old and ailing by taking on the administration of the venerable St Bartholomew's Hospital, while Christ's Hospital gave refuge to poor orphan children. Now visibly able-bodied vagrants and petty criminals were to be squeezed back into work deemed socially useful – supervised labour anticipating so-called 'work-fair' schemes today. From its inception Bridewell was multi-tasked, training children of the poor, the recovering sick, criminals and prostitutes. Only after punishment such as whipping or a period in the stocks did the Bridewell regime begin, with a levy on the richer guilds to pay for it. Queen Mary I's lack of full-hearted enthusiasm for secular charity meant that during the last year of her hapless reign it was merely a punishment block for prostitutes and vagrants. A treadmill was fetched in for the disgraced to grind corn by generating the power, and also a block on which prostitutes beat out hemp with heavy wooden mallets. Marian misgivings were partly the result of clerical concupiscence, while the place was equally misliked by well-placed men for so reducing their choice of whores. Occasionally a raid would be mounted to 'liberate' women to return to prostitution as a 'Bridewell baggage'. In the winter of 1576/7 the Bridewell bench boldly took it upon themselves 'to police immorality in the city'. And to do this they targeted brothels, highly visible premises able to lure moral defectives; among these were 'weak' husbands; serving-men (especially those who took to theft to satisfy their lust); and even youths hot with frustration that the economy of carnality held them at bay. As for the whores – they excluded themselves from civil society by their freedom from religious and ethical constraints. So Bridewell was a 'godly foundation' that would have punished Mary Magdalen had she been available.

These righteous efforts represent an early form of the communitarianism that has sprung up today like a mushroom in the darkness surrounding the supposed demise of society. Both forge an evangelical thrust, the language homiletic, and they 'deploy tones both moral and conservative to disarm opponents'. In the name of the community 'individual rights are curtailed, agencies empowered to intervene, and the State encouraged to regulate'.[6] The political reality of this is that a well-meaning exterior obscures coercion. In the England of the first Elizabeth those most affected could resist because of the non-conforming aspects of prostitution which was not dominated by a violent male criminal class. Some women trawled through premises like waterfront taverns, others loitered encouragingly in gardens and even great churches like St Paul's. Some women worked alone, on call to favoured repeat clients who paid a householder a fee to lodge the woman 'favourite'. A steward of the French ambassador had this snug arrangement, as did Sir William Brooke.[7] Such a manner of working by women suggests limited economic objectives and a partiality for sex. This

The gift of King Edward VI to the city of London, Bridewell was to be a house of correction for mendicants, the light-fingered and light of morals. Whipping of men and women for 'lewd and light behaviour' was routine.

coincides with the slant of the severest male commentators on female sexuality – that once unshackled it takes on a despotic imperative detrimental to patriarchal society: the engaging simile becomes a threat, especially to monogamy.

One of the participating householders in the sex economy was John Shaw, who took rents from women, including 'favourites'. He had five houses in Finsbury, Thames Street (close to water), Whitefriars, St Lawrence and Bishopsgate. Paul Griffiths has linked Shaw to twenty-three prostitutes, and even if they drifted out of prostitution over time for a variety of reasons, there were others to follow. Doubtless Shaw made a handsome living, and he actively frowned on any diminution of activity, shunting off one lodger who became pregnant. She likely finished up in Bridewell, where the bench probably grimaced each time they heard Shaw's name, just as they became familiar with Thomas and Ely Fowles, Anne Wilkes and Alice Dunsley who let out rooms. The prostitute Anne Smith told the bench she had used 'Wattwood's, Marshall's, Jane Fuller's, Martyn's, Shaw's and other naughty houses'. When business was very brisk at one house a call might go out for auxiliaries to come in and the messages were generally conveyed by pimps like the notorious Henry Boyer. These men were the assistant stage managers of the sex market rather than the impresarios. Combining this work with other jobs they sought to arrange slick conjunctions of lechery and availability. Foreign merchants might need particular guidance to the erotic life of the city, and though there were few resident ambassadors embassies were often crowded and 'fishmongers' (pimps) were well employed in such company. Boyer presented prostitutes to the Portuguese ambassador, as well as to foreign merchants, and members of the aristocracy.[8] In Philip Massinger's *The City Madam* Shave'em and Secret, a dirty duo, refer enthusiastically to the arrival of two ambassadors from France and Venice: one of the clarissimi/A hot-rein'd marmoset. . . . Says Shave'em: 'They indeed are our certain and best customers' (III, ii, 25–9). In Shakespeare too, monkeys (aristocratic pets of the day), represented animal lechery. Prostitution involves an elementary business transaction between vendor and client. However, arrangements could vary, so that some habitués of brothels paid a fee to the bawd (procuress) and to the prostitute, while others handed over cash to the prostitute who then paid house fees. If this was inverted then the keeper of the brothel would take the fee and give the prostitute a dole: this was what happened at Captain Carewe's brothel in Smithfield with Margaret Warren. Tariffs for sex varied; one man paid Marie Donnolly £10 over several weeks, which was a considerable amount but easily surpassed by Thomasine Breame's client, a short man with a burly physique, who paid her that for an afternoon. Ten shillings was a more likely fee within a bawdy house with the luxury of a bed, perhaps a chair and a retainer to fetch drinks. Ambulant whores excluded from premises by cost might accept as little as 2d. Also the rate for city apprentices seems to have been set lower or negotiated as an exceptional offer, although not all apprentices were needy and from a low social class. In *The City Madam* young Goldwire and Tradewell are both the sons of gentlemen and set to learn the business of being a merchant from Sir John Frugal. Shave'em values Goldwire because of his liberality in sex 'He parts with his money/So civilly and demurely, keeps no account of his expenses' (III, ii, 89–91). The key word is clearly 'expenses', a punning reference to what Goldwire gives to the bawd in coin and to the prostitute in sexual tribute; the young man is conforming to the code of the day by declining to hoard coin or semen. A client would always pay a higher price for a virgin, rarity commanding a premium and the merchant Paul Mowdler willingly handed over 40s to Mistress Corbet when Katherine Williams became first available. Indeed, Corbet was very likely better provided for than the whores in her premises because keeping was generally much more lucrative. From her six bawdy houses Mistress Blunt took a minimum of £6 per week in rent and this ignores possible tips. John Shaw as we know had five houses; others did tolerably well by allocating a room to a woman, such as Gilbert East at Clerkenwell who lodged Jane Lewis.[9]

For apprentices a whore might be an object of desire, but rarely of affection. By the early seventeenth century antagonism was channelled into the Shrove Tuesday uproar of attacking brothels.[10] The reasons for this may have had more to do with class than sex, because the bawdy houses fared best with a gentleman clientèle. A witness to the visitors at Mrs Farmer's premises in St John's Street noted 'divers gentlemen with chains of gold' – evidence of conspicuous consumption. Happy Mrs Farmer. Less happy Mary Donnolly, abused by 'gentlemen and wealthy men with velvet gaskeens and such apparel and not for the common sort'. John Shaw's wife sought out the Steelyard merchants, probably because ignorance made them freer spending, like Japanese businessmen in Manila on a spree after business. So in terms of financial sinew the apprentices, groggy with libidinous urges, were at a disadvantage, effectively shunted aside by a powerful swarm of merchants, gentlemen at the Inns of Court, servants to important courtiers, prominent citizens and embassy staff; Boyer got 5s for conducting Elizabeth Donnington's maidservant to the Portuguese ambassador. Occasionally a rare deal was exposed to scrutiny: in January 1579, for example, the governors of Bridewell were given surprisingly frank details of the sexual peccadillo of a very wealthy public figure by his servant. Gilbert Periam acted as pimp for Sir Horatio Palavicino, a leading financier in London who for years was an adviser to the Lord Treasurer Burghley and useful co-ordinator of spies in Europe for Elizabeth's greatest spy-master, Sir Francis Walsingham.[11] Palavicino was minded to secure a virgin and Periam waggishly reported to him that there was no available virgin in the entire city. Hence he was given 10s and a horse for a trip to Guildford in Surrey to continue the hunt there.[12] Palavicino brings us near (appropriately given the latter part of his name) some of the great men of the court. A Holborn brothel keeper in the mid-1570s, John Hollingbrig, gent. wore the livery of Lord Ambrose Dudley, Earl of Warwick, whose own brother, Lord Robert Dudley, had intervened years before when Helen Andrewes was indicted by the wardmote inquest of Cheap. The indictment of John Thrush in 1564 had a cluster of privy councillors led by the Earl of Pembroke writing on his behalf. Given the grandiose scale of some of the Thameside London mansions of the aristocracy it becomes almost inevitable that sometimes within the structure a brothel could be found. Mrs Higgens's brothel operated within Worcester House, and instead of being grateful when the City constables closed it, the earl countered with suits in King's Bench against the officers involved. So civic efforts against prostitution were hampered by the way in which certain brothel keepers could muster countervailing actions by courtiers.

As a consequence, Bridewell found itself under renewed scrutiny and its officers centred in conflicts of interest. In 1577 a London goldsmith of substantial means, Anthony Bate, filed a bill in the court of Star Chamber with the accusation that the treasurer of Bridewell, Robert Winch, had made an improper charge against him of sexual misconduct. It was asserted that Winch had gone about gathering evidence by improper means. Henry Boyer was himself held in custody for five days and complained of time spent on a hard floor with only a thin gruel and black bread for nourishment; not the diet of a prospering pimp. He was also made to witness the whipping of a prostitute with forty lashes and was told he would receive the like punishment every Saturday until an incriminating confession was squeezed out of

Sir Horatio Palavicino, descended from Genoese nobility, was an energetic and very rich merchant who followed Sir Thomas Gresham as chief financial advisor to the Crown, and aided (so he intended) Walsingham in matters of espionage abroad.

him.[13] In the event, Bate had been caught out and his counter response was to launch reprisals against Winch. By this very public antagonism he succeeded in convincing many well-placed men that the Bridewell itself was corruptly administered, and that their drive against prostitution was corrupt and futile. The pimp Richard Rolles spoke at length to Sir James Croft, privy councillor and Controller of Household, and as a consequence boastfully took the view that Bridewell was fatally undermined. The trouble the case caused Winch was exemplified by John Richardson's assault on him as the unfortunate administrator sat quietly in the doorway to his house in Cheapside.

In John Donne's *Satire I* (On London Society) the voice of the poem remarks on the 'plump muddy whore, or prostitute boy', two representatives of the transgressive sexual partners available to men in late sixteenth-century London. They are yoked together without distinction because they represent sexual activity without promise for society. Nor was the man who dallied with one excluded from dealings with the other. The Elizabethan man of fashion or dandy is anatomized in the neo-classical satires of Everard Guilpin, and in his *Skialetheia* (1598) we find a fellow who diverts his lady with music, singing and general frivolity, goes daily to a play and every night has supper with his 'ingle' or boy friend. The man is 'unmanly in that he has no constancy', except perhaps to extravagance and selfish pleasure. There is a tendency in contemporary satire like that of John Marston to collapse distinctions between whore and boy, so that the latter becomes as available as the former. Evidence for the existence of male brothels is extremely meagre, although it has been suggested that a property in Hoxton owned by Lord Hunsdon was one. Might ladies of wealth and fashion find a discreet premises to which they could venture if their husbands proved tedious? One undated manuscript conjecturally ascribed to *c.* 1615 and possibly written by Francis Osborne does have a very intriguing reference to just such an establishment set up to bring in wealthy women. At one point in the play based on the infamous court scandal of the murder of Sir Thomas Overbury (d. 1613), and called *The True Tragi-Comedie Formerly Acted at Court,** two women, Mrs Turner and Lady Frances Howard (widely believed, when still Countess of Essex, to have contrived Overbury's murder), are disguised as prostitutes for a visit to Simon Forman. Such a 'disguise' tempts male observers and Mrs Turner claims that dressed so she will often be accosted for her 'commodity'. Lady Frances then refers to places where men and women meet socially: St Paul's, Madame Caesar's 'or the Captain's wife, in Aldersgate Street, that was the first who kept a male stews: whither the greatest she's in England came under pretence of eating Apricocks ungelt . . .'. In Renaissance England a number of foods were ascribed aphrodisiac traits, usually because of some modest visual correspondence between the item and genitals. So asparagus, grown in the neathouses (literally cowhouses) to the west of Vauxhall bridge, and formerly widely noted in classical erotic writings, was later acknowledged by Culpeper as a means to stir up 'bodily lust in man or women'. The a/*pric*/ot (or a/pricock) is also an erotic fruit. Not only does it allow the pun on the name, but by calling them to be visualized Frances Howard surely aligns them with the testes. The joke pivots on a complicated pun; gelt suggests geld, but true masculinity requires the testes to be in place – ungelt – whereas fruit like the apricot has to be pulled from the stem for swallowing. Shakespeare too has apricots – 'young dangling' in *Richard II* – but substitutes damsons (dark-hued and smooth) in a passage in *Henry VI* (II, i). Aldergate was close to the brothels that had been established around (where else?) Cock's Lane in the Smithfield-Newgate area. The reference to the Captain's wife seems even more particular since, as has been noted, Captain Carewe's 'bawdy' was in Smithfield. There may, of course, have been more than one captain in the sex economy, but it seems quite possible that his wife ran an establishment devoted to the pleasure of ladies. This need not necessarily have been a place devoted to sex for rich, bored women employing male prostitutes, although for a writer like Jonson a brothel and a bath house were essentially the same (see *Epigram VII*). Perhaps for men but need we assume that the same was true for women? In *Westward Ho!* Birdlime (a white but grubby product) plans to excuse her presence in the merchant Justiniano's house by pretending to be a hot-house keeper there to return his wife's dirty linen (1, i, 8–10). Given the upper class

* BL Add. Ms. 25348.

fixation with white skin signalling freedom from sunlight toil, such women had to spend time luxuriating and cleansing in the bath house, where they could also enjoy gossip and snacks at leisure. In *Measure for Measure* a pregnant woman's craving for a particular food is given as a reason for going to the hot-house. Did men easily insinuate themselves there and would they have been prostitutes? It seems unlikely, so better perhaps to regard them as sexual opportunists who saw a clutch of near-naked rich women as splendidly available and availed themselves.

As for *Measure for Measure*, it was probably being written as the old queen dominatrix was dying and James VI of Scotland was preparing to enter his 'hortus paradisus'. The play was presented as part of the 1604 Christmas celebrations at the court of the new monarch, with Duke Vincentio linked to the king himself, not identically but purposefully. Following the festivities, in January 1604, James presided over the Hampton Court Conference on the Church, with representative divines. This coincided with a torrent of sermons beseeching action – godly or temporal – against the brothels that still flourished long after Henrician legislation had supposedly shut them down. The response of James was stern, calculatedly so, because he was actually trying to hold off going after disgruntled Catholics. Already a disaffected cluster was devising ideas to try to kill him. James had the examples of Tudor legislation against brothels, but he set his in particularly lurid terms. 'R' for rogue was to be branded on the forehead of a first offender, while a second offence was a felony that merited death.[14] So to pick up the topic for a play was likely to snare the attention of a theatre audience, and Shakespeare added levity and piquancy. He made the sub-plot and the underclass a witty even charming challenge to the prevailing views of strait-laced puritan clerics. The bawds are genuine, even candid, while most of the main plot characters are hypocrites – like the seemingly pure Angelo – a name freighted with irony. The invisible playwright was nudging king and council with the mild view 'that fornication, adultery, sex outside marriage and stews – law or no law – will exist'.[15]

CHAPTER SEVEN

THE CASUAL CORINTHIANS

Corinth in the eastern Mediterranean around AD 100 was a cosmopolitan city heaving with a daily business tumult. It was famous for its heterogeneity and 'a byword for immorality', stirring with urgent, contradictory expressions of faith. It abounded in mystery cults, and freedom was presented as an initiation into the knowledge of higher mysteries. Not content with Elizabeth as Astraea, Aurora, Belphoebe, Cynthia, Deborah, Diana, Flora, Gloriana and so on, in the *New Arcadia* Philip Sidney merged Queen Helen of Corinth with Elizabeth, the former having miraculously 'made her people by peace, warlike; her courtiers by sports, learned, her ladies by love, chaste . . .'. Elizabethan London was a Corinthian city and the political and social fate of the country rested on it to a far greater degree than any other nation state. One of the mystery cults of London was that of the virgin female; Anthony Gibson in his *A Womans Worth, defended against all the men in the world* (1599) quotes Vigo as his authority for stating that the eyes of a dead virgin have a special efficacy against charms. A brass candlestick placed over the eye will cause all apparitions to vanish. Virginity 'and in particular female virginity, continued to carry a powerful mystique after the Reformation'.[1]

What was the consequence of this for the virgin male? Given the evidence of rampant sexuality about him the young urban male was probably frustrated and angry, but defying social conventions was always a risky business – tender girls may have irate fathers. There was the infamous double standard that chastised her for sexual experiment but expected him to latch on to it. Privileged young men in the universities and the Inns of Court may have had sisters and female cousins but family duty commended them to defend them if fathers failed. Moreover, their own primary dealings were with other young men leading to bravura exhibitions for each other. Apprentices too had the same impulses to fight, drink and rouse the watch with ludic excesses. One possible answer to sexual drought was to marry very young and the authorities in London at the beginning of Elizabeth's reign felt they had begun to notice this as a social problem. Some woefully impoverished households began to be remarked, with early parenthood bringing the most dismal consequences; 'Venus gloves' (condoms) were beyond their means. In 1556 London's Common Council effectively barred early marriages by restricting the city to those over twenty-four years. Local society was more tolerant allowing juveniles to kiss and touch within limits, especially at dances and calendared festivities.

By the mid-sixteenth century social commentators were discerning s̲o̲c̲ ̲ ̲dislocation on a shocking scale as it seemed to them. Rural depopulation, decaying towns, spasmodic food shortages and price rises forced many people to quit their homes. Yet the trend in population was upwards, a somewhat perplexing effect that led many to believe, as did Sir Humphrey Gilbert, that 'England is pestered with people'. In the opinion of the jurist William Lambarde population growth encouraged poverty and in 1594, just as a succession of plague years was about to set in, he reckoned the absence of plague and earlier marriages were creating a new class of poor people. As they entered the labour market the real wages of urban workers fell, and this conspicuous lack of economic power deprived them of sexual power too. For the desperately undereducated girls who had escaped the sexual attentions of fathers, brothers, uncles and neighbours, there was one commodity to be sold once: their virginity. As the opening lines of *Two Noble Kinsmen* by Fletcher and Shakespeare had it:

> New plays and maidenheads are now akin,
> Much followed both, for both much money gi'en.

This premium was widely understood by mothers and daughters, and no doubt it reduced the prospect of early sexual contacts with young women for many young men who were competing with Palavicino and his ilk. Move away from towns with a brothel or two (or more) and for many boys and young men sexual activity with a girl would have been long deferred after the expected age of the late teens. For some in the remotest parts of the country it likely never happened, for others sexual experiences with women would have shadowed the year's festivities and the consumption of drink. A cluster of partners might be followed by a long period of latency.

Simon Forman allows an uncommon glimpse of the sex lives of lower-class men and their women in his diary. Forman's servant, John Braddedge, stayed with him for four years, after starting an apprenticeship in 1594 when he was twelve years old. Like many then and now he was gracelessly self-willed and stubborn, a youth who took more pleasure from idleness and gambling than working to the requirements of an older man. By 1600 Forman had evidently wearied of the 'junior trainee's' ways and his resistance to curbs or even bribes. Braddedge was released to allow him to go off to fight in the Low Countries (a designation that caused some amusement then in the manner of the town of Condom in France today). He went after Forman had prepared his astrological chart hoping to establish that he would not suffer great harm. Astrology did not as it happens completely fail the undeserving former servant – he did return to England unscathed, albeit poor and indigent. Then in 1603 he crossed again to Ostend, and in 1607, aged twenty-five, he married. His sexual life with women had actually begun some nine years earlier; now his wife was a lame Dutch girl. The following year, for reasons unclear – perhaps a heartless exasperation at his wife's lack of mobility – he returned to England and poor lodgings in Lambeth. So how fared an illegitimate child of his born during the time when he had soldiered in the so-called 'English' regiment of the Cardinal-Archduke Albert? Braddedge seems to have been a Catholic.

Simon Forman had led a markedly different and gruelling life. Born in 1552 in Quidhampton (Wilts.), he had long been an autodidact desperate to establish himself in a financially secure career. He had held back from women and sexual opportunities, which may have been few since he rejected paying and claimed never to have visited a brothel. He was, moreover, a rather unprepossessing and runtish individual. Then in 1582 he made a macaronic note, 'first time in sum that ever I did halek cum muher'. A.L. Rowse in his swarming book on Forman has noted that 'halek' is the code word apparently used for sexual intercourse; he missed the fact that 'muher' is merely a phonetic rendering of the Spanish for woman – mujer.[2] So who was the woman haleked? She was Anne Young, who in February 1584 became his mistress and gave birth to their son, Joshua, on 27 March 1585. Yet she did not marry Forman, instead choosing one Ralph Walworth. She died in May 1600 and Joshua moved to live with his blood-parent in mid-1602. He died abruptly in October 1603 when a stomach ulcer and the plague formed a hideous conjunction in his blood stream.

Simon Forman had no advantage in the world based on his background and appearance. He was undersized and although of yeoman stock his own father's early death meant that Forman's education was curtailed rather than rounded in the manner to which he aspired. After five years of a hated apprenticeship he got the chance to go to Oxford as a servant attending two better placed young men. No doubt he envied the cousins, Robert Pinckney and John Thornborough (later bishop of Worcester), who at that time were but lightly preparing for the Church. Forman had some Latin, the privileging language of the day, and after his Oxford experience was allowed to teach. The grounding in Latin was truly indispensable to anyone with social aspirations, and an Elizabethan schoolboy learned his masculine identity while pouring over the highly gendered Latin grammar.[3] The teaching regime then may have been complacent, stale in its repetitiveness and occasionally brutal, so that the weak faltered and the tenacious flourished, but it was a sharp and usefully early inculcation of the message that striving might bring rewards and that the greater world is adversarial. This was the great grammar school tradition that lasted hundreds of years until ambushed by two shrilly destructive women Secretaries of State for Education. Competitive élites were swamped by comprehensive failure under their control.

Latin, early taught from William Lyly's grammar textbook, did admit the occasional female like Lady Jane Grey, Lady Jane Lumley, Princess Elizabeth. The latter became, as it were, an honorary male, and when near the end of her reign she rebuked an impertinent Polish ambassador in a Latin extempore speech, her male courtiers were swift to praise her. If the queen had indeed been a man then they might not have made

Simon Forman, perhaps unwillingly, delayed the onset of his sexual life, but for such an unprepossessing little man he proved later immensely successful in serial seduction.

so much of it since Latin was the first language of diplomacy, international commerce and law. It was also the language of sexual knowledge, even jokes about the topic, and the more licentious writers – Catullus, Martial, Horace and Ovid – remained a coterie pleasure. Ovid had been the most popular Latin author in England since at least the time of Chaucer, surpassing even Seneca. Only those who had been admitted to the club of readers in Latin had the means to go beyond what had been censored by diligent school masters. Then the cosy conspiracy of generational discretion began to fold: Arthur Golding's translation of the *Metamorphoses* was printed in 1565 and George Turberville's of the *Heroides* in 1567. Both proved popular enough to go through several editions by 1580, and not long after the breezily iconoclastic young poet Christopher Marlowe translated the *Amores*. It was quite a precocious effort on his part since it was probably done before he left Cambridge University for London. He was democratizing the text by translation, opening the secrets to readers male and female in English. Marlowe was the grammar school boy *par excellence*, having made his way to Cambridge through scholarships; his father, John Marlowe, was a Canterbury cobbler. As a poet and playwright Christopher Marlowe sought his career and the advance of his reputation in London, among the better educated. Meanwhile in the provinces, the less learned, the first or second generation of readers, often hankered for items that chimed with their unaffected tastes, and Elizabethan journalism set out to cater for them.

Much of Elizabethan fiction was meant to be read aloud; this could shift it from a private pleasure to a group entertainment. In 1590 a booklet appeared aiming to please this amorphous public: *The Cobler of Canterburie*, 'a farcical medley of verse and prose'. This was not high culture underpinned by classical learning; it was what the author said – a compilation that the farmer can have read to him on a winter's evening by his son to raise a good belly laugh. 'The old wives that wedded themselves to the profound histories of Robin Hood . . . may here learn a tale to tell amongst their gossips.' A popular verse piece by Samuel Rowlands was called *''Tis Merrie when Gossips meete'*. In this he gives voices to women in a tavern – a widow, a wife and a maiden – who discuss men and marriage. Rowlands was a prolific writer of verse tracts, some pious and some satirical. *''Tis Merrie . . .'* is a buoyant naturalistic piece in six-line stanzas in which he weaves wittily together all the standard complaints that women regularly aired to their friends about the failings moral and physical of men. Gossip with its parochial, domestic or sexual connotations was always something done by women. In 1599 Emanuel Van Meteren, the Dutch merchant-scholar, found gossiping a notable characteristic of Elizabethan women. Men supposedly did not gossip, they conversed on altogether weightier matters. Gossip was boosted by alcoholic drinks since tea and coffee were not yet available, the primary lubricant being ale. A proverb of the mid-seventeenth century noted 'Gossips are frogs – they drink and talk'.

Other foreign visitors to London constantly remarked on what they considered the freedom of English wives to order their own lives. One habit that intrigued them was kissing on the lips. 'Were kisses all the joys in bed, One woman would another wed.' So thought one evidently male writer who was ignorant of female erotic life, its experimental base and range of affective possibilities. One writer not so ignorant was Shakespeare, for *A Midsummer Night's Dream* and *As You Like It* (a teasingly bold title) 'both present two pairs of female characters whose initial erotic investment is in one another'.[4] The young woman in each who defends such same sex-bonding, Helena and Celia, does so in terms of defiant nostalgia, apparently forced by the playwright to recognize the end of possibility in that direction. Their future is phallic, if wives or mistresses, yet it is still possible to discern an autonomous popular culture based on female friendship. This gynosocial clustering took place about unregulated gossip, a diversion and form or exchange that had the power to remove women from the home and their husbands on a daily basis. In the case of Lady Rich, the subject of gossip, it was she who removed herself from her marital home as often as possible, and despite having an exigent male lover she was constantly supportive of and available to other women. The only woman she regularly avoided was Elizabeth, who was an honorary man.

In Renaissance drama there is a pervasive sense that a company of women represent a threat to male security. In contrast, Anthony Gibson, writing in 1599 and paraphrasing Plato, says that 'womens society hath made civil the most outrageous conditions of mens lives'. When the gossips meet in Henry Parrot's *The Gossips Greeting* quite a lot of their conversation has to do with food preparation. Ben Jonson in *An Entertainment at the Blackfriars* recorded the proverbial characteristics of the midwife, a key figure in childbirth, the most mysterious aspect of the lives of women: 'Many a good thing passes through the Midwifes hand, many a merry tale by her mouth, many a glad cup through her lips, she is a leader of wives, the lady of light hearts, and the queen of gossips.' Gossip had the means to make women convivial, as tobacco did gentlemen, but the joy of the former was that it was free for all ages and classes, nor did it necessarily involve a group activity like sewing. Groups could meet in each other's houses and also in the alehouse or tavern. Whether they had a room designated solely for their use is not clear, although if their gathering was daily then it might have been worthwhile for the tavern keeper. In a late ballad (*c.* 1630) *Foure Wittie Gossips*, the women do meet in an alehouse 'to drink and pass the time away' – their tipple being sherry and their defence for being there the very reasonable one that the night before their husbands had been in the same place drinking beer.[5] Other ballads have husbands complaining of the drinking and the company kept, with the suspicion that it did not always exclude 'merry blades' as the drinks are poured. Perhaps the fundamental male concern which induced anxiety and nervous laughter was the notion that such wives might look for and find sexual partners other than their husbands. Male mistrust lingered even without a shred of evidence, because such a betrayal was too shaming. Cuckolds were in a special group themselves as targets of lewd humour and derision stemming from male powerlessness. The view that every married man was a potential cuckold, and hence vulnerable, was widely held. Male insecurity also extended to what was said by gossips about them, notably about their aptitude (or failings) as lovers.

Male solidarity did not extend to those lacking vigilance and for the young man of this period cuckoldry was the source of coarse and triumphant amusement. Roving free outside the commended state of marriage with its comfortable complacencies, the young interloper with adultery in mind could challenge the dominant male. He knew that pain and distress might be caused but the thought of the married woman, luxuriating in her experience and possibly willing to share it, was enough to smother prevarication. Alas, he might then begin to worry about his ability to satisfy her sexual inclinations. In his lewd imaginings he was a priapic god given to heroic strength, but in reality he might only be up to 'one moment's fading mirth'. The gap between imagination and reality admits mirth. Poets were ready to exploit this for the delectation of readers. Bawdy popular verse was not new, so when Thomas Nashe wrote *The Choise of Valentines* (dedicated to Lord Strange), he was following in the robust Chaucerian tradition. The opening lines recall the freedom with which young men disport; no such weakness in sexual matters was allowed to the girls under the intrusive jurisdiction of church courts. Nashe's male protagonist is Tomalin (Tom ailing?), whose trawl for female companionship takes him to a brothel where he finds his lover, Mistress Frances, engaging clients for startling amounts. Tomalin promises to pay her bawd in gold, and like Jupiter to deliver a 'golden shower' upon Danaë. Once assigned a room the erotic disrobing of the girl leads to his (most un-godlike) premature ejaculation, and Tomalin requires a fricative sexual caress for a very brief coupling that leaves his partner unsatisfied. She completes the encounter with a sex toy that

> will refresh me well
> And never make my tender belly swell.

The result for Tomalin is a dent in his male self-esteem. But how had he before this learnt with his contemporaries about sex?

In an agricultural country like England a sketchy knowledge of procreation would have early been acquired. Even children that rarely witnessed a bull among cows, or a stallion in action among mares, would often enough have seen domestic pets with the male mounting the female. If a boy was unable to shift from the agricultural to the domestic without help, then an older male could be questioned although that could entail some risk, since boys were widely regarded as sexually available for men. Those who could read might find restrained references in a book written by an Oxford don, Thomas Cogan, whose popular manual was reprinted seven times between 1584 and 1636. But the total of volumes sold cannot have been more than a few thousand; *The Haven of Health* had the sub-title *Chiefly gathered for the comfort of Students*, and in the section 'Of Venus' the author gives some attention to sexual desire in young men. If they read it and passed it on or sold it later the total number of readers still cannot have been that for a top-selling paperback instruction manual today. Cogan offered the advice of a presumably celibate don; essentially three rather comfortless modes of behaviour. There was prayer in the manner of St Paul, a rather arid business; celibacy; and preparation for life (presumably including sex) with disciplined hard work. For Cogan youthful sexuality was an infirmity of nature and marriage the only passage to good health, wherein was balance. The hot-blooded male should take steps to cool his ardour – he should sit on a cold stone, like marble, or periodically plunge into cold water or douse his genitals in strong vinegar.

According to the ancient Greeks, Pan, the compulsive god of Nature and of coercion, was lord of panic and sexual excitement. Puberty in boys is a sustained state of subliminal panic, as well as a time of high, irrational (because often undirected) sexual excitement. This flux of perturbation and arousal happens day and night, and the unseen, unpremeditated nocturnal emission is a particular cause of agitation. Bed-wetting has (usually) been left behind only to be replaced by a new phenomenon causing unease, and just at the time when masturbation itself becomes a productive option. Among his attributes the god Pan lists being the inventor of auto-eroticism, a 'fact' affirmed by Ovid, Catullus, and Dionus Chrysostomus, who cited the testimony of Diogenes the Cynic – that rarity – a man who would masturbate in public (hence 'cynic friction'). Aristotle and Galen had both taken a benign view of it as conducive to physical and psychological health. In the Italian Renaissance rediscovery of classical texts their views had been taken up by Fallopius and others. Yet Cogan and many of his contemporaries viewed it as a sullen diversion from procreation, so devoid of purpose for the species and society. In *As You Like It* the phrase 'weakness and debility' apparently refers to it disparagingly. In this manner Shakespeare appears to be continuing with the tone adopted in the *Sonnets* (the so-called procreation sonnets, nos. 1–17). Recently dubbed 'autofiction' by an American critic, perhaps 'auto-erotic fiction' would be better since the sonnets are evidently the poet's 'jerks of invention'. The pressure of bawdiness is undeniable, and Robert Crosman is indeed correct to see sonnet 1 as 'virtually one long double entendre'. Like his contemporary Cogan, Shakespeare is unwilling to reflect on the 'usefulness of masturbation in culture and creativity'. He is conflicted about it and coyly chides the 'tender churl' who 'mak'st waste in niggarding' – as if every emission of semen could be procreative. Sonnets 4 and 6 also mildly rebuke, but overlook the sexualization of the imagination, the conjunction of mind and body and the intensification of the moral conscience. Why shouldn't the young man addressed be 'self-willed'?

Many Elizabethan boys entered puberty in a disorderly milieu, and found protection in the homosocial group or the shared bed. Pornography was increasingly available to those who could read and students were not prevented by law from buying it. If they wanted violence with sex then by 1591 they had the *Life of Robert Duke of Normandy*, which begins with the baby boy biting off the nipples of his nurse, and when the wild child has grown up a Mother Superior is forced by him to parade her younger nuns naked. He selects and rapes one and then later amputates her breasts, which has a kind of formal logic given his mammary maiming years before. Naturally good comes out of evil and when he is converted he vows to eat with the dogs and moves in with one of the Emperor's pet greyhounds. Thomas Lodge's piece of grand guignol anticipates Shakespeare's most violent and bookish melodrama *Titus Andronicus*, in which a key prop is Ovid. The *Metamorphoses* remained Shakespeare's favourite reading, a pursuit very firmly established in his schooldays. There he found genial candour, tenderness and authority; Ovid was viewed by his defenders as a 'most learned and exquisite Poet', but by his detractors as master of a most desperate carnality. Yet they were not afraid to borrow directly from him. Stephen Gosson, like Donne in the Elegies, shifts Ovid into the contemporary world of London with which they were familiar. For anyone with the mildest interest in the theatre, especially as a mixed social gathering, Gosson presented inadvertently an intriguing *aperçu* based on Ovid's scene of the chariot-race from the *Amores* – the conjunction of theatre with sexual glances, hints and innuendoes. Not only on the stage, where human desire took protean form, but also in the main 'body' of the theatre where a large audience encouraged physical closeness. This was evidently based on his own experience too, because Gosson went to plays and took a comparatively sceptical attitude to the experience. Jammed into the space the object of desire must be touched – will he, nill he. The man who quit the theatre for a visit to a brothel left one performance for another in which he played a key role. Reading Ovid's *Ars Amatoria* he had come across empirical advice on the physical adroitness necessary for simultaneous orgasm, for the *Ars* is about the purposeful fashioning of the plain case individual as a multi-faceted lover. This can be the cause of hilarity when Bottom (a fundamental joke) becomes an ass and yet still ensnares a starry-eyed Titania. Or there can be a darker hue to the matter, for Ovid is not above suggesting the invention by the would-be lover of a bogus persona – the one who promises whatever is necessary as he clears a choking path to fulfilment; 'by promises girls are caught' and as you make them, Ovid advises, invoke any God you like since Jupiter is amused by the many perjuries of lovers.

CHAPTER EIGHT

'UNTAM'D DESIRE'

The Elizabethan fashion for the song book and the epyllion roughly coincide, although the latter had diminished in favour after some twenty years. It began around 1589 when Thomas Lodge had published *Scillaes Metamorphosis*, and so set in motion a sequence of publications by other writers in this new genre. Epyllion was not used at that time but it usefully signals in one word an eroticized narrative poem using the mythology of the Italianate Ovidian tradition. Hitherto a very large percentage of the secular reading matter bought by the English public had been translated from Greek, Latin, French, Italian and Spanish sources. It was the French and Italian blazon – 'a poetic set piece detailing the various features of the poet's mistress' – attached to the Ovidian features which gave the epyllion its erotic appeal. It was 'soft-core pornography' with a special feature of voyeurism given a distinctive twist – the older woman in ardent pursuit of the experienced beautiful boy, 'using the more subtle expressions of sexuality such as metaphor, hyperbole – even fantasy'.[1] This was given an added piquancy by examples in court society. Was there a *soupçon* too of derisive male laughter at the queen herself seeking to awe and dazzle every young man new at court? She had lost the Earl of Leicester in 1588, shortly after the triumph over the Spanish invasion fleet. He had introduced at court his stepson, the Earl of Essex, now embarking on a startling public career. The growth of popularity of the epyllion kept pace with the inexorable rise of Essex, and the decay of the genre set in around the time of his execution in 1601. By then, of course, Elizabeth was an old woman, and having been fixated with her hitherto, poets of the day now found rhapsodizing about her to be difficult, if not nauseating.

In a sea–girt nation of mariners it is not surprising to find water is the commanding element of many epyllia. It comes from a variety of sources and in varying quantities – sweat, tears, streams, rivers, seas and oceans. A poem by Ralegh (not, as it happens, an epyllion) begins, 'Our passions are most like to floods and streams'. In *Scillaes Metamorphosis* the tears of the narrator are a 'strong shower', and the second line of Shakespeare's *Venus and Adonis* (1593) has the morning weeping. Indeed, on the title page it had a quotation from Ovid's *Amores*:

> Vilia miretus vulgus, mili flavus Apollo
> Pocula Castalia plena ministret aqua

> [Let the throng admire base things, but let Apollo
> serve me cups filled with the purest spring water]

In fact, the throng that immediately admired *Venus and Adonis* was rather select and not at all ill-bred. Nowhere was there a greater collective regard for it than at the Inns of Court, and it achieved a headlong success. Within a year smart young poets were displaying its influence, and the most galvanized of the lot was Thomas Edwards. An admirer of Marlowe and his friend Thomas Watson, Edwards was a Shropshire lad, born in 1567, who after Furnival's Inn had shared a chamber at Lincoln's Inn with John Donne's friend Christopher Brooke, and who at the time of Marlowe's death was employed in some junior capacity by the Latin Secretary, Sir John Wolley.[2] Not long after that lamentable fracas at Mrs Bull's, Edwards produced *Cephalus and Procris*, entered in the Stationers' Register on 23 October 1593. The edition has not survived and the only copy still existing dates from 1595. William Covell, fellow of Queen's College, Cambridge, and the tutor of the poet John Weever, alludes to the poem in that same year. In *Venus and Adonis* resistance (male) meets ardour (female) in high comedy that Edwards evidently appreciated and strained to reproduce:

> He striving to be gone, she pressed him down;
> She striving to kiss him, he kissed the ground.

From the first stanza 'rose-cheek'd' Adonis is hunting, but scorning love. His sport is venery, her venery of the amorous sort and her anxiety to engage in its mutual pleasures is so strong that she yanks him from his horse – the inference being that he should mount her.

Shakespeare, Marlowe, Donne, Edwards and others skirt around explicit descriptions of erotic preliminaries and coition by using analogies. So in Shakespeare the horses, whatever aspect of sexuality they represent, be it 'lust or natural procreation', are synecdochic extensions of the goddess and her quarry. Marlowe uses a grand equine simile to show Leander's startling willingness if reined in too far to smash into the sea. Between them Marlowe and Shakespeare gave the epyllion a formal perfection that others could only struggle to emulate.

Among those who tried was a Cambridge man, Thomas Heywood, aged about twenty, who seems to have arrived in London with his epyllion based primarily on *Heroides* XVI, XVII. *Oenone and Paris* was surely calculated as an open letter of introduction to the literary world. It was entered in the Stationers' Register on 17 May 1594, and shows an almost slavish desire to imitate Shakespeare, although the pastoral location is elaborated. Heywood was a life-long associate and admirer of the older man and both had the peeving experience of being selected by William Jaggard for his 1600 edition *The Passionate Pilgrim*. The problem Heywood set himself with *Oenone and Paris* was that Oenone is trying to win back her husband from Helen of Troy, and this domestic triangle offers few surprises as she fails; Paris is no longer interested in sport at Oenone's 'fountain'. Heywood himself was intrigued by Shakespeare's lively exploitation of red and white as signalling emotions and physical attributes simultaneously. When Venus plucks Adonis from his horse and lodges him under her arm and over her ample hip, he blushes 'red for shame', while she is 'red and hot as coals of glowing fire'. As Katherine Duncan-Jones has said, when stretching beyond his skills of imagination Heywood stumbles; virtuoso eroticism and high comedy are difficult.[3] The remarkable image in which the prostrate form of Venus becomes a rolling verdant deer park, and Adonis a stag browsing over the covert places of her champaign body (venery indeed), becomes a scene envisaging water sport. Oenone says:

> Oh be my sternsman, I will be thy barge,
> It's not thy weight that can me overcharge.

It is so unflattering to Oenone herself that Paris laughs at her, and for the reader too the effect is risible.

Shakespeare's goddess 'is confusingly multi-faceted.'[4] She can be languorous or animated, but mostly Venus is with Venus enflamed, believing all that she articulates, almost delirious with desire but yet still able to articulate this frantic yearning. And all to no avail despite being a goddess who need not plead at all; it is Adonis who has free will in this pagan territory and his preference for boar-hunting over love leads directly to his death. There is after all a thread of irony in the poem; the natural order of things is disordered. Thanks to the goddesses Cynthia* and Venus, the course of true love never will run smooth, and the discourse on this state of affairs offers variety, with wit and sexuality. Enough to set the blood pounding in every young blood's chest, for the rhetoric of courtship was an intoxicant, sexually stimulating, and no one paid much heed to the failure of Venus. Indeed, the poem set off a remarkable surge of excitement in literary London, and Gabriel Harvey, who became more conservative as his career as man of letters was rubbished by Thomas Nashe (see Chapter Thirteen), remarked some time after 1598 that 'the younger sort [thereby excluding himself] takes much delight in Shakespeare's *Venus & Adonis*'. It seems to have provided too something of a bonanza for publishers with no less than six editions by 1599 (and the possibility of others unrecorded).[5] It was Richard Field who originally obtained it, selling on the rights to John Harrison in June 1594. Given the competitive interest among publishers for epyllia it is at least odd that when John Wolfe purchased the rights to *Hero and Leander* shortly after Marlowe's death in May 1593 the text was not published until 1598. He delayed too on the publication of Thomas Edwards's *Narcissus*, the beautiful

---

* Cynthia = Diana, the moon goddess.

youth who has captured many hearts but loved none until he falls in love with his own image in a pond and, becoming so fixated, watches until he dies. Edwards gave the story a high camp ending, substituting the hero dressing in women's clothes before deliberately drowning himself.

The transvestite dive of Narcissus is only one example of the strongly bisexual tone of the epyllia. It is evident too in Marlowe's treatment of Leander (deriving from the *Heroides*), although the portraits of the boy and girl as sexual individuals are not fudged. Both are extravagantly beautiful and Cupid cannot differentiate between Hero and his mother Venus. Leander's beauty is of a kind touched by the gods' 'immortal fingers' marking out the 'heavenly path' of his spine, and causing confusion among men, like the otherwise obdurate Thracian soldier who can resist everything but the boy – 'was mov'd with him, and for his favour sought'. Others think Leander a girl in men's clothing, and everything points to Marlowe wanting to link Leander to Adonis, who through his affair with Venus has become a bisexual figure identified with the procreative energy of Nature and hence the sun, which, with water, gives life to all things. It is not Cynthia or Venus who kills Adonis, but the hunted boar, and theirs is a primary collision of life and death. Adonis is Adam before Eve – the perfect androgyne beauty from whom she will be plucked.

The most thoroughgoing attempt to make the epyllion a vehicle for philosophizing was by George Chapman in his *Ovids Banquet of Sence*. Whereas the Latin poet in his fifth *Elegy* (translated with gusto by Marlowe) retreats from the midday sun of summer to lay on a bed before the entry of his lover, Corinna, whom he disrobes swiftly to embrace her naked, Chapman's Ovid is himself in Corinna's garden, feeding as it were his senses. In each a transformation takes place as he experiences 'the metamorphosis of the potential of sense into spirit'. As the sun animates the earth with its warmth, beauty operates within the world of the senses to animate the soul. The lofty drift of Chapman may have been half or even wholly understood by avid readers of the genre, but offered a tour of the garden or an hour with Corinna and the lady triumphed. Reading an epyllion gave the male reader at an Inn of Court respite from the severe tedium of reading law texts; like masturbation which likely followed eager reading and re-reading, it stirred the erotic imagination of young men who had hitherto probably not seen a naked woman save in voyeuristic circumstances, and in the epyllion often art imitates life with clandestine perusal of a body and extravagant enthusiasm for the most erotic parts. The sweep of the eye of the reader down the page mimics the strategy for looking of the poet, from the head downwards.

The lust-wish of the students and their 'devotional' reading of such secular texts could be mildly parodied as in the 1599/1600 Christmas play performed at Cambridge that year. Adonis (or his young substitute) has a perfectly formed young man's body of matchless grace, and this flawless creature anticipated the so-called Uranian cult of the late nineteenth and early twentieth centuries. The *Narcissus* poem of Thomas Edwards brings out that the boy mesmerizes 'a bevy of paedophiliac ladies' and no later image better captures this sensibility than that of Baron Wilhelm von Gloeden (1856–1931). The body of the idealized boys and youths in 'classical' grottoes is never muscular beyond possibility; they are not yet men so toil and effort has not formed them, and their skin is smooth. In the epyllion *Salmacis and Hermaphroditus*, the boy is fifteen, on the cusp of manhood:

> He knew not what love was, yet love did shame him,
> Making him blush, and yet his blush became him:
> Then might a man his shamefast colour see   (659–61)

Gloeden's boys and youths (one or two of whom look demented) may be pale skinned or tanned since he photographed them in Sicily. In the epyllion Elizabethan authors always have the couple daintily pale like Meissen figures of shepherds and shepherdesses. In Weever's *Faunus and Melliflora*, Venus coming upon Faunus and mistaking him for Adonis, throws off her clothes to reveal an ivory skin tone, and when Venus takes the hand of Adonis in Shakespeare's poem 'so white a friend engirts so white a foe'. In *Hero and Leander* the 'ivory skin' is that of Leander.

Early Christian art had been at best ambiguous in its attitude to the body and its portrayal.[6] Official Christianity recoiled impatiently from pagan cult images, often of the human body in sculpted form, wishing to destroy them. So having annexed and smothered so far as possible the pagan in festivals like Christmas and Easter, there was an inclination to do the same to inherited artistic motifs. There was a period in late Roman and early Byzantine art when the man called Jesus was presented as the perfect Apollo figure, but when the dominant weird power of asceticism ruled most of the Christian world, and the monastic orders appeared in its wake, the human body slipped from the pinnacle of idealization, no longer glorified, but an ill-regarded vessel doomed to condemnation and extinction unless swamped by faith.

With the energy gone from the monastic movement by the late fifteenth century, replaced in part by the more worldly, energetic Jesuits (who still belittled their own bodies with the tormenting excitement of flagellation), the old constraints on thinking and representation were gradually removed even if veils were painted over genitals in frescoes. Through humanistic and scientific scholarship there was a dramatic surge in interest focused on the long-neglected human body. By the time of Elizabeth the anatomical studies of Andreas Vesalius were well known to John Dee, owner of one of England's finest libraries, and royally patronized. Men had not only rediscovered Greek texts through teachers and grammarians like Manuel Chrysolaras, who moved to Medicean Florence in the early fifteenth century, but also the Greek ideal of the body with particular emphasis on the male physique. This happened so much later in England that the shift with its prestige coincided with the last years of Elizabeth's reign. Richard

Barnfield, who very likely was personally acquainted with Shakespeare, included a verse tribute 'A Remembrance of some English poets' in his last book (1598):

> And Shakespeare thou whose honey-flowing vein,
> (Pleasing the world) thy praises doth obtain.
> Whose Venus and whose Lucrece (sweet and chaste)
> Thy Name in fame's immortal Book have placed.
> Live ever you, at least in Fame live ever:
> Well may the body die, but Fame dies never.

In that year too came a late published reminder of the genius that had been lost forever in that clumsy ruckus with knives in Deptford in 1593. *Hero and Leander* was only published at the height of the vogue for wanton poetry, and possibly it convinced the new men that to make their mark in the literary world with an epyllion meant devising something naughty and novel.

John Marston of the Middle Temple was a young man who sought to cultivate a personality that bellowed unconventional. When he wrote his mocking epyllion, guying the genre and also teasingly erotic, is not known. It is possible that it circulated among the select in manuscript or that it was put out in an edition which has not survived, but in 1598 it was the lead poem in his earlier extant publication *The Metamorphosis of Pigmalion's Image and Certaine Satyres*, entered in the Stationers' Register on 27 May and issued anonymously later that year. Does suppressing his own name signal a bout of nerves? It is peculiar because if he wanted genuinely to succeed Marlowe, Shakespeare and Donne – whose *Elegies* (thoroughly Ovidian) were in private circulation – then his own naughty piece had to be given to him. There is, incidentally, no proof that Marston had read deeply in Donne's poetry before 1598, but how could he have avoided the reputation of the man? As to his own in the immediate future he may well have calculated that the minor secret of his identity was hardly likely to remain so within the ferment of the inns. Naturally the poem achieved an almost immediate and scandalous success. Such a celebrity indeed that in *Salmacis and Hermaphroditus* (by Francis Beaumont jnr.), Marston's short poem based on a story from the *Metamorphoses*, X, 24–97 is identified as forming part of a courtesan's library so that her gentlemen could 'stand and deliver'. We have every reason to think of Marston as cunning as well as dirty-minded. Much of the subordinate business and digressions of epyllia is omitted and there is a particular focus on the moments when Pygmalion, who has sculpted a statue in ivory of a radiantly beautiful woman, by the torrential force of his passion brings her to life. The inert female is so charged with male intensity and swamped with his libido, part of his prayers to Venus, that she comes to life, sharply reversing the direction of *Scillaes Metamorphosis*, where the sexually torpid woman is turned to stone for her unresponsiveness.

Marston's somewhat brittle defence against charges of salacity was made in *The Scourge of Villanie*, his next volume and reprinted within a year. In it he devoted eighty lines of the sixth satire to his touchy assertion that he was coolly satirizing the clamour for such erotic pieces. What Marston did (in effect) was caper between the lines and in the margins, signalling a highly personal tone even in the abbreviated narrative. Marlowe and Shakespeare rarely intrude and if their poems in the genre were anonymous 'one might hesitate to assign them to the authors of Dr Faustus and Hamlet'.[7] Marston ruffles up eye-catching nods and winks, and as the story nears its (rare enough) happy conclusion, he squeezes in lines to suggest that if his naked mistress lay beside him as resistant as stone, she would soon be transformed by his sexual attentions. This smirking boast is part of his weaponry to puncture the Petrarchan mode by juxtaposing Pygmalion and Galatea against an actual physical encounter. The ironic timbre of such boasting becomes clear when it is recalled that he (Marston the poet) has invented his own response to an event in fiction. This is as phoney as his synthetic outrage in *The Scourge* which he invents in order to attack lubricity in Ovidian narratives.

Marston's underlying mockery of the reader is confirmed in the next stanza, where he rounds on the 'wanton itching ear' – a misplaced itch that listens 'with lustful thoughts'

> expecting for to hear
> The amorous description of that action
> Which Venus seeks, and ever doth require,
> When fitness grants a place to please desire   (195–98)

This would have meant much more to Elizabethans than it does to us, for the young customarily shared rooms and beds, and so could not help but hear any fumbling in the dark. Inadvertently they became 'ausculteur' – an erotic eavesdropper. The conventional Ovidian style poet would trip into 'the amorous description'; Marston sets up the expectation but then claims it is enough for the reader to substitute mentally for Pygmalion in his own erotic imagination:

> What he would do, the self-same action
> Was not neglected by Pygmalion   (215–16)

Realistic asides underline Marston's own high judgment of himself as a connoisseur of human ineptitude; especially in erotic exchanges:

> I oft have smiled to see the foolery
> Of some sweet youths, who seriously protest
> That love respects not actual luxury,
> But only joys to dally, sport and jest   (109–12)

The worldly maturity of this is actually an amusing, self-gratifying pose because if Marston was born in 1576, a disputed date, then when he wrote the lines he was about twenty years old – yet who would have thought it? Satire assumes the unwillingness or inability of the collective to discern and live with truth, suggesting only individuals can do this. For success in its own terms satire requires an acute awareness of the chasm between the ideal and empirical reality, and Marston, a Christian satirist, not a pagan like Martial, developed a precocious awareness that a romantic juvenile insistence on the ideal can only lead to absurdity. So conventional raptures about ivory breasts, are in Galatea's case, happy for her breasts are indeed ivory.

After Tom Nashe's *Choise of Valentines* and Marston's *The Scourge of Villanie*, Francis Beaumont took no chances with *Salmacis and Hermaphroditus*; it appeared anonymously in 1602. Nashe's work remained in manuscript because publishers flinched at its unblinking, unblushing sexuality; Marston's works ended up on the list of banned works issued by the bishops in June 1599. Beaumont's caution may have been general or even particular because his father was a judge. Francis and his brother John resided in Inner Temple at the end of the century and they competed in the writing of Ovidian and mock-Ovidian poems. This story reverts to *Metamorphoses* IV (285–388), and the exemplary pursuit of an innocent, Hermaphroditus, by the sexually rapacious Salmacis. Their one-sided sexual collision destroys the potential for full masculinity in the chaste boy, and creates out of the union in a pool a single bisexual being. This story has lurked behind virtually all Elizabethan epyllia. It had, as has been suggested, 'a latent paradigmatic status' and to develop it with refined gusto Beaumont is sensual but not salacious. The myth is that of the water-nymph Salmacis enraptured of the beautiful boy Hermaphroditus, who is androgynous and effeminate long before he is merged with her in the pool. Male power is at its lowest ebb in Hermaphroditus and in the poem's preface Beaumont audaciously suggests 'I hope my poem is so lively writ/That thou wilt turn half-maid with reading it'. This would certainly cause many of his male readers to wilt because the prospect of being 'half-maid' would scarcely be welcome.

Salmacis fails in her wooing, the boy remains a boy, and she pretends to go away but actually hides. Hermaphroditus approaches the pool supposing himself alone, but voyeuristically regarded by Salmacis who watches him test the water with his toe, a tentative sexual gesture, before stripping 'his soft clothes from his tender skin'. The form of his naked beauty after the striptease is too much for Salmacis, who has borne acute frustration and agonies of desire. Indeed, this is a body that would cause the moon to quit her path if she could. With a shriek of 'He's mine', Salmacis sheds her clothes and leaps on him in the pool, signalling the victory of water over the sun on the boy's body. She invokes heavenly intervention to allow them to remain together and with stunning literal-mindedness that is what they deliver, merging male and female, like the female praying mantis masticating the boldly foolish male who impregnates her. The implicit warning of the poet is that the idea of men and women growing together in love to the point that individual gender is submerged is only a metaphor. If it happened in reality it would be calamitous, smothering profound distinctions and leading ultimately to sterility and extinction.

In the meantime Beaumont's readers, perhaps a little disconcerted by the perfunctory ending, could exercise their gender prerogatives by re-reading a skittish, even subversive poem.

CHAPTER NINE

'UNSTAID DESIRE'

English love poetry of the Elizabethan period, love of the exalted, literary kind, was written by men for a mixed audience. Their aim was verbal as well as physical mastery. Prince Pyrocles in Sidney's *The Countess of Pembroke's Arcadia* silences Philoclea by kisses and she never succeeds in relating her narrative to her amorous young listener. Writing on marble stone exposed to the elements, her poem praising chastity is nearly erased by the flow of moisture, a distinctly sexual procedure. Composing a new poem to compensate for this loss Philoclea, lacking a pen and ink, never commits it to paper. What it would have recorded was profound unease at her initial blotting of the unstained surface of the marble itself. So in both cases, 'Philoclea's words are pervaded by an over-whelming sexuality which precludes any sustained role for her as author'.[1] Writing, with its dipping and sliding across the page, was an activity most suitable for men when they were not preoccupied with male diversions requiring superiority of sinew and muscle. It was unsuitable for women to write because their social and marital status became suspect; women's words were freighted with sexual meaning, and their circulation, whether spoken or written, not approved. To avoid this women minded to write often substituted translation and correspondence, but there were sonnets, elegies and even pamphlets from the boldest, most driven women who did also read books of love, and did sometimes defy their censorious husbands.

Still, there were some few women and more men able by instruction and education to respond with critical approval and alert seriousness to innovation as well as formulation: 'Elizabethan poetry is neither "classical" nor "romantic".' Given the exclusive circularity of the reading group within London (though with provincial outposts like Wilton), before the modest unfurling to the democratizing lottery of publication, certain writers achieved an unsteady credit long before wider public recognition or acclaim. In his *Palladis Tamia* (1598), written while he was living in Botolph Lane, Francis Meres, later rector and schoolmaster in Ring, Rutland, made some important private jottings on the sonnet writers of the period, 'the most passionate among us to bewail and bemoan the perplexities of Love'. He begins with Henry Howard, Earl of Surrey (d. 1547), whose view of the happy life in the poem so named includes health, a quiet mind, an equal friend and a chaste wife. Among later poets he lists Sidney, Sir Walter Ralegh, Edward Dyer (knighted in 1596), Spenser, Daniel, Drayton, Shakes-peare (sic), and others like Thomas Churchyard and Nicholas Breton now regarded as minor. Thomas Nashe in 1591 saluted *Astrophel and Stella* as the mirror of passionate melancholy, and its publication unfettered a striking surge of

Petrarchan sonnet sequences. Passion may be sanative in its heartfelt 'forcibleness'; it is the rhetorical devices that need purging, because mere verbal trickery is not persuasive. 'To impose a form on measureless passions was almost a moral duty for Sidney's generation.'[2] To exalt it was to align it with civility. He wrote toughly of poets who 'so coldly apply fiery speeches that, if I were a mistress, they never would convince me, that they were in love'.

Whereas for erotic-mythological fantasies (see Chapter Eight) the Elizabethans had an abundance of classical examples to find as source and inspiration, the sonnet could not be so directly imitative since Ovid and Virgil had not known the form. Still, writers in Elizabethan England were so saturated in classical literature that the lack of a precise model was not a source of concern to Thomas Watson, whose sonnet cycle *Ekatompathia* is dated to 1582. It is possible that while he lodged in Westminster his sonnets in manuscript reached the poet Edmund Spenser, whose literary connections included Dyer, Gabriel Harvey and Sidney. 'Listen, then, lordings, with good ear to me.' So wrote the latter and there is no doubting that they did, but the most obvious aspect of the sonnet cycle *Astrophel and Stella* is that there is but one person it seeks to bestir. It is a performance of huge animation just as the revival of the tourney was before Elizabeth. It was a glamorous tradition of the past and was intimately linked to Italian fashions at the end of the sixteenth century. The tradition began with Dante and Petrarch, whose formal distinction as sonneteers established the conventions which became permanent. The poet as lover is harrowed by his pursuit of an elusive woman whose beauty attracts magnetically, but whose virtue remains unbreachable. The woman is blonde and a cause of acute distress in the man whose unrequited love leaves him trapped by his passion.

Sidney was doubly qualified to undertake a sonnet sequence. Under the influence of his sister, Wilton House became a famous centre of art and learning. It was Nicholas Breton who elevated the Countess of Pembroke to a position above the Duchess of Urbino as a patroness of literature, and as nearly as possible the house sought to emulate the liberal culture of the Italian courts. The trend in such circles was towards an increase in the freedom with regard to sex which has been identified as characteristic of Elizabethan literature. Secondly, Sidney had travelled to Italy to study in Padua, one of the great university cities of western Europe, and he had also visited Venice in company with Griffin Madox, a family retainer, and Lodovico Bruschetto (englished as Lodowick Bryskett). Venice was the city of golden-haired beauties who were courtesans, the pinnacle of the prostitution hierarchy. In Renaissance Italy the cultivated prostitute was valued and sought after. Her task was not only to sexually enthral her client, but play the lute, sing, write sonnets and so on. Not only did they pose for artists, but sometimes they became works of art themselves, as happened with Lady Penelope Devereux Rich. In every respect she was the finest aristocratic translation of a Venetian courtesan to England, acknowledged by society and even more fortunate than them because rich without effort. Not only was Lady Rich proficient in the arts, but like Italian Renaissance courtesans she was able through her powerful connections to converse intelligently on matters of policy in the tenebrous world of late Elizabethan politics. As an ornament of society Lady Rich enjoyed extraordinary freedom after the mid–1580s.

The dizzying numbers of courtesans in Venice made for an extreme diversity, and they became an identifiable part of the state's apparatus for encouraging foreign merchants and tourists. In the carnal city the visitor did not have to scratch about for information, even if local gossip eluded him. There were catalogues acting as guide books to the brothels and the courtesans. Intended for the most part to denigrate, they provided free (if not altogether accurate) tariffs of pleasures and prices.[3] There were also albums with illustrations of lovers sexually cavorting, intended not only to stimulate but also to instruct the tyro. These were popular from the sixteenth century onwards and an inquisitive English youth entering manhood might have been slightly incredulous at all that was available for money, but it would have braced him for participation. Born in 1554, Philip Sidney was around twenty years of age when he stayed in Padua and Venice. We have an image of him that has become falsely mythologized; the compassionate wounded soldier was not the whole man. In a city swamped with every king of erotic pleasure it would have required a moralistic and prudish young man to resist. Sidney was not such a man. Although he had a dominating routine of study he still did have time for enjoyment and his companions, although older (Brushetto was born in 1546), had no reason to prevent this. Sidney's awareness of the opportunity offered by a Venetian sojourn is also highlighted by his choice of Paolo Veronese to paint his portrait. Exploring the city by boat and on foot, constantly aware of the traffic in commercial sex, men out for a spree would not avert their eyes, whenever they stopped to quench their thirst or dine, from the portraits of courtesans which were frequently displayed in the city in serial form. When the men bathed in public baths the evidence of women of pleasure being available would have been condoned. This advertising mode spread through Italy, the Netherlands and on to England, where Shakespeare noted that Elizabethan bawds kept portraits of available women to engage clients.[4] Confirmation of this manner of advertising can be found on the engraved title page of *Le Miroir des Courtisanes*, executed by Crispin de Passe II (*c.* 1597–1670). It seems very possible that Sidney, with his looks marred by the childhood illnesses of measles and smallpox, had his first full sexual experience with a Venetian courtesan, an essential preliminary to his ardour for Lady Rich explored in *Astrophel and Stella*.

After his return to England from the civilized city of courtesans, Sidney was continuously lapped with the waves of golden opinions of his contemporaries. Despite this expectant regard very little of consequence happened, although in 1577 Sir Francis Walsingham regarded him as a 'great hope'. It was this widespread expectancy which became the troubling keynote of Sidney's life and without resolution in some form this delaying of self-gratification can lead to psychological confusion and frustration. This was given an edge by the queen being (as it were) his mistress, with mastery over him signalled by his sardonic New Year gift to her in 1581 of a jewelled whip. Penelope Devereux again insinuated into his emotions by being at this time his intended mistress. 'The love-game enacted in the sonnets is a struggle between her and Sidney for control not only over their relationship but over the poems as well.'[5] All this mimics a pattern that characterizes the political forum of the Elizabethan court. There is a contest of wits going on, leading to the muddling of language by 'the force of erotic desire'. The struggle between the reader and the writer, Stella and Astrophel, favours the former but leaves the loser without consolation. It is an incomplete experience, a stage in development, just as had been the sexual encounter with the Venetian courtesan since it was just one episode. There is no evidence of Sidney having had any sexual affairs after Venice and preceding his marriage to Frances Walsingham in 1583.

In the interim, Sidney's pent-up energy exploded onto paper in the domestication of the Petrarchan mode in the sonnet cycle. It was done with great virtuosity and immediately set many others to emulation. *Astrophel and Stella* exalts passion which has the power to send language spinning out of control, or lurching into silence. Sidney works up the whole sequence from that first emission of seed in Venice. For that experience to be grounded (in England) he collided it in his subconscious with the tenderest feelings for Penelope Rich. But for the world and its ways she might have married him, just as he might have fought a duel with the Earl of Oxford if majesty had not ruled otherwise. When Sidney gave way to pressure it always caused a blessure. Privacy was the rarest, most precious item for courtiers, and during 1581, before her marriage to Lord Rich, it is doubtful if Penelope, barely more than a child-woman, spent more than a few minutes alone in his company. Little time to woo in Venice, or in London, where far more time was taken up with the marriage negotiations of the Duke of Anjou and Elizabeth. How right it seems that when taking part in a great celebratory joust in May for the French party, Philip Sidney appeared with four other knights as the 'Four foster-children of Desire'. Marriage would have legitimated his sexual desires which came to be acknowledged in the sonnets. In sonnet 71, after praising Stella's virtue and beauty for thirteen lines, he closes with the unmistakeable voice of Desire calling for an end to his sexual famine.

The lover in Petrarch in a vein that slides between 'restrained wooing and distant adulation' admits the possibility of union only in dreams. Sidney's sonnet cycle is variously toned in its erotic urgency; there are many sexual puns, some obvious, others more recondite, but also a rejection of the idea of substitution, sexual experience with anyone other than Stella. While he has been unchaste, she has not and he regrets this double standard. His past experience seems to hover as he considers a sex shock with Stella in sonnet 68:

> O think I then, what paradise of joy
> It is, so fair a Vertue to enjoy.

Alan Sinfield has teased out three meanings in the pun on 'enjoy'.[6] Firstly, being so good must be a wonderful thing; secondly, to have sex with such a virtuous person must be superb; and thirdly, that it must be gratifying to be able to draw comfort from insisting on your honour (while I suffer). If we continue to scrutinize the vocabulary two more words take on close meaning. They are 'paradise', a word often deployed by sense-saturated English travellers to Venice, and 'fair', meaning beautiful and blonde, that essential hair colour for so many Venetian courtesans, and the natural hair colour of Penelope Devereux Rich. The sonnet cycle does not offer any solution to the immediate problem of his rejection of the idea of a platonic relationship, which is what, if anything, they have had hitherto. 'Leave love to will' (sonnet 10) sounds like a cranky self-admonition; he is dragooning his reason, and makes use of that frequent pun of the Elizabethans on 'will' meaning genitals. But rejecting a platonic relationship for a would-be sexual one serves no purpose either because 'I crav'd the thing which ever she denies,' – she is quite resolute in denying him her bed. She represents unspotted authority; he is the libertine who spends his wealth idly in pursuit of self-gratification:

> And which is worse, no good excuse can show,
> But that my wealth I have most idly spent   (sonnet 18)

Alert readers will have noticed the sexual puns on 'thing', 'wealth' and 'spent'.

In all Petrarchan sonnets elements of pleasure and pain are fused, and in seeking to emulate and perhaps even outdo his great Italian precursor, Sidney avails himself of strands of his public and private life. The former is under an uncaring mistress, his queen, the woman for whom his own mother had unstintingly sacrificed her facial beauty to nurse through sickness in the early 1560s. This collides with a melancholy obsession with a remote beauty, but Astrophel and Stella can decouple from such hindrances and personal riddling. To readers then no doubt that riddling was as teasing and vital as the many sexual puns in the text, offering a privileged glimpse as it seemed of court life and loves. The sonnets circulated by hand, sextexts. Three unauthorized printed editions appeared in 1591, and in 1593 in the preface to the folio *Arcadia* it was announced that the Countess of Pembroke was planning to publish more of her brother's works. The speed with which the sonnet cycle became a fashionable literary genre is remarkable. This may in some part be attributed to the fact that it was Sidney, dead in 1586 after taking a battle wound, who wrote them, and that Lady Rich was a striking figure in court society. More weight should probably be attached to the view that the vitality of such cycles came not from real life 'but from the multiple significances inherent in . . . female figures who symbolize all that is desirable and unobtainable in human life'.[7] In the 1590s at least twenty sequences were published dealing, with varying degrees of bookish candour, with secular love of women and men. Since the literary world pounced on *Astrophel and Stella* and every sequence that subsequently appeared in manuscript or print, the sonnets naturally show a conspicuous sameness of temper and emotion. Imitation, of course, was not seen as a disabling flaw; indeed, in Renaissance poetics, expert imitation allowed pronounced similarity to give a scholarly burnish to the artefact. Petrarch himself in writing to Boccaccio had made a critical recommendation in the mid-fourteenth century that the 'proper imitator should take care that what he writes resembles the original without reproducing it'. Mimicry and pastiche were not favoured and Petrarch went on to emphasize that similarity should be 'planted so deep that it can only be extricated by quiet meditation'.

So, is there anything significant in the silence of Marlowe? There was, after all, a 1592 edition of Samuel Daniel's earliest collection, *Delia*, fifty sonnets, with Hero and Leander appearing in sonnet 38. Since Renaissance poetry was not primarily aiming at 'self-expression' or the confessional truth, perhaps not. Given Marlowe's towering confidence in his own genius, if he had wished to write a sonnet sequence no personal aspect of his sexual inclinations need actually to have underpinned the text. Instead he chose the topic of Hero and Leander for an epyllion, forfeiting the opportunity to write a sonnet sequence before his sudden death of 30 May 1593, which left the former work apparently unfinished. Marlowe may give a pronounced homo-erotic swerve to the description of Leander but the greater text is concerned with heterosexual consummation. Neptune's optimism that Leander is really fond of him and will succumb sexually proves to be false: 'Leander made reply:/"You are deceiv'd, I am no woman, I".' Homosocial high jinks appear bubbling in *Love's Labour's Lost*, when Shakespeare found the opportunity to joke about poetic and sexual fashions; the King of Navarre and his little academy pen poems to their ladies and are mocked for so doing. The sonnet 'If love make me foresworn, how shall I swear to love', was written for Berowne, whom some have thought was acted on stage by Shakespeare and hence speaks directly private thoughts of the playwright. It appeared in *The Passionate Pilgrim* (1599), a miscellaneous volume put together by the publisher William Jaggard, who purloined several sonnets and put 'By W. Shakespeare' on the title page to bait potential readers already familiar with his plays. It was a ruse that worked for two editions until someone got wise to what he was up to and put a stop to it. Criticism of 'If love makes me foresworn . . .' is found within the play and given by Holofernes, who rumbles that it is poetry by numbers, and the true master of all writing on passion is Ovid.

Imitation by itself is not enough to command unfettered admiration – a view set out by Quintilian in his tenth book. Emulation, however, can strike a richer vein than imitation: the craft involved should not produce a clumsy replica, but should emulate – in this case, Ovid's elegance and facility. The sweetness of expression advocated by Seneca, and before him Horace, is likened to the honey-making of bees, and these tiny workers on wings are driven to their continuous efforts to service the queen and augment the hive by their nature. The writer of sonnets should fall into the same category, combining imitation and invention with a natural economy of effort. In sonnet 59 there is a rueful reflection that in writing nothing can be new, all that needs to be said has been said, our brains are beguiled. True today perhaps, but for many of his co-writers and contemporaries writing sonnets to beguile, Shakespeare's mild protest at the past pre-empting the future would seem genuinely quaint, the more so since he brought abundant invention and complexity to his own sonnets.

The Romantics, most famously Wordsworth and Coleridge, expounded the view that in his *Sonnets* Shakespeare wrote with a precious exultation and secret rapture that sprang unbidden from the hidden depths of his emotional experience. 'With this key Shakespeare unlocked his heart', wrote Wordsworth, and later Browning snorted in response, 'If so, the less Shakespeare he'. Romantics since have rejected the Browning version in favour of the 'lay bare his soul' school of thought, a matter of inclination rather than scholarly rigour. Why would the poet do such a singular thing? It is a proceeding entirely inconsistent with the writing of the playwright – could such an intellectual canyon exist in the man? In his plays there are few signs of private thoughts swimming in because Shakespeare was a box-office specialist, not a philosopher although philosophically inclined. Moreover, he had evidence that a sonnet sequence, even if initially written as a coterie diversion, was likely to garner a wider readership. Shakespeare was barely a public figure, his name hardly a household word when he embarked on this mould-breaking sequence. He was a man of no particular social standing who confessed in sonnet 110 to embarrassment about his profession; it provided him with the means to support a wife and family in Stratford, while he lodged periodically in London. What Shakespeare did was seize the Petrarchan mode, place it like a piece of iron in a flame and hammer it into an entirely new shape. The expected convention of writing soulfully about a beautiful women disappeared in a hundred thousand sparks derived from his sweat and effort.

In Harold Pinter's play *Betrayal* an affair is scrutinized backwards to its clumsy inception. Something akin happens in the *Sonnets,* where the first person utterance (or poetic 'I') treats the reader to a multiplicity of views about a strikingly handsome young man and a woman who betray the writer by becoming lovers. Just as each character he invents for his plays arises out of a source which may be factual or fictional, all that can be said of these two is that they could be prompted by people encountered by Shakespeare in his daily, routine life in London. Nor is it at all certain that the first person utterance is indeed Shakespeare the man, rather than a protective carapace making such an identification woefully misplaced. To many people it seems

What Hugh Clopton had built, New Place, Stratford-upon-Avon, the last home of William Shakespeare, Sir John Clopton had demolished in 1702. During the destruction this glass roundel was said to have been saved, bearing the letters W.A.S., for William and Anne Shakespeare, tied in a true love-knot.

much more likely that Shakespeare took on the task of imagining himself as the poet within the poems, ruefully dealing with ungovernable feelings. To do this successfully must heighten the formal difficulties and the satisfaction felt as they are resolved within the cycle. The story within the cycle is a commonplace one; it is not required to be Shakespeare's own personal story; surely we can allow him to brood, fantasize and invent. A love triangle is not complicated, because by definition it involves three people, not thirteen or thirty-three.[8] Robert Crosman frets that if 'the poet in Shakespeare's sonnets may not be taken as a self-portrait, then it is hard to know who he can be'.[9] This erosion of the poetic 'I' is a matter of time, and it means simply that we cannot read the *Sonnets* as Elizabethans read them. The documentation of feelings should be left to romantic poets – 'Renaissance poets loved to debate the powers and limits of art.' Shakespeare's art was to create fictions voiced as if by himself in a heroic act of ventriloquism. What Shakespeare did was to magnify under the lens of scrutiny the nature of rapture. The science of optics at this time in Europe was in its infancy, although in the year of the publication of the *Sonnets*, 1609, Thomas Hariot was studying the moon with a telescope. This great scientist was a particular friend of John Dee, the Elizabethan polymath who wrote about optics that it makes things far off seem near, and near to seem far off: 'Small things to seem great: and great, to seem small. One man to seem an army. Or a man to be cursedly afraid of his own shadow.'

The poet, the friend, evidently younger, and the mistress are nameless, and by this suppression Shakespeare has tempted many scholars and amateur literary sleuths to try to fill the gap that so teases them. The namelessness probably has more to do with art than a whimsical way with biographical facts. Shakespeare was intending to subvert a long-established tradition and he does this in a radical way. The sequence begins with seventeen sonnets on the theme of procreation addressed to a young man and 'love is for a long while not even mentioned'. Radical indeed, subversion of the accepted mode – certainly. After this the sonnets 'record constant revisions of attitude' – but one meaning of 'constant' is 'unvarying' which misdirects, so strike it out. Shakespeare's 'revisions of attitude' are variety; add exhibitions of wit, as well as a purposefully bawdy use of language, a dole of courage and a competitive, materialist streak. He did not lay bare his heart, but elevated his genius with a sonnet cycle unyoked to patronage. The epigraph, sometimes called the dedication to the mysterious Mr W.H., filches the notion of fathering to allow the man who handed over the *Sonnets* for publication to be called their 'onlie begetter'. The Stationers' Register entry of 20 May 1609 – 'a booke called *SHAKESPEARES* sonnettes' – tells us only that this collection has no title more evocative than this. Names had regularly marked publications before as a publishing blandishment. Sidney, for example, did not call his sonnet sequence *Astrophel and Stella* – the name familiar then and ever since – it was named thus by the publisher in 1591. Philip Sidney was a great public figure immortalized by his early and widely lamented death; that alone would guarantee sales. Shakespeare had no secure public reputation as a playwright until the late 1590s. When writing the sonnets it seems unlikely that he had any expectation that they would be published as a collection, although some seepage into print did occur before 1600 – after all, Francis Meres knew enough to heap praise on him amongst others.

Yet by 1609 the high fashion for sonnets had much fallen away, so Thorpe had Shakespeare's name (by now well known) on the title page in a quaint hyphenated form. Thorpe has often been called a literary pirate who likely purloined the text, though from where and whom is never stated. But the 1609 edition was surely formally organized, and who better to arrange the sonnets than the author. This time there was no effort to suppress the edition which must have had his agreement. He may, indeed, have sold them to Thorpe through the benign agency of Mr W.H. because he needed the money to support his comfortable manner of living, and theatre income had fallen off because of plague outbreaks. Shakespeare had a family and no interest in voluntary poverty. Katherine Duncan-Jones has shown that Thorpe was a publisher (for twenty-five years) of 'deserved status and prestige, handling works by close associates of Shakespeare, and producing in many cases, highly authoritative texts'.[10] Yet in his artful 1987 article, Donald Foster tried to persuade with the notion that Mr W.H. was a simple misprint for Mr W.S. or even Mr W. SH. It is an argument presented with great academic aplomb but it is still daft – plain wrong. What is worth hauling from the rubble and dusting off is one insight – 'initials were rarely used in Renaissance dedications unless it was perfectly clear to whom they referred.' Perfectly clear then and one man stands out of the throng as the agent for publication – the 'onlie begetter'. Mr W.H. was a literary contemporary and very friendly acquaintance of Shakespeare who had borrowed ideas and phrases from him as they looked over each other's work. The matter was solved in a footnote some sixty years ago, but no one paid any attention afterwards to Nicholas Breton, who used Mr W.H. among a cluster of initials. Breton had used W.H. before, in 1606, when instigating the posthumous publication of Robert Southwell's *A foure-fold Mediatation.*

Shakespeare made his greatest effort to lock the attention of his contemporaries onto his plays. Even so, it is very doubtful if he or Ben Jonson or Thomas Middleton could have confidently named one playwright even from the earlier part of the century, other than perhaps John Skelton. Plays looked ephemeral – the evidence for this was undeniable – but poetry lived longer and the famously bawdy Chaucer was a key example. In 1590 popular taste was offered a 'good read' in a booklet called *The Cobler of Canterburie*, which in low verse and prose declared its kinship to Chaucer, a cheeky claim for a text exclusively concerned with cuckolds and faithless wives, and best read aloud, like most Elizabethan fiction. The 'inwardness' of the *Sonnets* and *A Lover's Complaint* (its companion piece and twin in feeling) marks an authentic sense of love's exaltations and desolations. The story of the *Sonnets* is akin to the jealousies and rivalries of Chaucer's *Knight's Tale*. Despite the keen references to the world and its transcendent beauty, the greater impression on the reader today comes from a sense of great forces compelling and compressing experience. This is chamber poetry, two loves in different rooms kept secret from the intrusive world, until an accidental breach admits betrayal.

CHAPTER TEN

THE PURSUIT OF
GANYMEDE

The procreation sonnets at the beginning of Shakespeare's sonnet sequence clearly constitute a warning to the narcissistic young man. The first person utterance is given over to a cool exposition of the necessity of marriage as the essential prop of house and family. The expression of sexual desire outside the monogamous marriage was subversive since its entire aim was personal gratification; without a life partner able to give birth to children the young man's patrimony will be fruitlessly scattered; the 'tender churl, mak'st waste in niggarding', which should alert the reader to the fact that these opening sonnets might be called auto-erotic fictions. The more important matter is: how seriously are readers meant to take a directive that may have a satirical purpose? The other love-object at the end of the sequence is a lady – the so-called 'dark lady', whose busy sexual schedule suggests she is a whore, either emotionally or professionally. The young man and the dark lady, top and tail, as it were, mark the illegitimacy of this passion, blasting apart the good conduct bromides of the very many domestic conduct books then on the market. In neither relationship will the poet (not emphatically Will, the poet) find love, though he tries through 'all the powers of language that his genius grants him to make two people love him'.[1]

To begin the sequence of sonnets with a young man and end them with a sexually rapacious woman signals the poet (again not Shakespeare in person) as a 'fop', the effeminate man whose sexual choices are not fixed by inclination or marriage. In Renaissance England effeminacy was not synonymous with a sexual preference for men. The fop is not designated a sodomite because he deliberately chooses to have sex with another man, but because having eschewed married monogamy and its relentless discipline of exclusivity, he can be expected to express his sexuality in unsanctioned ways. Indeed, the worldly woman entering the fop's life may actively prefer sodomy to vaginal intercourse since it prevented pregnancy. Sexual desire freely expressed 'was marked as subversive in that it alone led to a man's effeminacy'.[2] 'Vice steals secretly upon you through the avenue of pleasure.'

The fop will swing from sexual mode to sexual mode; he will entertain his lady, according to Everard Guilpin, and having taken in a play in the afternoon has supper with his 'ingle' or catamite. Pollio in *Skialetheia* (1598) has all the attributes of a Renaissance putto: 'wanton face', 'curled hair' and 'fat buttock'. In their readings of Greek and Roman literature the Elizabethans found poetry and prose lauding and anthologizing the many physical charms of the beardless boy poised sweetly on the brink of youthful manhood. The boy who wished or found it expedient to market this transient charm might be satirized by those quick to spot a social trend. To read about such things in classical texts was disturbing to many; to have the matter made contemporary, and in the public domain was actually quite shocking to many more. To pursue a sexual relationship with a boy was disreputable and might be punished. It was unfathomable that the Greeks in particular should write about it with such freedom and ease when they were apparently authorizing, as Sidney put it, 'abominable filthiness'. He had a special admiration for Plato and Plutarch, but he stated in the *Defence of Poetry* he would not recommend reading Plato's *Phaedrus* or *Symposium*, nor the discourse of love in Plutarch simply because of such unwelcome and unwholesome rhapsod(om)izing on boy love (pederasty).

The beloved boy is severely disadvantaged in a sexual relationship with a man. The man has experience, money and so power; all the boy can bring is freshness (at a premium as with the virgin girl) and cheerful naiveté. As age and experience erodes the advantages of the beautiful boy his chance of being discarded for another, younger than him, increases. Like the pederastic photographs taken in Sicily by Wilhelm von Gloeden in the late nineteenth century, poets learned to dress up their texts in pastoral disguises. As Simon Shepherd appropriately has pointed out, the 'classical reference is invoked in order to present the poems as imitation rather than expression of desire'.[3] The props of short shifts, sheep and wild places should fool no one; indeed, they heighten expectation that the love object may be male. From the myth of the passionate shepherd in Arcadia, a number of Elizabethan poets elaborated on the current meaning of passion – physical love. This allowed for erotic sighs, yearning for sex and gentle fumblings. Boys will be boys; these boy shepherds are not worldly men and their knowledge of carnality is rather limited by their dwelling in uncorrupted wild places. In Virgil's second eclogue the limitation is well marked by the failure of Corydon to woo Alexis into a fully sexual relationship. Abraham Fleming made a translation into English in 1575, and in his Argument before the poem seems relieved that this was so. Corydon is aroused and passionate but there is no reciprocation; 'Alex regards no gifts' and the wooer's dream subsides into a dull little fantasy, ending with something more realistic than transfiguring pleasure.

In Marlowe's *Come live with me, and be my love*, written perhaps a decade or so after Fleming's translation, the seductive urgency of the shepherd is woven into his offerings – no smelly sheep run for these two when they become lovers – and the shepherd seems so masterful yet tender that few can doubt that this time they will. 'Beds of roses/and a thousand fragrant posies' will usefully mask the natural animal reek around them. This time imagination triumphs over reality because there are no dead ewes corpsing legs up in the sun; even the bird songs are magicked into madrigals which often then had an erotic content. The dizzying effect of all this will cause a swoon:

> If these delights thy mind may move;
> Then live with me, and be my love.

Actually, the appeal is not to the mind but the body since 'delight' was sexual pleasure given to a partner, an intention that was further developed in Marlowe's play *Dido, Queen of Carthage*, in which sexual love is given central weight and authority. There is a very important opening scene in which the seduction of Ascanius by Venus is easily achieved; just how easily is made explicit by the first lines of the play yoking together the seduction theme of the Passionate Shepherd with two other leading themes; the defiance of Time (*carpe diem*) and the horses of the night (*noctis equi*).

Jupiter, father of the Gods, is wooing Ganymede, a name evoking for Elizabethans the boy whore:

> Come, gentle Ganymede, and play with me
> I do love thee well.

The word 'play' invokes sexual frolics and after reassurances that the goddess Juno will not again frown on Ganymede without Jupiter constraining her, the boy is encouraged to ask for some benefaction. The god woos the boy under the premise that they are supremely privileged, but actually it is the god that has the privileges which he transfers benignly to the beardless boy. So the bearded (manly) god courts his 'ningle' or 'ingle' – the boy favourite who in theory can reject this role. The future prospects for the lad who does refuse his body are not guaranteed, for his particular charm lies in being a willing subordinate. Terms like 'ingle' and 'ganymede' in Elizabethan England 'reveal the power differentials common to early modern organization of service and homo-eroticism'.[4]

Unlike terrestrial lovers having to be vigilant in noting the passage of Time, Jupiter and Ganymede are supremely privileged, literally having all the time in the world. The seduction is sought and urged not because time is against the seducer and his toyboy, but because Time itself can be controlled and work for them; there are no sheep to round up, no predators to keep at bay, nothing can mar their joy. It seems to be Marlowe's view that the gods have a sublime advantage over humans in that they can seek pleasure, defer it, and to find pleasure in that. It is impossible for humans to do this graciously, a pleasure deferred is a pleasure confiscated by Time. The gratification of the precious instant is what rules the calamitous decision of Faustus to sell his soul. In Ovid's *Amores* the lover with the loved one in his arms begs the horses of the night to slow their pace. Marlowe of course translated the *Amores* and too shifted the horses of the night to his plays *Dr Faustus* and *Dido*. In the former the quote is used with bristling ironic purpose since Faustus pleads for a few seconds more. In *Dido* the irony is almost festive since Jupiter and Ganymede are free of the shackles of Time; the horses can, as it were, gallop endlessly on the spot and advance not at all.

Being a god means Jupiter has privileges galore on earth and in the heavens, and his slyly seductive offers to Ganymede reinforce this. Vulcan is to dance for the lad's amusement, and exasperating as it is for Juno, she has to forfeit her marriage jewels for him – 'trick they arms and shoulders with my theft.' Like a rent-boy today hankering for a gold watch Ganymede wants a jewel for his ear and a fine brooch to put on his hat: 'and then I'll hug with you an hundred times.' This seems bland enough, but 'hug' in Elizabethan England is erotic – this is undoubtedly an embrace with a sexual component. The 'female wanton boy' evidently has a low imaginative threshold (like Faustus); Ganymede may be male but his fee for erotic availability is actually quite modest and Jupiter does not need to muster a great amorous argument. In dramatic contrast are Dido's efforts to secure the love of Aeneas. In the heavens the rules of love are transgressed at no cost, but on earth the love of Aeneas for Dido is contrary to the will of heaven. The gods themselves behave absurdly, ungraciously, transgressively. Marlowe's overall comment seems to be one of ironic mockery for the authority of heaven, which destroys the love of Dido and Aeneas. The airy puerility of Jupiter and the simpering cupidity of Ganymede are held up surely for derision and in performance would have received just that from a knowing Elizabethan audience. Marlowe may be making a general point by working up a view widely held in society, or he may have in mind some particularities from his time as an English government spy. In France he likely heard stories of the notorious travesties at the French court, where Henri III would, it was said, don women's clothes and where his male mignons were exclusively favoured.[5] The word was anglicized to 'minions' and meant a male favourite of a king. In *Edward II* it is the enemies of the king who distinguish between the favourite, whose whims had power to damage the nation, 'and the ideal of male friendship as exemplified in certain classical rulers'. Even ideals can become disturbingly slanted and friendship became a notion in some disarray. Michel de Montaigne in his essay on 'Friendship' cited the inequalities to be found in androphile relationships in ancient Greece and was critical of them. 'Friendship' is actually a problematic word because writers then used it of sexual and non-sexual intimates.

Montaigne's views may have been influenced by his own cordial dealings with Anthony Bacon, elder brother of Francis Bacon. The possibility is enhanced because although the connection between Montaigne and the English traveller and spy is not detailed in their correspondence, and only a few references to them as friends survive, we do know now that Bacon kept a boisterous household of 'wanton boys' and young men. In the town archives of Montauban are papers relating to sodomy charges.[6] The first seems to have accused him of having sexual relations with one of his page boys, and another of tolerating such activity among the young men and boys employed by him. The charges were serious and the outcome required in 1594 that Richard Barnfield made the dedication of his miscellany of subversive poems *The Affectionate Shepherd* which takes up the theme of *Come live with me*, as well as Virgil's second

Eclogue and so cunningly combines the classical and the sexual in a text strewn with double meanings. Three pastoral *Eclogues* revel in the erotic reverie of the 'fair Boy':

> If it be sin to love a lovely Lad;
> Oh then sin I, for whom my soul is sad

And the 'lovely' lad's name is Ganymede, and Daphnis anticipates Walt Whitman by a sexual fantasy of two boys imagined clinging together; 'Barnfield's text invokes a taboo and produces sexual pleasure'.[7] The high fun is not only that a sexual frisson is provoked by artful language that has an innocent camouflage, but also that the friendship invoked is itself erotic and transgressive. Barnfield's readers in the fraternity of the Inns of Court would have fallen on this gleefully, but others may have taken offence so when his second volume of poems, a collection entitled *Cynthia*, appeared he took the opportunity to write a defence in his preface saying that *The Affectionate Shepherd* was simply an imitation of Virgil. Even so, the second volume also comprised sonnets supposedly written by Daphnis to Ganymede, and again Barnfield used double meanings to test the alertness of his predominantly male readers. One of these was thoroughly familiar then, 'stones' being used for testes, or properly in this case since these are boys – testicles. Another invokes the 'coral lips' at the very tip of the penis; one night a dream of this prompts a wet dream.

Such male–male bonding does not lock out women. Having dedicated the text to perhaps the second most famous woman in the kingdom, on his own Barnfield goes beyond Virgil, where women are written to the margins, by introducing a competitive female called Guendolen. Barnfield specifically imitates writers of his own period and her introduction as the sexual raider who threatens to destroy the boys' idyll may be a parodic element. Ganymede is so handsome that all the shepherdesses have a tender yearning for him. One love triangle is not enough for Barnfield and if he is parodying Shakespeare's *Sonnets* he makes the matters of the heart more complicated and amusing by making an old grey beard Ganymede's rival for Guendolen. This comes about when Cupid and Death get drunk and mistakenly claim each other's arrows. Death fires and the old man is smitten by one of Cupid's arrows, rather than falling dead in the expected manner. Death's dart when fired by Cupid kills a 'fair and beautiful young man', with whom Guendolen was already enamoured. If Penelope Rich ever read this, what might her response have been? Was it blithe, amused, or tenderly self-reflective since not so many years before a poet who claimed to love her had died young?

The uncertainty of her future is echoed in the uncertainty at the heart of these poems. For the sake of his own future Ganymede must curb his audacity, and Daphnis who loves him unrequittedly takes on the role of wise old counsellor. The shift, as Bruce Smith has indicated, is more political than moral; the would-be seducer returns from the field with an empty seed-sack having sown his wild oats. In my view,

Barnfield is playing elaborate games and the sequence reflects deliberately the personal histories of Anthony Bacon, Essex and Lady Rich. When Bacon returned from France some years after the Montauban hearing he was much subdued. Distance from England had once protected him from scorn, but such an escapade would have been even more dangerous in England since Elizabeth took a moralistic and even hostile attitude to men who preferred men or those who preferred boys. Perhaps as a consequence Anthony Bacon avoided the court as much as possible and used his physical infirmity as an excuse. By the end of Barnfield's second *Eclogue* the rhapsodomizing of the first has been replaced by a judicious anthology of advice – the sort that Francis Bacon gave to Essex:

> Swear no vain oaths; hear much, but little say;
> Speak ill of no man, tend thine own affairs,
> Bridle thy wrath, thine angry mood delay;
> (so shall thy mind be seldom cloyed with cares;)
> Be mild and gentle in they speech to all,
> Refuse no honest gain when it doth fall.

Daphnis advises Ganymede to marry. Essex had already done so in 1590, but the advice goes further; he should embrace his wife but 'live not in lechery', a notion that Essex found difficult to comply with. So who in the period might be the old man wounded by Cupid who becomes a comic rival for Guendolen's favours? The answer is that this ridiculous figure was Barnfield's joke at the expense of a new, foreign arrival in England, the posturing, flattering, self-abasing Antonio Perez, an emissary sent over by Henri IV of Navarre and France in the spring of 1593. The queen declined to give open acknowledgement of Perez being in England but he found a comforting welcome in the Essex circle and he made himself acceptable by extreme flattery and a squirmy devotion. Although an outsider without any English language skills, Perez was observant enough to realize that many of the men about Essex were men who preferred men or boys. Lady Anne Bacon, mother of the brothers, regarded Perez with outright contempt – 'that old, doting, polling papist', and 'Bloody Perez'. On whom did the old chap dote? Penelope Rich and Essex.

English law gave stern directions against a man having genital contact with another man or a boy. Yet the noble and dignified friendship or love between men could never exclude such a possibility, while the accusation that a man had had sex with boys was a damaging one that the courts would punish variously. What they seem to have resented most was the thought of coercion on the dominant man's side; the teasing and frisky charm of boys capering before an older man or youth was overlooked since Elizabethans as pre-Freudians averted their gaze from manifestations of junior sexuality. That was regarded (if at all) as transitional. Even Elizabeth finally learned to ignore

Antonio Perez, a worthwhile intelligencer to Philip II of Spain, was ejected from the inner cluster of royal servants and forced to flee for his life taking state secrets with him. Arriving in England for the first time in the 1590s he amused and intrigued the Essex circle.

pederasty with the promotion of Francis Bacon, whose many talents had long been frostily resisted; and there was a sting too, in this advance, for Bacon was required to lead the public prosecution of the Earl of Essex after the rout of his rising in 1601. For many Elizabethans pederasty could be a symptom of social and political unreliability, and the men involved wayward and wild. A prominent example was the Earl of Oxford, whose dealings with a pederastic coterie at court led to accusations and a blotted public career. A kitchen boy had no one to defend his interests and was immediately dispensable. The much more public boys of the theatre companies who had to take on roles like that of Ganymede were probably better treated and protected from sexual predators if that was their wish. Certainly they had a great following in the theatre-going public and among this mixed crowd there were doubtless men and women who found the boys sexually alluring. This does not mean that all the boys were sexually improvident or untroubled by attempts to make assignations, but given the sophistication of the plays they were asked to perform in, with their insistent double-entendres, the boys must have realized that they could create a stir, in costume or in their daily working clothes. Salomon Pavy in his woefully short life became famous and Ben Jonson wrote his epitaph when he died; so far, I am not aware of Sam Shepherd doing the same for River Phoenix, a pan-sexual icon today whose experiments in sexuality are legendary already. A video of the late actor playing a female role in a high school Shakespeare production would no doubt become a vitally sought-after item by collectors.

Sir Francis Bacon was a servant to two sovereigns, but it is noticeable that his public career achieved a much greater impetus under James I, and his fall from the king's favour had most to do with suspected financial peculations, rather than a liking for handsome boys.

Within the enclosed, highly masculine world of English Renaissance theatre companies the boys were susceptible to cajolery, teasing and their own curiosity. In Anthony Bacon's household in France it was not just the master accused of sodomy but a much younger adult, Isaac Bougades, who attempted to penetrate the boy, David Brysson, causing the boy to cry out at the pain, bringing the intervention of another servant. If the boy players with the greatest charm or sweetness of expression were sexually abused by male actors, or if they were regularly seduced by male theatre-goers, how is it no charge of buggery was ever made against an actor or play-goer? For the young man studying at the Inns of Court the thought itself might be father to the act, and there was indeed a good chance of escaping prosecution, but to find out more about the law regarding same-sex offences required some pertinacity. The implication was, of course, that a case involving sodomy between two men was rare and in a lifetime at the bar a lawyer might never have to mount a defence.[8] The only legal authority to confront sodomy textually was Sir Edward Coke, and to secure an indictment he sought a threefold sequence of events: violence leading to penetration followed by ejaculation. Sodomy becomes a version of rape, and in Coke the law only takes an interest if the person subjected to these carnal actions is a boy. Humphrey Stafford was tried by the Court of King's Bench (1607–8) for just such a crime and executed. 'A lewd consumptive fellow', according to Simon Forman, his mistake was to choose a sixteen-year-old.

Historians have tended to treat the Elizabethan audiences as unanimous in their responses to plays and players. Given the numbers over the years who poured through the box office paying to be amused, diverted, stirred and shocked, such a sustained collective view is impossible to establish. There is the view that they accepted boy actors as actresses 'without confusion or feelings of sexual ambivalence'; alternatively, that they accepted it because it had become the convention of the day which as outside agents they could not challenge. Besides, better to have a boy mimicking unseemly behaviour of any kind than a woman; women constituted a large enough minority in the audience and male dominance of them was hard enough to establish to the patriarchal society's satisfaction. If boys played women the actions seen on stage need not stir real women to disconcerting and provoking replication. Going to the theatre then was not an act of quasi-worship, it was a way of seeing the world – the greatest of them was called the Globe – and the plays there purposefully called up the familiar and unfamiliar. The play was the 'thing' and the play on words is this time redundant. The 'thing' the boys possessed with which to capture the attention of a noisy, improper audience was not genital, but a thorough grounding in acting techniques. Any failure before an audience would make life harder for the senior players and management. The apprentice players were there to learn and if they developed a following like Pavy no one would have denied them that right on the grounds that there might be a sexual component in the admiration. It is perhaps an exaggeration to suppose, as some writers recently have, that the primary pleasure for the mixed audience then was a raging and covert yearning to bed the boys. It is akin to suggesting that spectators today at a football match are most concerned with the Laocöon-like writhings of a goal-scorer and his team, a bundling of bodies that might lead to cautions or arrest if conducted in a public park or on a beach. It is licensed homo-erotic behaviour by men who outside the stadium would scorn men who prefer men.

For a boy or youth to represent a woman successfully on the Renaissance stage, to move an audience to suppress their knowledge of his gender, required an unbroken or alto voice as well as a costume. These latter were evidently very important and in the inventory of Philip Henslowe, pawnbroker and theatrical entrepreneur, the examples of women's costumes suggest that companies made every effort to dress the boys appropriately and convincingly. Consider at the same time that there was too a stage outfit with a remarkable function – 'a robe for to go invisible', which did not make the wearer invisible any more than a dress miraculously made a boy into a woman, save in the imagination and for a limited time and purpose. Neither of the items taken from the wardrobe for a performance had meaning outside the space of the theatre. The robe did not allow its wearer to pillage merchant premises in Cheapside; no boy (so far as is known) patrolled the Bankside late in Cleopatra's finery. However, the celebrated actor of female parts, Richard Robinson did in a real life situation act the part of a lawyer's wife, a triumph mentioned in Jonson's *The Devil is an Ass*. English theatre then was not organized like late kabuki theatre in pre-Meiji Japan.

Despite the general exclusion of women from Elizabethan theatre companies, there is some evidence that very infrequently one or two squeezed through the barriers. Earlier in the sixteenth century a clutch of women performed in the shows of 1523 and 1534 in London for the new Lord Mayor. The evidence for this was found by Glynne Wickham and before him two researchers found two girls acting in a pageant in 1519, 'and in 1534 four ladies played the Virgin Mary and her three attendants'.[9] With the headlong assault and battering on the Roman Catholic Church in England begun by Protestant reformers of the evangelical bent, the lauding of Mary shrivelled in all but a few pockets of resistance, and as a result women were very quickly marginalized as performers; no cross-gender invasions were permitted, and a new tradition of having boys play the late female roles grew very quickly. It is my view that the consolidation of what may have begun satirically took place with the growth of the professional travelling troupes, and that the establishment of purpose-built theatres with no concessions to the requirements of female hygiene made the boys invaluable. The theatrical tradition of Catholic Southern Europe was markedly different; so says Stephen Orgel. In France, Spain and Italy, actresses remained on stage, while in the Netherlands and parts of Germany theatre itself was banned. England's countervailing position actually encouraged experiment and there was no call for women on stage, which to the Calvinistically-minded remained a lewd venue.

Since 'insatiable lust' and 'lewd behaviour' were part of the erotic nature of women it is no surprise that Spenser wrote that women often seemed to prefer the personified lechery. Some years later, in the early 1620s, Edward Elton argued that a woman had to avoid all activity that incited lust. For John Rainolds the most pressing reason for closing theatres was that it would bring an end to lads dressed as lasses, so inviting same-sex lusts, but no one in the plays written for the public stage showed any unease about such matters. Likewise, foreign visitors simply accepted the convention and appear to have thought little of it. In 1599 Thomas Platter, who was a student visitor to London, saw *Julius Caesar* in a production on the South Bank, and when the play was over enjoyed without any apparent sense of incongruity the dancing of two boys dressed as men and two as women – 'as is their wont'. Almost at this very time, many thousands of miles away in Japan, an unfamiliar theatre form known as kabuki was about to appear. Ironically, given its later history, kabuki is credited to an actress, Izumo no Okuni, and in its original form was a dance – nembutsu odori/'prayer dance' – of short duration. It became vastly popular all over Japan in the performances of courtesans, and when the Tokugawa shogunate adopted the strict moral code of Confucianism, kabuki and its performers were denounced as immoral, and legislation passed to protect public morality. In 1629 women's kabuki was banned, and in 1652, shortly after all theatres in England had been closed by Cromwell's government, young men's kabuki was also banned. If this theatrical structure was to survive it could only be as an all-male drama enriched with narrative, and the best-looking actors were cast in the female roles – onnagata.[10] The alternative name was oyama, which had another meaning – courtesan. In the early period onnagata divided into two groups, wakaonnagata and kashagata, with the former designating the young parts played by young men: young ladies, princesses and courtesans. Before the Meiji Restoration (1868) onnagata dressed in female clothes off-stage as well as on stage 'and every effort was made by them to be like a woman in everyday life'.

CHAPTER ELEVEN

THEIR EVERY MOVE

By the end of the reign of Elizabeth I many hundreds of books and pamphlets had been written and published on the inexhaustible great topic of the late sixteenth century: the nature of women. Just as Elizabeth had tested to breaking point (even execution) the imaginative limits of her male courtiers, politicians and statesmen, so women in the larger society beyond the court began to move out of the milieu and social apparatus which had bound them for many centuries. The tumult of the Reformation had accelerated this, but women were still a mystery to men and to bridge the gap in the theatre, where invention and fantasy were given much more freedom than ever before, boys were employed in what became a transitional phase. Boys were not men; neither were women, so it was permissible for boys to play women when the nature of the latter created so many problems for the patriarchy. Women were considered to be set apart from men in many ways, beginning so it was thought in the womb because a male foetus grew on the right side, a female to the left. John Donne envisaged women as an eternal mystery, saying that women like the sun have a motion of their own, unfathomable to men. The shifts of this underclass could make the dominant partner nervous and apprehensive in a wide variety of respects. Like servants, and most women were employed as such, women could threaten insurrection by look or posture; a man's sense of his own authority and security could be easily undermined. Women were house-trained and familiar in the manner of a pet, but yet not wholly biddable even with curbs, for there were gender mysteries that they shared only among themselves. They were a class – but not a true one, so obscuring boundaries of eros and confusing categorization; the paradigmatic woman was therefore not Elizabeth, admitted with some grumbles to the ranks of men, but Lady Penelope Rich, who seized control of her own life after an arranged marriage that chafed her individual spirit.

The tension in the houses where Lord and Lady Rich spent any time together must have been like a vapour from the conduits for foul matter. Indeed, the tension in most Elizabethan homes, with the observed actions of each woman freighted with significance, was likely quite palpable. The pressure confused and irked men, young and old. In the domestic economy of sexual exchange it was still possible for the man to dominate, and he would want to do the same in the disposition of his household if he had to be absent for any length of time. Even in a genuinely good-tempered marriage such as that of Sir Robert and Lady Sidney, friends of Penelope and her lover Mountjoy, his will had to prevail, especially when duty called him out of the country to the Netherlands for long periods. She wanted to follow him; he wanted her to stay put and to reside in London rather than Penshurst. His agent, Rowland Whyte, was alerted to the requirements of his employer and found a house that Barbara Sidney was reluctant to move into. When she did move it was with some trepidation that it was going to be a costly business. So it proved and Sidney complained within three weeks of her arrival that the household was too large. He took the view that employing sixty people was extravagant, especially since he was not clear what they all did, including the eleven women about his wife. Some of them, he thought, only waited on the others, and there were two superfluous boys in the house called Robin and Frank. Sidney thought his son Will must have better chums available to play with so the lads were a pointless burden. She was to budget with rigour, 'for I assure you charges grow terribly upon me here', he wrote from Zealand. Sidney might have considered the cost of procreation, but evidently preferred not to and Barbara was more or less constantly pregnant like Penelope Rich. So, both were occupied.

Writers and readers alike of the period thought chastity a peerless virtue, and women should be heedful of it because there was little difference between being unchaste and being thought unchaste. In John Lyly's *Entertainments at Sudeley* a character asks why it is the man who always does the wooing, and the answer comes back it is because men are the least chaste and most inclined to venery. This last word sports two meanings: first, the pursuit or sport of hunting, especially deer, but other game creatures as well; and second, the pursuit and practice of sexual pleasure. Men, of course, dominated both and even the queen's hunting in the first category was limited in scope and activity. The killing tended to be a massacre rather than the inevitable end of a furious hunt. Venery in the second meaning contained within it a profoundly unsettling core. It was possible to buy instant sexual gratification almost at the moment of stepping into the street. A man saw sexual availability in every aspect of town and city, and if he remarked it then it was certain that other men had done the same. They might be able to outbid him, and it is quite clear that Elizabethan men were absolutely obsessed with where women bestowed their bodies – in which bed and with whom. Could wives themselves be clandestine whores when there were so many about? Did their wives have secret lives elsewhere? Did women meeting to gossip denigrate men? And to prevent such a thing, were there chores enough within the confines of the house to keep women occupied?

'Occupation' (and its derivatives) was a word heavy with sexual overtones. Pompey in *Measure for Measure* speaks of 'your whores, sir, being members of my occupation'. Lusty punning of this kind saturates the drama and comedy of the day and in this case three words out of eight have a sexual meaning. In conduct books for the middle classes the advice to husbands often took the line that no temptation should be offered to a wife by the introduction of his male friends into the home. Only his best friends should visit and caution should be maintained, for a man 'may show his wife, and his sword to his friend, but not too far to trust them'. To avoid the social and sexual calamity of being cuckolded requires vigilance, and in Jonson's rank high comedy *Volpone* one man's answer to this perceived threat is to show a Mediterranean caution by never letting his wife leave the house. To smother the inclination to do this means controlling her wardrobe. Theoretically this was done by the State in sumptuary laws which made formal the links between personal attire and social rank. However, like so many such laws their passage through Parliament and royal assent could not in themselves guarantee a rigorous observance. There was frequent testimony in publications (written and produced by men) that most wives were inclined to press for what they wanted even if it ruined their husbands. Bishop Pilkington wrote, 'it is to be feared, that many desire rather to be like dallying Dinah than sober Sara. And if the husband will not maintain it, though he sell a piece of land, break up house, borrow on interest, raise rents, or make like hard shifts, little obedience will be showed.' Clothes then could signal defiance as well as deviance. It was well known that the Jesuit missionaries from the 1570s onwards made clandestine arrivals in clothes intended to mislead and render false names. The shifting in and out of names and clothes became a key aspect of traitorous behaviour in plots against Elizabeth.

Disturbances in fashions, especially for women, were not regarded lightly by commentators who were willing to denounce makers and wearers. The tailors were easy targets because they aided and abetted rampant social climbing (which involved climbing over someone else) and the market for consumer luxuries. Moreover, by spending so much time in female company, pandering to female demands, the sexual jokes about tailors will portray them as simultaneously effeminated and inclining to seduce their clients, the ladies of fashion who required an eye for details and speed of application. Both connive at superfluity and extravagance, not simplicity and comfort. Barnaby Rich teases the woman who complains she has nothing to wear and so refuses to leave the house: 'how woebegone is that poor woman, that is out of the tailors trim, that is out of the embroiderers trim, that is out of the haberdashers trim'. A proper and modest woman would dress herself any way as long as it was decent, not too expensive for her status, did not put her in debt, and was not given to her by some man other than her husband. To disconcert a man in Elizabethan England, to undermine his public and private confidence and to drive those who spoke for him into raging denunciations, warning of calamities named and unnamed, a woman only had to discard what was 'proper and modest' in female attire and decide that superior comfort could be found in men's clothes.

Just as pink shirts, flared hipster trousers, personal jewellery and long hair mystified and alarmed fathers in England in the late 1960s, so a similar kind of unease plagued commentators in the late sixteenth and early seventeenth centuries. A yardstick of masculinity then was conformity ('yard ' being the literary term for penis); once short jackets, tight hose and the codpiece (also used as a pocket) had instructed the beholder's eye. The projection of bulk seemed to declare – behold the man. Yet this was changing by the end of the sixteenth century when the bulging codpiece and bulging calf began to slip on the inventory of erotic stimuli. The painter of the portrait (*c.* 1585/6) of the Earl of Leicester in Parham Park shows the late middle-aged masculinity of the man aided by military trappings. In many ways the picture can be read as transitional since on the one hand Leicester rests on an arquebus, while on the other his hand rests on a knight's helmet from a suit of armour: the courtier at war. The Bodleian Library portrait of Lord Burghley shows an elderly gentleman in cap and ample gown that covers his feet, apparently riding a mule side-saddle. Did the painter intend to deride his sitter or was the incongruity of the pose with the politician's high offices merely accidental? Broad-skirted coats, fur collars, lace collars and wide breeches, jewelled buttons, feathered hats, long cloaks were part of 'femenish' fashion around 1600. Another gender marker hitherto had been the trim, barbered hair of men; by the 1590s it had become fashionable for men to let their hair grow. The famous Hilliard miniature of the Earl of Southampton, now in the Fitzwilliam Museum, shows him with a mane of light brown hair swept from his forehead, arranged in bunching curls on the ears with the remnant hair falling beyond his lace collar onto the black doublet. This example of 'femenish' appearance may suggest Southampton's almost fatal inability to grow up. It was at a time when little boys and girls were not so clearly decked out in gender-specific clothes. But then at about five or six years the boys were abruptly thrust into breeches to symbolize their entry into the great world of men. The separation from their mothers was sudden and disturbing.

In the 1580s Barnaby Rich criticized a whole swathe of Londoners, the wealthier gentlemen, for wearing clothes 'more new fangled and foolish than any courtesan of Venice'. This is a fairly typical and representative piece of grumpy exaggeration, but it is interesting because once again it yokes upheavals in fashion with eros. Another former soldier, George Gascoigne, an early example of the gentleman who sought a career in writing, made one of the very earliest satirical comments on masculine women in *The Steele Glas* (1574). If this comparatively (as it seems) new phenomenon had not achieved any sort of notoriety by that date then the comment would have been jejune. The question is, as Jean E. Howard recently put it in a striking article: how many people cross-dressed in Renaissance England?[1] Her answer, that we have no way of knowing empirically, any more than we know the numbers given to bestiality (apparently very few), may seem rather blunt and disheartening, but lack of numbers does not preclude an investigation because the polemics against it 'signal a sex-gender system under pressure'. Social cross-dressing adopted by some bold women was not derived from theatre practice. It was a transgressive choice that chimed with the 'femenish' fashions and challenged the buttons and bows and farthingale subordination of women. Class frictions were revealed in the overpowering sense that clothes were

The woman in the chair is about to have her hair cut in the formerly masculine mode (which was actually changing at this time), while her female companion assesses the impact of her short hair and hat in the mirror.

social markers of great significance, raising hackles in a manner that perhaps only fur-wearing causes today. No one cares if a woman spends thousands of pounds on a Lacroix outfit to parade in Bond Street today, but if she wears a Fendi fur coat even on a freezing day in winter she will likely be harangued and maybe even spat upon. No one is recorded as having spat on Elizabeth or any of the great ladies of her court for having so many dozens of elaborate dresses with accessories. But such a thing was not beyond criticism and Philip Stubbes boldly put the question: 'Do they think that it is lawful for them to have millions of sundry sorts of apparel lying rotting by them, whenas the poor members of Jesus Christ die at their doors for want of clothing?' It is a caricature of Philip Stubbes to make him out to be solely an anti-theatre Puritan. He did not think well of the theatre certainly, but he was not a Puritan. He was a social critic with strong moral convictions and ideas for improving the social welfare of many. His reforming spirit sometimes nudged him into contradictions; luxury is an affront yet those of aristocratic birth can wear gold chains, silks, diamonds and pearls because they have been born to it. Whereas when common subjects trick themselves out in such things they are behaving improperly because they make it very hard to know who is noble.

Women offend Stubbes, yet clearly enthral him at the same time, by their passion for unguents, perfumes and powders, all part of body-intensive beauty culture,

> wherof the smell may be felt and perceived, not only all over the house, or place, where they be present, but also a stones cast of almost, yea, the bed wherein they have laid their delicate bodies, the places where they have sat, the clothes, and things which they have touched, shall smell a week, a month, and more, after they be gone.

Notice the small lexical stumble on 'yea', indicating the unease Stubbes feels in considering the intimate contact of bodies with inanimate objects. He was unwilling to concede choice in the matter of garments because God 'alloweth us apparel not only for necessity's sake but also for an honest comeliness'. When the latter is swamped by rivalry and vanity then a woman may be drawn to 'wanton, lewd and unchaste' behaviour. Stubbes was expressly perturbed by his difficulty in distinguishing between 'an honest matron and a common strumpet'. The stability of the social order was dependent on such distinctions, as well as those between aristocrat and yeoman, and men and women. When men dress in 'femenish' fashions and women dress as men then sexual chaos ensues. A man who dresses effeminately can only by said to 'adulterate the verity of his own kind.' A woman in man's clothes offends God-given distinctions of gender. 'To switch coats is to undo the work of heaven.'[2]

Several years later a country parson produced a relation of manners and mores, *The Description of England*, in which he denounced the direction of fashion. The tone was splenetic for he was dismayed by the decline he remarked in modesty and decorum. The women who behaved indecorously were a threat to formality and social observance, most especially when they elected to dress in a way that obscured their gender. Having had chances in London to observe such people Harrison admitted his own inability (or disinclination) to distinguish men from women. Therefore by this line of reasoning women who took to dressing as men must have a lewd purpose: they were 'trulls', prostitutes of the most degraded kind. Recent examinations of the Bridewell records and those of the Court of Aldermen have found that transvestite women between 1565 and 1605 who were apprehended and examined were often accused of prostitution.[3] Were they such? Men evidently found the action of cross-dressing disturbing and their presumption might easily be that such a woman was a sexual radical luring men into irresponsible sexual activity. Yet in 1569 a woman was whipped and detained in Bridewell for correction because she had dressed as a serving man to accompany her soldier-husband to war. And this martial note reminds us of Mary Ambree, who, in 1584, fought against the Spanish in the Low Countries. So adopting a variant of male attire could be entirely sensible and purposeful, as is evident in the biography of Thomasine Hall, who arrived in London aged twelve. She lived as a girl (despite the male component of her first name) until 1596 and the clamour surrounding the preparations for the Cadiz expedition. She ended the stable gendered years and enlisted as Thomas Hall in an apparently successful disguise, looking for adventure. Then for the next twenty years or so she veered from one gender designation to another and back again, crossing the invisible sexual boundary with nonchalance. Geography aided her. She sailed as a man to Virginia but on arrival in the colony only found work as a chambermaid – hence a change. When eventually commanded to give testimony before the General Court of Virginia to defend an accusation of being a transvestite, she claimed sweetly to 'go in women's apparel to get a bit for my cat' – a perfectly fine response as cat-lovers will agree. The decision of the court was equally neat: s(he) should signal her androgyny to the world by wearing a combination of male and female clothes – mostly those for men but under an apron. Applause for the sapience of this while wondering if the judges took their line from the native American Indians. Young men lacking fighting spirit were allowed to cross-dress through the social mechanism of *berdache*. They were then given female tasks and might even marry a warrior-hunter who needed wives of either sex to prepare hides and so on during the annual bison slaughter.

Thomasine Hall can usefully be characterized as a wandering cross-dresser, given to choosing the gender that most suited her situation. A woman resident in London in late Elizabethan and early Jacobean England who dressed continuously as a man risked opprobrium and punishment. Yet there were such women and one who became notorious for her brazen behaviour was Mary Frith, alias Mary Markham (the Roaring Girl), alias Moll Cutpurse. This last name is a particularly obscene pseudonym of the time involving complex puns. Just as Doll Tearsheet was a risqué catch-all name for one who tore the bed sheets as a romping whore, or one who caused them to be so torn by the sexual energy of her client, so Moll Cutpurse denoted 'a notorious baggage' who did indeed cut (i.e. steal) purses wherein might be found items beyond price given that 'purse' was cant for scrotum. So the lady had balls, and spoke in a tobacco-stained voice that 'challenged the field of diverse gallants'. She was born in the Aldersgate Street premises of a shoemaker in the mid-1580s, and since Dekker and Middleton considered her notoriety so great that they jointly wrote a play about her, probably written in the spring of 1611, she must have achieved this between the end of Elizabeth's reign in 1603, and the time of their collaboration. The better-known 'roaring boys' of that time were usually gentlemen, Inns of Court men who caroused away their evenings in taverns and ordinaries before spilling onto the streets to brawl with the watch, ordinary townsmen and themselves. 'Roaring boys' seem to have made up the 'damned crew', swaggering young gentlemen of good family who picked quarrels with the newly arrived Scots in London. Mary Frith was not of this class and so had no well-placed friends to defend her if her manner of presenting herself in public in doublet and baggy breeches, pipe-smoking and swearing, outraged citizen sensibilities. Yet the hectic life as it was recorded did not end prematurely. She died of dropsy in 1659 in Fleet Street, but had consolidated her fame before that by apparently robbing General Fairfax and shooting him in the arm during the Civil War. There was a frequently repeated story that to escape the gallows she handed over a vast bribe of £2,000.

Even if the details had become exaggerated in the telling as we may suppose, the holding off of retribution suggests that her life-long eccentricities (if banditry can be so called) were licensed and that she was allowed a greater freedom to fetishize. She had long collided with normative values; there was, for example, a performance by her in drag in 1611 at the Fortune theatre (which had been trailed in the epilogue to *The Roaring Girl*). The famous woodcut of the day shows her smoking a pipe, wearing men's clothes and carrying a sword to her shoulder. On stage she exchanged saucy banter with the audience like a stand-up comic today, and then sang a song to her own lute accompaniment. It seems probable that the lyrics were also saucy and the simple activity of plucking the strings of the instrument was erotically stimulating to the men. Women did not play in public and to do so was to scoff at convention. The follow-up 'performance' was noted later by John Chamberlain writing to Dudley Carleton in 1612. On 9 February of that year Mary was required to do penance for her evil living. At St Paul's Cross she had an appreciative audience who regularly heard the great preachers of the day perform a monologue (called a sermon) lasting some two hours. 'She wept bitterly and seemed very penitent, but it is since doubted she was maudlin drunk, being discovered to have tippled of three-quarters of sack.' If so, for what reason? Was alcohol necessary to generate the mood of self-accusation and high

Moll Cutpurse: that is, Mary Frith, alias Mary Markham, or the Roaring Girl; a gutsy female transvestite who shocked and amused generations of Londoners in almost equal measure.

distress? Was the whole thing a performance made all the more dubious by being fraudulent?

Mary Frith did not wear men's clothes as a temporary disguise in the manner of Elizabeth Southwell eloping with the young Robert Dudley. Although her choice was provoking to many, it allowed her to suppress her manifest discomfort with her gender and the concomitant expectations of society. But not wholly because, remarkably given her public self which might have frightened away the most dim-witted suitor, she was married. In 1614 she became the wife of Lewkner Markham, and although it was very soon evident that the whole thing was a pointless charade domestically, in law suits brought against her she countered the description of her as spinster with her lawful status as a wife. There was a mundane use for what was otherwise pointless.[4] By the 1620s, in her own account, she was the doyenne of the London underworld, working as a fence and a pimp (hitherto a masculine preserve). The scale of the sex 'industry' in Elizabethan and Jacobean London was discussed earlier in this book (see Chapter Six); what is of particular interest about Mary Frith is that she not only procured young women for men, but also respectable men as lovers for middle-class wives. The implication of cross-dressing then was that the woman was sexually riotous and uncontrolled. Yet Mary declared her own disinterest in sex, and channelled what might have been nurtured into a profitable business that satisfied many clients. She told the story of the cuckold whose young wife confessed to him before her premature demise that she had taken many lovers supplied by Mary. He was angry at the shame to his name and the charge to his pocket for numerous children that were not his. Mary claimed to have repaired the economic damage by leaning on the lovers 'procuring him round sums of money from his respective rivals to the maintenance of their illegitimate issue, which they honestly paid'; yet another surprise and a tribute to her negotiating skill. Indeed, characteristic of the anecdotes in the *Life and Death of Mrs Mary Frith* (1662) is the emphasis on private gain so that at the end of her life she could live as comfortably as any male householder in a house with spotless floors (despite her parrots and monkeys) which was maintained by no less than three maids.

'The stage drew upon, produced and reproduced more than a single sexual discourse.'[5] In *The Roaring Girl* Dekker and Middleton tinker with the heterosexual expectations of Sebastian Wengrave of his wife-to-be, Mary Fitzallard. They plan to marry against the wishes of Sir Alexander Wengrave, who regards her five thousand mark dowry as hopelessly inadequate recompense for the item he has to offer: a well-set-up son. At a late point in the play Sebastian invades his father's chamber, meeting Mary and Moll Cutpurse there, both women in male attire. When Sebastian kisses his chaste Mary he acknowledges the erotic frisson he feels at kissing a woman in drag. Mary looks like a boy; she is a boy for the stage performance and dressed as a page, an employment with erotic availability imprinted on it by usage. This is not a proposed marriage made in heaven but in confusion. Sebastian has grown up in a household excluding women, even his mother; this is the homosocial world of the gentry. Even the middle-class world of the sub-plot cannot exclude such connections for all that marriage is the maypole around which the couples hop and caper. In the marriages of the Openworks, the Tiltyards and the Gallipots, the wives are very visible and vocal, but their sexual desires are deferred or unfulfilled. Gallipot represents a form of effeminacy that is dysfunctional, being so besotted with every aspect of his wife that he surrenders all features of masculine dominance; in every respect he lacks weight, he is her 'apron husband' – 'so cookish; thou dost not know how to handle a woman in her kind'. She fares not much better with the man-about-town Laxton, and the pun on the name mischievously suggests the reason: he is 'a lame gelding'. The problem for Mistress Openwork is not that her husband is a capon, but that he finds his sexual pleasures with others. This explains her hostility to Moll, who enters their shop to buy a ruff. The speech of Mistress Openwork is heavy with sexual innuendo including the notorious pun on 'low countries'. Her conclusion seems to be that in the sexual economy she might as well close the shop 'for when I open it I take nothing'.

Ironically, it is Moll herself who is chaste by inclination and so naturally regarded as sexually incontinent by the men. She is, as Sandra Clark has noted, 'the one honest and truthful character amid a host of cheats and hypocrites'.[6] Appearances can deceive, as Middleton makes abundantly clear with the androgynous Moll, who resists male concupiscence. She is in male eyes a paradox – the whore who resists sexual advances – and so a sexual prize of heightened worth. Moreover, she speaks eloquently, at a time when sexual and verbal incontinence were twinned; at times Moll speaks a parodic version of the late queen's style – what might be called 'street regal' – 'I have no humour to marry . . . and am man enough for any woman'. In this last phrase the authors tease not only the other characters but the audience too, for Moll is either presenting herself as sexually able to satisfy another woman, or she is saying that in her male rig she can act convincingly as a man (although played by a boy). She is also challenging the governing view in the Renaissance about the domination of women by men, because discourses of gender were overwhelmingly hierarchical. The radical rage of Moll is dumped on Laxton, who has made the error of viewing her only as an erotic object. She is refusing the placid role of 'fond flexible whore' on all three counts. The representations of venery in the play are 'fraught with frustrations and antagonisms', as Jean Howard has said.[7]

CHAPTER TWELVE
THE MARRED MALE

Male impotence was a disturbance of sexuality so particular and dismaying to men in Elizabethan England that it is very difficult to find satisfactory evidence. In daily life male domination was for the most part unthinkingly accepted, and the silent expectation that opportunity would lead to erection was part of masculine self-definition. Failure was a profound diminution of obligation to the subservient partner; it suggested that an unseen instrument, something sinister and ungodly, was at work. Very likely the spiritual perturbation of demonic forces at work on the body increased anxiety. In the lyric by Thomas Campion, *If any hath the heart*, he dramatizes impotence by attributing it to witchcraft, as had the original text from which he derived his poem, Ovid's *Amores*, III.vi, but at least he does not shift the mechanical failure to the female's lack of erotic expertise:

> What hag did then my powers forespeak,
> That never yet such faint did feel?
> Now she rejects me as one weak,
> Yet am I all composed of steel.

Annulments of a marriage for reasons of impotence (or frigidity) were extremely rare. The incapacity may have plagued very many men and women then, but we will never be aware of it because it was extremely hard to prove, and discretion veiled it. For a woman to sue a man for marriage annulment on the grounds of a husband's incapacity to act as a fully sexual man in penetrative sex was even rarer.

One case of an aristocratic wife seeking the nullification of their childhood espousal on the grounds of his impotence is very well documented because it caused such a stir in society. Although it comes a decade after the death of Elizabeth the elements within the case are so ample and authentically Elizabethan in tone that the chronological blemish can be ignored. The more so because a great range of medical files of doctors and self-trained physicians do not exist, and hence material that is still available requires even more careful scrutiny. Fortunately Simon Forman did write up aspects of his practical work in the community, and even more useful, one among the heterogeneous throng that paid well for a consultation was the former serial seducer, now impotent, Sylvan Scory. The charmer who, like Bassanio in *The Merchant of Venice*, had dissipated his wealth (and possibly health) in pursuit of self-gratification was frequently found in London – Scory just added some baroque figures to the score, making himself notorious in society and the subject of sometimes sour gossip. John Scory, his father, was an ex-Dominican monk who became a Protestant bishop, so a prayerful realist who became Bishop of Hereford. Scory snr. was extremely avaricious, principally with the intention of passing wealth to his son. Sylvan Scory was always happy to spend such sums as came his way, and John Aubrey heard that the profligate son had been left an estate of £1,500, which allowed for some instant dissipation. Later, Scory became a friend and patron of Ben Jonson, which may explain quite simply the uncommon interest shown by the playwright in the subject of impotence, which had led Scory to consult Forman in 1598. The diagnosis was of a humour abounding in melancholy so Scory was no longer as 'tentiginous' as he had been. Unfortunately Forman had no cure, though doubtless he prepared various concoctions for a patient living in hope of a restorative. As Forman himself declined to pay for sex and was never impotent he may have been rather too relaxed and smug about the matter. One of his diary entries for 9 July 1607 suggests why. On that day, when he was fifty-five, Forman had sex at 8 a.m. with Hester Sharp; at 3 p.m. with Joan Wiseman and at 9 p.m. with his wife.

In any town, but in particular in a city as large as London, crammed with carriages, carts and horses, it was inevitable that men might at any time receive a disabling kick from a horse. An iron-shod hoof or wheel thudding into soft tissue was likely to cause severe physical damage, and the speed with which this damage repaired itself, or could be repaired by medical intervention, was altogether uncertain. Jonson's repertoire of impotence may well have included a case dependent on just such an excruciating accident. In 1561 a Devonian called John Bury had been declared impotent by his wife, Willmott. Prior to their marriage Bury had taken a kick from a horse with the result that his testes had been deformed. If both had formerly descended into his scrotum, only one 'the size of a small bean' survived the kick. The circumstantial evidence was enough to gain an annulment for his wife, and she remarried. Although legally debarred from marrying again Bury followed suit, and while his former first wife was still alive, his second wife gave birth to a son. In 1599 the son's right to his late father's estate was challenged by the man who was next in line to the inheritance – Mr Webber. If Bury was permanently impotent, how could he have fathered a son? Had his second wife perhaps found a lover or a donor for the pregnancy? Not in English common law which regarded all children of a marriage as those of their mother's husband.[1] So the argument made before the court was that the first verdict on Bury's impotence had obviously been defective because of the subsequent birth. This being the case, Bury remained married to Willmott and their second marriages both were invalid. Bury's son was therefore a bastard and not able to inherit. Cannily argued as the matter was, it induced long discussions and deliberations. Yet Webber did eventually lose on the grounds that no challenge to the 'voidable' second marriage had been made during Bury's lifetime – number two nuptial had not been annulled and so on appeal Bury jnr. won the case.

The absence of any other similar case may suggest that it was a very rare thing for a man to sustain such an injury. However, the Bury case only reached the court because of an inheritance and it is possible to imagine such an accident with grievous results for the man or boy would be quite frequent in an agricultural setting. If there was no property involved then the event would remain a private calamity. A decision on impotence was always difficult and if an annulment was sought there was always the suspicion that the two sides had selected it as their least worst option if the submission was uncontested. The court always had the utmost problem with evidence or lack of it. In France in the sixteenth and seventeenth centuries impotence suddenly took on more importance in the sexual directory – it was much referred to and also much contested.[2] Despite the French habit today of preening themselves for collective rationality, then French courts devised modes of investigation into impotence that were woefully unsound. The most bizarre was the so-called 'trial by congress'. This required a husband and wife taking to a curtained bed while court officials in a nearby room waited for an hour or so before scrutinizing the participants and the bed for signs of emission. The absurdities of this are many and obvious, especially if the couple had managed to agree on their tactic before seeking the court's acceptance. If the charge of impotence was actually contested then the husband who had to prove himself was under a severe burden of anxiety, while his partner could lie back, resist or deride his advances.

In England there was a thoughtful reluctance to admit such a manner of securing evidence. Such dealings were considered lewd and without support in ecclesiastical law. Instead, ecclesiastical courts in England substituted 'compurgation' by which the man declared impotent could present seven 'oath-helpers' (family, friends or neighbours), who would take an oath to support the court testimony. In England as in Europe, judges could require the couple should be physically investigated by doctors and midwives. This would in theory determine the degree of sexual dysfunction of the man and whether his wife was still a virgin. Impotence in the man was presumed to be permanent if in three years of living together after marriage there had been no erection, penetration and ejaculation. So what if the carnal famine only took root with the bodily presence of the wife? His generative organs worked but not with her, so he was *aptus ad generandum*? The wife would still be a virgin, but doctors then disagreed over the mode of investigating this for evidence. Some said that the hymen was always whole, but others pointed out the possibility of self-rupturing; even the exploration undertaken by a doctor, however delicate, might sunder it. And two eminent French physicians, Paré and Guillemean, who specialized in obstetrics, declared they had never found it intact – hence it was a fiction or social invention laid to rest by their autopsies and dissections.

The statistical observation of Lawrence Stone about the marriage difficulties of the English aristocracy was noted earlier (p. 1). Yet none of them sought to escape from a dead union by the means Frances Howard elected, after a few years as wife of Robert

Devereux, 3rd Earl of Essex. She had already witnessed the particular difficulties of her husband's aunt, Lady Rich, and her lover, Lord Mountjoy, when in 1605 a divorce had been granted to Lord Rich. The terms of it precluded remarriage, yet that was the course, as we have seen, taken by the lovers. The Church rejected this and it displeased King James mightily so that the earl and his new countess were forbidden to attend court. Their attempt to regularize their long-standing liaison was done to protect their children. Mountjoy, now Earl of Devonshire, had wealth and titles that he wished to pass undisputed to his sons even though they had been born before his marriage. His new wife had been allowed to take the precedence of the ancient Bouchier Earls of Essex, fifth in the kingdom, and she was a Lady of the Bedchamber to Queen Anne, so the earl argued vigorously and at length in a submission to the king that their marriage was legal and proper. It had taken place at Wanstead on St Stephen's Day, 1605, when Frances Howard, daughter of the Earl of Suffolk, was preparing to marry Robert Devereux at the end of the Christmas season. Born on 31 May 1590, she was likely a little older than her husband of January 1606.[3] Not that age mattered very much, for it was a dynastic and political union like those of her sisters, Elizabeth and Catherine, married respectively to the 58-year-old William Knollys (now a peer), and William Cecil, Lord Cranborne, teenage son and heir of the Earl of Salisbury.

As the historian Arthur Wilson later remarked of the Howard-Devereux alliance, they were 'too young to consider, but old enough to consent'. The masque written by Ben Jonson for the occasion was the high-spirited *Hymenaei*, freighted with allusions to the joys of the marriage bed, though this was contradicted by events. There was no post-ceremony intimacy between the couple because adult regulation kept them apart. By the early seventeenth century the view was taking hold that sex at too early an age was debilitating for the youthful husband, robbing him of vital strength. As for the young wife, it was increasingly held that her body would likely be too small for child-bearing at too early an age. So Frances, Countess of Essex, returned to her family, and her callow husband was sent off on a European tour between 1607 and early 1609. In three years the emotional growth of the couple had been apart and when Essex returned there was no happy union – his wife sought every means to avoid him. There were two key reasons; it seems likely that Essex was seriously ill with smallpox, and above all, she had fallen in love with the puppyish young courtier also adored by the king – Robert Carr, later Earl of Somerset. When the Essexes were together it seems to have been for visits disliked by her to his country home at Chartley in Staffordshire where lived his grandmother, Lettice Knollys, a former Countess of Essex and Leicester, and mother of Penelope Rich. If, as seems likely, Essex was impotent from the first, Frances did nothing to secure a remedy because she wanted him to remain so with her. Instead she turned to her confidante Anne Turner, Catholic wife of George Turner, a successful physician, who put her in touch with Simon Forman, the man with a reputation for expertise with love-philtres.

Frances Howard, Countess of Essex (to the 3rd Earl) and then Countess of Somerset, who was vilified for the annulment of her first marriage based on the claim that he was impotent. Later, she and her second husband were tried and found guilty of the murder of Sir Thomas Overbury.

These were sought to pinion the affections of the erratic young Scot as Frances hoped for an end to her marriage. Her husband meanwhile spent much of his time in male company, drinking, which he found convivial: 'and all the content he gives me is to abuse me, and use me as doggedly as before', which I take to mean ignoring her until minded to give her a pat or stroke. When Forman died in September 1611 Mrs Turner and Lady Essex looked for a replacement in Abraham Savery, once a distributor of Catholic books from Europe and formerly resident in Middleburgh.[4] The ladies hoped that with his arcane skills Savery could incapacitate Essex. Evidently Frances felt herself on a knife edge, uncertain about an unconsummated relationship with Carr – whose own sexuality was rather wobbly at this time – and desperate to be free of an unmanned and unmannerly husband. How long, it may have occurred to her, before Essex would be goaded into a sexual assault that would be akin to rape and then all her hope of an annulment would be gone. She does not appear to have considered the Turner solution, which offered interim pleasure and good company. Mrs Turner was a wife, but also a mistress of Sir Arthur Manwaring, who was much younger than her husband; she also supervised supper parties for Sir Thomas Monson, a former client of Forman, and a long-time client of the Howard family – a connection that may have a bearing on the case.

When Frances, Countess of Essex, chose the most difficult and fraught procedure of annulment to rid herself of her husband she could not do it representing herself. Her father and her uncle, Henry Howard, Earl of Northampton, represented her position in the drawing-up of a so-called 'libel' or petition. The intention was to reduce as far as possible the strife between the estranged couple, but the rarity of the situation ensured that private distress and personal aggravations became an unseemly public entertainment for those with prurient minds – the nation. Perhaps there were none present among the commissioners headed by George Abbott, Archbishop of Canterbury, assisted by the Bishops of London, Ely and Lichfield, together with six lawyers and judges from the upper judiciary. The case for Frances was that as a woman and wife the best that she could muster in sexual availability and preparedness had not been enough to induce her husband 'to have that copulation in any sort which the married bed alloweth'. She deposed that she was still a virgin and, perhaps not so surprisingly, had not been aware of Essex's incapacity prior to their marriage. A final clause was a disclaimer; she had never made public the cause of her marriage breakdown, and but for the contemptible false rumours of her adultery she would never have done so through the annulment statement.

In the text of the 'libel', Essex tried to underline the particularity of his impotence. He said he 'hath power and ability of body to deal with other women' but try as he may, 'with his best endeavour', he had not been able to consummate the marriage 'no not once'. So he tethers his impotence quite specifically to his wife when Abbott had expected a general plea of infirmity. Witnesses testified that the marriage bed had

The Illustrious Lord, Robert Deureux Earle of Essex and Ew. Viscount Hereford Baron of Ferrers of Chartley. Lo: Bourchier & Louain, &c.

VIRTVTIS COMES. INVIDIA.

BASIS CONSTATIA VIRTVTVM

If Bounty, Courage, Curtesy Desert
Of noblest choice, could haue bee shew by Art
This one Piece had exprest Them All in This
Liues what perfection can or Bee or Is.
Essex; heyre to his Father: by his blood,
His birth, his honours Great his virtues Good.
What Time can add to Meritt for approu'd,
In Essex must last happy. that's Be
LOV'D

Robert Devereux, 3rd Earl of Essex, the apparently sexually impotent son of a philandering father. It was a dysfunction so irksome that he could not bring himself to admit it in the annulment hearings.

indeed been shared, but when Essex was called he would not admit openly, according to what seems to have been agreed beforehand, that he was impotent. Instead, he tried to disguise his mortification at this public embarrassment by blaming his wife. In England and Europe alike judges could command that a man said to be impotent, along with his wife, should undergo physical examinations to test the degree of his incapability, whether it was a stray incident, and to test her for virginity.[5] So Abbott and his fellow commissioners elected to have Frances appraised by ten matrons and six midwives, although, in the event, this cohort was reduced to a handful of matrons and two midwives who found her hymen intact, but no other manifest physical obstruction to childbearing. Despite the issue turning on Essex's impotence he was never examined; male solidarity and high unease protected him. Instead, witness submissions were made by Worcester, Knollys and Suffolk that Essex had been candid with them, and Frances on oath declared his sexual torpor. Abbott himself sought to counter all this with contradictions because of his reluctance to annul. A friend had told him that while in bed one Sunday morning, chatting with his cronies, Essex had stood up and lifted his nightshirt to show them the risen member, a cue no doubt for noisy applause, toasts and derision of Frances, the languishing virgin.

Still, since Frances was not present this meant nothing much, and when asked why only she occasioned his failing as he claimed, his response was equally feeble. When alone together 'she reviled him, and miscalled him, terming him cow, and coward, and beast'. In fact, in male company Essex could have a superfluous (if welcome to him) erection, but not with his first wife, and very possibly not with his second wife either.[6] It may be that this young man did not realize or simply repressed the fact that his sexual response was induced in male company. At Chartley – that 'vile place' as Frances referred to it – he may have felt more relaxed and less pressured in the homosocial group of drinkers. His wife's sharp hostility was enough to depress a flickering heterosexual obligation to his family and society at large, the society sniggering at his chagrin. He must by the familiar requirements of the day be a bull, not a cow, but later his second marriage also collapsed and although there was a child, his wife Elizabeth had taken six years to conceive so that the suspected father was her lover, Sir William Uvedale.

There was a political shading to the challenge made by the countess to the matter of male sexuality. Her father and uncle used it to dislodge a key opponent, Sir Thomas Overbury, admired by Carr and well versed in the latter's dealings with Frances. Overbury was keenly hostile to the Howard faction and when he turned down a royal offer of an ambassadorial post he fetched up in the Tower in April 1613. The Lieutenant of the Tower, Sir William Waad, was ousted from his post and speedily replaced by a Howard man, Sir Gervase Elwes, while Overbury's keeper was a former servant of Mrs Turner, Richard Weston, recruited at the promptings of Lady

Essex.[7] Even as Overbury sickened during the summer, the case tilted away from Frances and stalled. The commissioners held back from a candid investigation of Essex's ability and so could not properly reach a conclusion. Abbott and James became embroiled in an argument about satanic involvement – the plea of *maleficium* – and in discussion with the commissioners James said that 'the Earl was once purposed to have gone to Poland to have tried whether he might be unwitched'. Abbott's response was to declare his requirement of legal proofs in these matters. Indeed, the annulment would not have been granted without the brusque intervention of the king, keen to gratify his favourite laddie. James did this by adding two more bishops to the commission while the unfortunate Overbury decayed in his chamber cell. He died on 14 September 1613, and the nullity for Lady Essex came through eleven days later. At the conclusion of the proceedings the archbishop was prevented from delivering a speech of summation; he had been out-manoeuvred by the Howards and their faction.

The two great losers immediately were the unfortunate Overbury, probably the victim of a murderous Howard plot, and Essex. The bishops had flunked the possibility of viewing privately Essex's 'privities' and instead they had posed questions that added greatly to the gaiety of the court, city and country. Mockery and ribald commentary was rife; so was suspicion of a fix.

> This Dame was inspected but Fraud interjected
> A maid of more perfection
> Whom the midwives did handle whilst the knight held the candle
> O there was a clear inspection.

The very fact that for modesty (as was claimed) Frances had sought to be veiled during the inspection suggested that the whisper of a substitution of Sir Thomas Monson's daughter for herself might not be false. On 3 November the royal *valido* Robert Carr, Viscount Rochester, became Earl of Somerset and on 26 December 1613, he and Frances were married at court. All of which led to a deluge of satirical comment, but without newspapers to run with the story a great deal of the satire would have proved ephemeral, except that this time much of it was saved by being copied nationwide into commonplace books. As a pithy comment with extra meaning, Thomas Campion wrote into his masque for the wedding night:

> Some friendship between man and man prefer,
> But I th'affection between man and wife.

Did he mean James and Carr, or is there a buried comment on Essex here? Diagnostic evaluations of Essex after nearly four hundred years may seem insubstantial, yet work

by recent researchers on testosterone suggest that he had a male hormone deficiency.*
Hypogonadal men, low in testosterone, in a research group before treatment reported
feelings of edginess, anger, irritability and aggression. It is known that Essex during his
lifetime showed all these behaviour traits, leading to quarrels and threats of duels. The
group treated with male hormone had many of their symptoms abate, with increased
optimism and friendliness.

Although pre-dating the Essex case by a few years, there are two early plays by Ben
Jonson that unleash a mordant commentary on the nature of sexuality – especially male
sexuality and the insidious, demoralizing threat of impotence. *Volpone* opens with a
bedroom scene, but one with a subversive kick. Volpone wakes alone in his bed (that
crucial prop of Renaissance theatre), and when he leaves it he stands squandering his
early-day emotions over the golden hoard of items amassed from rapacious fools and
gulls who gamble that his death is imminent. They defer gratification in their perverse
dealings with him. No production of this great play that I have seen has begun with
what would be a striking gesture by Volpone – directing a golden stream of urine on
the hoard. It is a sterile liquid and to splash it onto the items squeezed from clients
who have become deformed by greed seems highly appropriate. Even without this
coarse gesture an audience some four hundred years ago would quickly have gathered
that sexuality in this magnifico's household is deviant, commercial and sterile. The play
is deliberately set in Venice, the city most associated in English minds with luxury
trade, courtesans and role-playing sodomites. In the opening scene Volpone himself
remarks on how each day new clients arrive at his house, 'Women, and men, of every
sex, and age,/That bring me presents, send me plate, coin, jewels . . .'. They fawn on
him like lovers with a new object of desire while he explores and exploits, prostituting
his talents like a whore, but with a dexterity that relies not on health and vigour, but
on potential collapse and breakdown. Volpone may be 'the true father of his family' as
his dandy aide-de-camp suggests, but this prompts the question – how could it have
happened? Apart from Mosca (the fly – a creature of foul habits,) parasite and narcissist,
those in Volpone's 'family' are Androgyno, Castrone, and Nano – three distortions of
natural sexuality. The first is hermaphrodite, like the man reported in 1583 by the
Spanish ambassador as living in Beaumaris, formerly a married man with children who
'changed his functions' and became pregnant. 'It seems contrary to nature that he
should both conceive and engender.'[8] Castrone is mutilated and without potency, and
Nano is so small that sex seems an impossibility, although court dwarves did marry and
have children occasionally. The question is whether these creatures are human at all,
appearing like carnival figures; naming in Jonson is 'an act confirming the moral

---

* Research report by Dr Christina Wang to the Endocrine Society AGM (1995).

qualities in people'. The sheen on Mosca delights and deludes Volpone, which explains in part why he dallies so long with an unruly servant and ignores the muffled call of patriarchy to take a wife even now and beget an heir. The hopes of the 'animals' about him rest on this failure. Easy intimacy, tenderness and generosity of spirit are put down, and Volpone trumpets his intention of being more sensual in his pleasures than the harem-commanding Turkish Sultan, ancient enemy of Venice and ruler of the Ottoman Empire where addiction to sodomy was regarded by other nations as a hateful scandal. When Mosca produces an account of Celia's beauty this litany becomes an aphrodisiac that sends Volpone spinning from lechery into crime, proposing her rape. That attempt occasions a court scene in Act IV in which Celia's good name is defiled by lies and by the appearance of Volpone before the court 'as impotent'. Voltore's defence of his client (role-reversal) is artfully worked out. To present the court with irrefutable evidence of impotence requires the sort of scrutiny Abbott and his fellow commissioners would later eschew in dealing with Essex; on this point life imitates art. Volpone says nothing in his own defence and swings into a routine of outward manifestations of old age – a shrunken body, dull eyes and limp hands. He mimics a lack of easy virility which is yielded to young Bonario. Corvino's jealousy, his flagrant misrepresentations of Celia's sexual appetites, has him embrace a fantasy of cuckoldry, while Volpone's immediate public biography is of a striking detumescence. As has been pointed out in a subtle reading of the play, 'they enact an abdication of masculine power and privilege so astonishing that unless they are telling the truth their behaviour seems inexplicable'.[9]

Volpone has used sexual infirmity to plunder the pockets of other men, but what he has filched from them is immobile and it is locked away. This hoarding betokens the true coldness of his spirit; he spends nothing when in the language of venery 'spend' equals emission. Yet he tickles himself with notions of what he intends to do: 'live free/To all delights my fortune calls me to.' The impossibility of this is later proven because each increment in self-display and performance makes the auto-pleasuring less satisfying – and it cuts him off from social as well as fully sexual intercourse. Like a petty despot Volpone has his own favourites within his household, including Mosca, who skips away from his employer's more exuberant sexual propositions. If Volpone imaginatively straddles both genders (and he allows the audience a glimpse of his performance as Antinous years before – Antinous whose beauty captivated the Emperor Hadrian), many who come to court him are de-sexualized, or have to invent a sexual persona for themselves. Voltore (the vulture) is one of the former because it was held in popular thought that the bird lived a sexually isolated existence. Corbaccio and Corvino do not bear such instantly revealing names so the text spouts their impotence. The former is introduced as more impotent than Volpone can even feign to be, dismissing and disowning his own son in a symbolic act of self-mutilation. By proclaiming to society that his son is not his son, Corbaccio embraces sterility.

Corvino's sexual confusion is self-induced, like the grotesque delusion that his faithful wife is unfaithful. When she is responsive to Volpone in the guise of Scoto, Corvino's punishment is alarming, yet related to that inflicted on adulterers. They were paraded backwards in public, and the perverse tone of Corvino's backward retribution is underscored by his notion that his wife's pleasure thereafter will be so. This would have confirmed, as many in England then thought, that sodomy was the highest rated sexual pleasure in Catholic-dominated Italy.

The woman who invents a sexual persona for herself is Lady Politic Would-be, who claims to know everything about everything important, and who makes unseemly advances to Volpone and Peregrine. Having elbowed aside her fumbling husband, whom she finds with a man she believes to be a transvestite prostitute – (it is Venice) – she becomes aggressively sexual in the mode formerly assigned to a man. At that time her torrential style of speech-making, verbal incontinence, signalled sexual incontinence too. The female with the galloping tongue, uncurbed, figures proverbially in English Renaissance writing, and in *Epicoene* Jonson again satirizes 'hermaphroditical' talking women. Before writing that play Jonson seems to have particularized his anti-feminist satire in *Epigram on the Court Pucell*, a poem mocking a contemporary lady at the Stuart court. I say 'seems' because the slant of the poem is not straightforward; Jonson himself admitted that his poems can scamper free of facts. Overriding the notion of veracity is the notion of finesse; the epigram is lively and insulting, but it is finessed by his *Epitaph on Cecilia Bulstrode*. Either may be accurate but not enough is known about her to tell which. She was the daughter of Edward Bulstrode, of Hadgerley Bulstrode (Bucks.), and was baptized on 12 February 1584. According to James Whitelocke in a family autobiography, his sister-in-law was a Gentlewoman of the Bedchamber to the Catholic Queen Anne of Denmark, wife of James I. The older brother of James was 'Captain' Edmund Whitelocke, a shameless society sponger who dined with Henry Percy, Earl of Northumberland, on the eve of the Gunpowder Plot in early November 1605.[10] Suspicion that he was involved in it ruined the earl; did, as has been suggested, Cecilia act as conveyancer of the news of the plot to Robert Cecil, Earl of Salisbury and chief minister to the Crown?[11] If it was thought by Jonson that she was the 'leaky vessel' it might explain why briefly he was so angry with her, for he had himself been a Catholic and in the aftermath of the plot was quick to spy for Salisbury in order to protect himself. The first line of the epigram is certainly intriguingly mysterious:

> Do's the Court-Pucell then so censure me
> And thinks I dare not her?

Did Cecilia Bulstrode, an intimate of another former Catholic, John Donne, denounce Jonson for his clandestine efforts? Epigram CVII, '*To Captayne Hungry*', suggests a comment on Edmund Whitelocke:

> Do what you come for, Captain, with your news;
> That's sit, and eat: do not my ears abuse.
> I oft look on false coin, to know't from true:
> Not that I love it, more, than I will you.

In *Epicoene* it is Morose who hates ear abuse, but his solitude is suspect, being akin to reclusiveness. His luxury is privacy; the chink in his armour is that he is unwilling to allow his nephew Dauphine to inherit from him. Jonson's contemporary Anthony Nixon quoted the view that there are only two good days in marriage: the wedding day and the day the wife dies. For Morose marriage is an unmitigated disaster, because like his sex his expectations shrivel. The wedding festivities become a mock wedding masque immediately after the exchange of vows, with Epicoene's friend Truewit as master of ceremonies. Desperate to escape from the marriage, Morose offers to mutilate himself; he will lose an eye, a hand 'or any other member'. It is Dauphine who replies: 'Marry, God forbid sir, that you should geld yourself to anger your wife' (IV.iv. 9–10), as it was he who duped Morose into a transgressive marriage with a woman who is actually a boy in drag. By doing so he clinches his inheritance, brings low the sexually boastful fops claiming Epicoene as a sexual partner, and sees off the collegiate women – true epicoenes who threaten for a time the triumph of the hermaphrodite. Dauphine's triumph is because he uses his intellect; the boy is not merely a toy whether or not he is actually Dauphine's sodomitical plaything.[12] He is a gentleman's son and loyal withal to his employer who may (or may not) have had sex with him.

A robust nosiness and noisiness erupts into the provocative stillness of Morose's household. Hitherto like Quarlous in *Bartholomew Fair* he has excluded women from his life because he fears aptly their unfathomable ability to effeminize men. They are unwilling to accommodate the whole man and will always seek to neutralize, denigrate or dismember him. The richest irony of the play is that Morose panics before the silent woman who penetrates his retreat from the world and is another man (albeit much younger), and before he knows this Morose has to confess to impotence: 'Utterly un-abled in nature, by reason of *frigidity*, to perform the duties, or any the least office of a husband.' (V. iv. 46–7) He may be lying, but this is a confession made to the world, (something that later the Earl of Essex simply could not bring himself to do); and this sexual disorder stands in for his disregard of social order, the authentic claim of Dauphine to his estate. Morose panics – 'I am no man' (V. iv. 44) – a realization that his predicament is self-inflicted. This makes all the more galling the revelations to the judges in the court proceedings of the last act by Epicoene's 'friends', that s(he) is sexually liberal, meddling and given to gossip. Morose had not had sex with Epicoene, but 'a sodomitical effect has been created in the absence of homosexual sex'.[13]

A number of critics have pointed out that the virility of all the main characters, not simply Morose, is constantly debated in an atmosphere of high unease. That this debate went on beyond the walls of the theatres so much is clear. In a play that eschews farce but seeks tragic heights Shakespeare himself itemizes and re-enacts the effeminization of a warrior, Antony, who 'gives his potent regiment to a trull'. Maecenas is speaking bluntly to Octavia, then wife of Antony, and is referring to the genitals. In the play there is even a speaking part for a eunuch, Mardian, a name cannily recalling 'marred' and 'maiden', one who symbolizes the dismembering power of women. Cleopatra's power lies in her theatricality, a characteristic attacked vehemently by those who saw the perversion of self resulting from boys wearing women's clothes. To signal the surrender of masculine potency before her scorned 'infinite variety' she seizes hold of Antony's sword for which, boyishly, he has a name – Philippan. Phallic Phil, like all swords, is meant to penetrate the flesh of others unto death. By seizing it Cleopatra has stolen, as he bemoans in the scenes that follow, the emblem of his masculine power; his passivity is un-Roman, 'a very serious moral, or rather political infirmity' correctly identified as such by Shakespeare. The Roman self of the un-manned Antony can only be retrieved by a clumsy suicide and in death his entire body will uselessly stiffen. That is true impotence.

CHAPTER THIRTEEN

TROUBLE IN MIND

Censorship in England of erotic printed material has long been erratic, fumbling, ultimately pointless – and so it has remained. Writers in Elizabethan England had an even more difficult time, since trying to anticipate a reaction from censors who were high ecclesiastics closely involved in government matters, while simultaneously seeking to liberate the erotic imaginations of readers, was a troublesome task that could lead to self-censorship. No wonder that the promising career of a man as well placed as George Gascoigne (1542–77) was messily derailed, for he was too candid, as it seemed to some, in his 1573 masterpiece *A Hundred Sundrie Floures*. Its frank sexual discourse displeased the bishops. Even so, Gascoigne did find more work, but directly commissioned by the Earl of Leicester for the Kenilworth Festivities in 1575, the same year that Gascoigne tried to sneak *The Posies of George Gascoigne* past the censors. This was a slightly edited version of his earlier book, prologued by his claim that the text was now castrated, 'gelded from all filthy phrases'.[1] He had not had much luck in what seems to have been his appearance as an *hombre salvagio* at Kenilworth; when he broke the small tree he was carrying over his thigh and hurled it aside the pieces barely missed the queen's horse and it shied. Elizabeth retained her seat and indicated she was not upset; but Gascoigne had made an error in frightening the horse and the bishops – identified by him in a chagrined phrase as castrators. This pithy exposure of them led to the confiscation of the *Posies* in 1576, and so the most provoking part of the text, *The Adventures of Master F.J.*, a study of a sexual affair that may have been autobiographical, came close to oblivion. Gascoigne's difficulties came from his breaching of decorum, not only sexual but social, for he published his own work and had sought a wider readership than courtier-poets hitherto. Perhaps he had not intended to libel anyone, but by setting an amorous, sexualized narrative before the lower orders, he took the risk that it would be read so: 'a loose allegory of courtiership as a form of courtesanship.'

Even as Gascoigne was being neutered by prim definitions of what was proper to be published, an Englishman was in Italy learning about publishing and the improper. John Wolfe was in Florence in 1576, and after returning to England he began a printing business in 1579 that was to make him a prominent publisher for twenty years. His speciality was Italian literature, including items by Machiavelli and Pietro Aretino that had been banned in Italy, and he was cautious enough to bring them out with false or fictitious places of printing in Italy, a procedure that might also boost sales. When he brought out Aretino's first and second parts of *I Ragionamenti*, there were

George Gascoigne (1542?–77) was of gentry parents and so educated at Cambridge and the Inns of Court, yet he was one of the first to seek to use writing as a career in itself.

John Florio was the Italian-born lexicographer and language instructor, whose translation of Montaigne's Essays *appeared with a dedication to Lady Penelope Rich.*

enough buyers of Italian pornography in England to justify the 1584 publication; buyers, readers and imitators. Englishmen working on epic poems consciously sought out Italian models and so too did those seeking to broaden the range of erotic writing. If his command of Italian faltered then he could turn to the London Italian, Giovanni (John) Florio, language teacher and lexicographer whose influential Italian-English dictionary, *A Worlde of Wordes* appeared in 1598. Florio took great pains to make contemporary Italian literature, 'especially learned erotica and pornography', available to English readers.[2] Indeed, by the 1590s Aretino had become famous among educated Englishmen, especially the worldly young fellows at the Inns of Court, for his collaboration with Giulio Romano, mannerist painter, and Marcantonio Raimondi, engraver, on a salacious text called *I Modi* (The Positions); this was a series of prints depicting in detail the positions of heterosexual penetration, and accompanied by a set of sixteen equally explicit sonnets. The artwork and *Sonetti Lussoriosi* achieved a pan-European notoriety far beyond their actual availability, which had been limited by the seizure of all copies of the first two editions, destroyed thereafter on the orders of an outraged Pope Clement VII. Apparently only one copy of a subsequent counterfeit survived.[3] So their rarity made it very unlikely that many Englishmen had seen sets of the prints or tried to read the sonnets; it was the thought of them that set off libidinous imaginings and Aretino's reputation came to be that of a true pornographer, 'the symbol, the very type of venery'.[4] Yet it had not always been so; Sir Thomas Wyatt in

Pietro Aretino, whose pungent reputation in Renaissance England was soon exclusively that of a pornographer, author of texts which had first aroused and scandalized Catholic Europe.

his *Penitential Psalms* had drawn on Aretino's *The Seven Psalms of David*, the Italian having produced a cluster of pot-boiling religious works to fill his pockets and maybe protect his back from irate churchmen like Giberti, the papal datary. Aretino had died in Venice in 1556, but for years before that had been a key figure in Venetian cultural life, particularly close to Titian and Jacopo Sansovino, the architect. It was only some time after his death that continental critics had begun chipping away at his reputation; such efforts were eventually to reach England.

The comments of English critics like Gabriel Harvey on Aretino were not always harsh and disgusted. Before the change in attitude Harvey admires the novelty and extravagant verbosity of the Italian, and had been so taken with things Italian that he had planned a lengthy trip to the country. Writing to Edmund Spenser about the intellectual life of Cambridge, Harvey, with a certain bemused satisfaction, noted that many there were acquainted with Aretino. But then his approval began to be undermined and the force behind this retreat seems to have been his own brother, the Revd Richard Harvey. In his pamphlet *A Theological Discourse of the Lamb of God*, the puny parson echoed Roger Ascham's earlier attacks on things Italian and Italianate Englishmen, and was blunt about the scandalous reputations of Machiavelli and Aretino. A contemporary of the Harveys, the satirist Joseph Hall was unhappy that English writers seemed to be attempting to go beyond Aretino, and it was this point that launched the Harveys into their war of words with Thomas Nashe, who made his first reference to Aretino in *Pierce Pennilesse* (1592). Gliding over the supposed godlessness of Aretino and his willingness to be anatomical, Nashe praised the satirist, the modern Juvenal who would take on high and low. Nashe was, of course, a Cambridge man like Harvey and Marlowe. The latter was at Corpus Christi, and several years ahead of Nashe, who became an ardent follower and friend of the brilliant young writer and spy. Whether either of them had actually read for themselves Aretino's works is open to doubt, although Nashe was a friend of Florio's and may have taken his instruction on what to read and what to skip over. What Nashe certainly knew in detail was Aretino's witty, daring, salacious copy and extravagant mode of living. Aretino had had a genius for self-promotion and Nashe would happily have annexed that all for himself; as a literary predator Aretino was a role model.

Nashe went boldly after him with his *Choise of Valentines*, which readers and non-readers alike agreed was a strikingly lascivious piece of writing. Although it only circulated in manuscript form it attracted new readers and Nashe achieved what he wanted – notoriety, since it may be 'the most obscene Elizabethan poem known to us'.[5] It is indebted to Chaucer but principally to Ovid's *Amores* III.vi, which Marlowe had already translated. Nashe's intention was surely to mock the male pretence that at every opportunity for sex he would never fail to get an erection, a pretence that the reader holding the text in his hand would no doubt noisily proclaim. The speaker of the poem is Tomalin; his lady is Frances, both names freighted with meaning, and although Tomalin does get an erection it is comically mistimed. As a professional with an obligation Frances does her best to revitalize his sullen member, but the dominant thought is of her own pleasure. When he flags after a second orgasm – 'I faint, I yeald' – Frances finds comfort in a glass dildo (possibly made by Italian immigrant glass makers in London), and thus confirms the male view of female sexuality – consuming and slow. David Frantz is accurate in calling the *Choise of Valentines* 'one of the few unadulterated pornographic works of the English Renaissance'. Its purpose is explicit and even today when pornography relies on the prying lens rather than the acute pen, it remains as bright testimony to the urgent imagination of the writer who had no moral purpose, and many then (and now?) will have preferred the humour to the towering grossness of Aretino's pornography. In the verbal skirmishes with the Harveys the 'English Aretine' showed an extraordinary flair for sexual insults and scatology, so it was perhaps fitting for a clumsy woodcut in Richard Lichfield's antagonistic pamphlet *The Trimming of Thomas Nashe* (1597) to show him as a felon mired in filth. Lichfield has Nashe as a recidivist with not one prison in London unpolluted with 'Nashes evil'.

It is an image that takes no account of Nashe's startling ability to flit from one Harvey failing to another, unleashing a flurry of counter-punching insults, bruising the tenderest spots and leaving Gabriel and Richard wheezing in his wake. In some ways fate played into his hands because the Harveys were too apprehensive about the world's opinion of them. Nashe exploited, for example, the sexual imbroglio of their sister,

Mercy (or Marcie), with the young Philip Howard, Earl of Surrey, and after 1580 Earl of Arundel. He had been married when twelve years old to Anne Dacres, who was the same age. After leaving Cambridge in 1576, he arrived at court to live extravagantly for a time while his wife lived at Audley End, some 3 miles from Walden and the Harvey home. Seeing Mercy in a field one day Howard attempted to seduce her, and but for Gabriel's positive intervention might have succeeded. The story was gratefully seized upon and reworked by Nashe, who artfully offers the suggestion that her behaviour stemmed from lack of a dowry. Richard Harvey is ridiculed as the 'unclean vicar', and in the same text, *Strange Newes* (1593), Gabriel was charged with sexual impropriety. In September 1592 he arrived in London on business with letters of introduction to the Dutch merchant-scholar Emanuel van Meteren (known as Mr Demetrius). The letters were from Christopher Bird of Walden and writing to him later Harvey explained that in the absence of van Meteren, he had handed over a letter to van Meteren's wife, 'whom I found very courteous'. The detail is winkled out of Harvey's *Foure Letters*, and by hoisting it into public scrutiny (while pretending to protect Mistress Demetrius) Nashe raises doubts about the propriety of Harvey and the unfortunate housewife who is exploited in and out of parentheses.

When Nashe wishes to insult the Harveys in the most coarse-grained way his humour becomes lavatorial. Given the charmless function of the Elizabethan privy, equating the works of the Harveys with what was left there had a particularly gross pungency, albeit lacking subtly. The scatological tradition goes back at least to Chaucer's *Miller's Tale* and *Friar's Tale* and forward to Jonson's *Alchemist*. It was so traditional and English that a court variant could be found. It was the work of Sir John Harington, one of many godchildren of Elizabeth, but among the most gifted. Harington was not a court jester, but he had, as it were, a licence to amuse and he did so with rather risqué humour that veered to the Rabelaisian. Moreover, he never pressed for preferment and seems rather to have relished his role as epigrammatist, translator and inventor. His epigrams were well known through manuscript circulation, most of them written between 1585 and 1603. They were about quotidian life:

The whore: Lesbia doth laugh to hear sellers and buyers
              Called by this name, substantial occupiers;
              Lesbia, the word was good while good folk used it,
              You marred it that with Chaucer's jest abused it;
              But good or bad, how ere the word by made,
              Lesbia is loth perhaps to leave the trade.

Here the epigram turns on the double meaning (already noted, see p. 112) of 'occupy'.[6]

The cuckold: What curled-pate youth is he that sitteth there
So near thy wife, and whispers in her ear,
And takes her hand in his, and soft doth wring her,
Sliding her ring still up and down her finger?
Sir, tis a Proctor, seen in both the Laws,
Retain'd by her, in some important cause;
Prompt and discreet both in his speech and action,
And doth her business with great satisfaction.
And thinkest thou so? a horn-plague on they head:
Art thou so like a fool, and wittoll led,
    To think he doth the business of the wife?
    He doth thy business, I dare lay my life

(No. 335, p. 280)[7]

The courtier: A courtier, kind in speech, curst in condition,
Finding his fault could be no longer hidden,
Went to his friend to clear his hard suspicion,
And fearing lest he might be more than chidden,
Fell to a flattering and most base submission,
Vowing to kiss his foot, if he were bidden.
My foot? (said he) nay, that were too submiss,
But three foot higher you deserve to kiss.

(No. 275, p. 261)

The lady: A vertuous lady sitting in a muse,
As many times fair vertuous ladies use,
Leaned her elbow on one knee full hard,
The other distant from it half a yard.
Her knight, to taunt her by a privy token,
Said, 'Wife, awake, your cabinet stands open'.
    She rose and blushed and smiled and soft doth say,
    'Then lock it if you list: you keep the key'.

(No. 404, p. 312)

As a translator Harington worked long over Ariosto's *Orlando Furioso*, which was completed in 1591 and which was the first English book to be illustrated with copper engravings. His next book was *The Metamorphosis of Ajax*, which he presented to Elizabeth in 1596, causing something of a stir as it described a water-closet (or 'jakes') which he had invented and installed at his home near (appropriately) Bath. The topic itself was not what troubled the old queen, who could cope with something witty and basic, but Harington mocked any number of his contemporaries in cheeky allusions which often veered towards the libellous. The book was refused a licence for publication, but Harington, with his usual insouciance risked it anyway and three editions were entirely sold out within a year. We might say he had hit pay dirt – or made dirt pay. What it cost him was an exile from court to Ireland where he soldiered.

The fundamental things of the body appear in the epigrams of John Heywood, grandfather of the poet and churchman John Donne. Heywood had a rather wayward celebrity as a musician, comic entertainer and poet from early in the reign of Henry VIII.[8] It was lucky for him that the king got the impression he was only a harmless poet, for a plot to bring down Archbishop Cranmer on a charge of heresy failed, and the plotters, including Heywood, were tried and condemned to death. Years later it was Harington who recalled that Heywood had ''scaped hanging with his mirth'. Yet few of his epigrams would raise a smile today and those of his grandson, written in Latin originally, seem sententious and even crabby for a young man, with a whiff of the lecture room about them. For laughter the Elizabethans would turn to jest books; the first collection had been printed in England in 1525 and the demand remained until well into the next century. Sexual jokes could be indulgent or gleeful, even innocuous in terms of their humour, but there were a good many that were ruder and cruder, and as David Frantz has noted this often means cuckoldry. The humour arises from the failure of the individual to remark just what it is that is causing noisy guffaws in the group. Marriage was a relationship of unequals, and cuckoldry marked a profound shift in the power relationship; an artful wife and a sharply opportunistic lover stole freedom from a dominant figure and this loss of control was funny. 'Ridicule was central to Renaissance comic theory.' Laughter was occasioned, according to Thomas Wilson in 1560, by 'the fondness, the filthiness, the deformity and all such evil behaviour as we see to be in other(s)'.

Transgressive wit was just as likely to land a writer in gaol as bawdiness or obscenity, between which Joseph Hall and John Marston tried to draw a distinction. Ironic then that Hall thought Marston (whose name invited insult since 'stone' equals testes) a candidate for castration, the best cure for his lumpishness. And both found themselves proscribed by the bishop censors of the Elizabethan press in 1599. On 1 June Whitgift and Bancroft suddenly ordered the Stationers' Company, with its monopoly of licensed printing, to corrall certain named texts, including a new edition of *The Fifteen Joys of Marriage* (1509) by Antoine de la Sale. This was not as it might sound, a sex handbook, but a cheerful compilation of the way many marriages took shape: bankruptcy, bawling children and redundant in-laws. The bishops' ban meant that nearly a dozen of London's leading writers had the unhappy experience of knowing (if not seeing) their work torched, with a further injunction on reprinting; the burning of the texts took place at Stationers' Hall, and was so thorough that most of the original editions disappeared and very few copies of any of these books survive. The episode was symptomatic of the decay of confidence that had taken place after the lucky triumphs of 1588. The country at large was waiting for Elizabeth to die, queasy at the succession prospects, while its greatest city was boiling with an extraordinarily dangerous melange of religious ideas – Catholic, sectarian and church Puritan. And all the while 'printing technology was simultaneously spreading beyond any immediate control'.[9] Even the date, just before the turn of the century, may have played a part in setting the bishops on this course as they saw apparently some imminent threat to stability. Thomas Nashe, who was on the list, was rarely more than a stride ahead of official retribution and Marlowe was some time dead. What seems to have jabbed the bishops into action as well was the satirical treatment of erotic or salacious subjects, since satirists and churchmen alike regarded a large body of popular literature as obscene. John Davies, Middle Temple lawyer and poet, was on the list; the author of very many epigrams he deserves recognition here for his flagellation epigram, one of the few Renaissance poems in English to mention whipping. Scenes of flagellation with erotic overtones occur from time to time in Italian Renaissance art. Lynne Lawner illustrates the point with an engraving from Agostino Caracci's *Lascivie* series.[10] In the epigram the satyr and nymph are much more like real people:

> When Francus comes to solace with his whore
> He sends for rods and strips himself stark naked:
> For his lust sleeps, and will not rise before,
> By whipping of the wench it be awaked.
>> I envie him not, but wish I had the power,
>> To make myself his wench but one half hour.[11]

Everard Guilpin, the satirist, was also on the list, being one of those who wrote bawdy epigrams:

> Since marriage, Faber's prouder than before,
> Yfaith his wife must take him a hole lower.

The inference seems to be that before he got married Faber had been limited to anal sex by his lover on contraceptive grounds. Another common euphemism for anal sex was 'back-door' and since the practice was regarded as suspect and even tinged with degenerate instincts, the phrase 'back-door'd Italian' came into use to allude to sodomy and pederasty, both these in English eyes characteristically Jesuit and hence papal: Thomas Middleton, Thomas Dekker and John Marston so use the phrase. In the latter's *Insatiate Countess*, two close friends in one of the sub-plots marry two Italian merchants who are frank enemies.[12] The men decide to seduce each other's wives, but Abigail and Thais are alert to what goes on and Abigail proposes that old stand-by, the bed-trick. Being naive or hesitant, Thais has to have the proposal to defeat their husbands repeated:

Thais: But you mean they shall come in at the back-door?
Abig.:   Who, our Husbands? nay, and they come not in at the fore-doors, there will be no pleasure in't.

'Going to the back-door' was even used in a deposition about the transgressive behaviour of the Earl of Oxford by his friend (turned enemy) Charles Arundell. His testimony was that Oxford often had sex with a kitchen boy:

I have seen this boy many a time in his chamber, doors close-locked, together with him, maybe at Whitehall and at his house in Broad Street. Finding it so I have gone to the backdoor to satisfy myself, at which the boy hath come out all in a sweat, and I have gone in and found the beast in the same plight.

Whatever the interpretation of this then (and now), what is clear is that the sexual narrative provides a potentially hostile grounding for satiric attack. Sexual metaphor is threaded into an aggressive discourse, and after Nashe with his narrow target of the Harvey brother, comes Marston with his defiant grasp of the pornographic. One advantage he had over his jostling contemporaries in the scrap for an 'aggressively sexualised form of distinctly English literature', was that his mother was Italian and that he spoke the language rather better than his shaky Latin. In his play *Antonio and Mellida*, probably written a few months after the bishops' ban, an important section was written in Italian, and he would have been aware (like Nashe) that Aretino had been designated 'il flagello de principi' – the scourge of princes. The notion is rehearsed in Marston's title *The Scourge of Villanie*; admiration and imitation are not incompatible with finding a new, raucous voice for, in Francis Meres' phrase, 'lasciviousness and petulancy'. This volatile mixture soon went into a second edition, evidence that he had struck a chord with the reading public. In *Metamorphosis of Pigmalion's Image . . .*, Marston's presentational technique for the sexual components is to push them forward and then whisk them back as if ill-disposed to them. The intention is evidently the arousal of the reader (male), and it is done with the pouting cunning of an erotic dancer in a bar-club today. This brinkmanship eventually leads Marston at the end of *Pigmalion* to clobber his own readers as 'lewd Priapians' (Priapus being the Roman god of male virility). The abrupt reversal may have amused some, especially the author, who liked to 'dally with my excrement', as Armado says in *Love's Labours Lost*.

This evidently gave pause to John Weever (born *c.* 1575), who arrived in London from Cambridge with literary ambitions and his *Epigrammes*, which were printed after the bishops' ban. His publisher was the tough Valentine Simmes, a member of the Stationers' Company, who ignored the requirement of the censors in 1599 that 'no satires or epigrams be printed hereafter'.[13] The text worked up by Weever for publication with praise of living poets was dedicated to Sir Richard Hoghton, who was knighted in June 1599, so printer and author flouted the authority of the bishops even before it became clear that the authorities would not apply the new regulations too rigorously. But Weever decided to be more cautious than this suggests because before the bonfire he had wanted to emulate Marston's success by writing an epyllion and some satires, and when this plan was frustrated he cobbled together what he had and published it as *Faunus and Melliflora* (1600). The following year Weever had published anonymously *The Whipping of the Satyre* in which he attacked his former role model Marston for writing 'that which should not be spoken'. Weever calls him a 'sin-monger' and a purveyor of 'foul-mouthed speeches'. Weever may have recoiled, and Jonson ridiculed him as Shift (alias Signior Whiff) in *Every Man out of His Humour*, which reads like a double hit at the pushy homosexual, but others found Marston's new coarseness in the sound of the language and its semantics particularly stimulating. Playwrights at the turn of the century were much better placed than Gascoigne twenty-five years earlier. The sometimes rasping, sometimes insinuating voice of the libidinous Renaissance imagination quit the page for the stage. Their mucky/murky complexities were delivered on stage in Jacobean drama. As the bishops went in for literary criticism that literally scorched the pages, a new venue for plays was being completed – the Globe – built for a mass audience of some two thousand. By the time it burned down in 1613 there had been a startling shift in the culture from poetry to theatre, that is from print to performance, incorporating aspects of 'Italian bawdry' that sexualized the English theatre thanks to the father of modern pornography, Pietro Aretino.

CHAPTER FOURTEEN

THE FIRES OF VENUS

The sexual culture of Renaissance England was found in sundry places, not all risk free or cost free. The primary risk was venereal disease – the pox – a long and shameful evolution of disintegration in places lubricated by natural secretions: nostrils, eyes, mouths, uvula, urinary tract. Modern medical opinion is divided on the first appearance of syphilis in Renaissance Europe, and the true ground zero from whence this destructive calamity came, probably at the end of the fifteenth century. The problem is compounded by the correspondences between leprosy (so-called) in Europe before 1500 and syphilis, which appears discretely in published writings soon after the return of Christopher Columbus and his crew men from the Caribbean, prompting the 'Columbian Theory'. The Unitarian (or African) theory sets out the view that syphilis and other systemic diseases caused by the spirochaete *Treponema pallidum* are intimately related, forms of a single disease spread by hefty population shifts such as slavery. This view suggests too a disease of some antiquity and evidence may be drawn from the Old Testament, classical and medieval literature. Finally, the theory settles for the opinion that a torpid strain of *Treponema* mutated late in the fifteenth century and became highly active among the shifting population thereafter. The speed with which syphilis took hold in Europe was bewildering but evidently assisted by war, with soldiers playing a crucial part in its pan-European advance. The papal physician Giovanni de Vigo in 1514 published his famous medical text *Pratica copiosa in arte chirurgica*, which summarized the surgical learning of the time. In the fifth chapter of a book that went into fifty-two editions he looked at the supposedly new disease and drew attention to its spread by sexual contacts. His treatment naturally included surgery – excising the chancre by knife leaving a wound to be cauterized by a hot iron. No doubt the trauma of this immediately killed more than the slow individual progress of the disease. The second book in English on syphilis was a translation of Vigo by Bartholomew Traheron published in 1543.

Johannes Fabricius, drawing on a wide range of contemporary sources and recent research, has made a very strong case for contending that syphilis was sweeping England by the mid-sixteenth century.[1] This argues against the view of Lawrence Stone, put forward in the mid-1970s, that syphilis was, unlike gonorrhoea, rare. In fact, its momentous eruption into the nation's health had a consequence for the organization of medicine. The act of 1540 which incorporated barbers and surgeons into the Barber-Surgeons' Company was very likely a response to their hope for a monopoly of venereal treatments when there was a continual surge of clients. This guaranteed an income for the barber-surgeons who for a century served as the consultants to the poxed. Other physicians were ruffled by this and viewed such rivals for fame and funds with rancour, since the dead could not rebuke them and those who lived advertised barber-surgeon skills – which we might call random luck.

Simon Forman had a brief tangle with the company in 1593, but nothing came of it, because the barber-surgeons were engaged in their long-running dispute with the Royal College of Physicians, and because Forman had well-placed friends who could bring pressure to bear for him. His treatment was routine for the pox – an austere diet, followed by purging and salves for the stinking ulcers. Given Forman's formidable sexual appetite and his many fleeting partners his avoidance of the pox was remarkable, as was his recovery from the plague, for in July 1592 he found plague-sores around his genitals and later his feet. Forman's self-treatment required his sores to be lanced and a herbal concoction to be drunk; the success of this for patients beyond his household secured his fame. By 1593 the terror of the times, rampant city-wide sickness, had Thomas Nashe quacking and in September he had a licence for publishing his series of contrite reflections on metropolitan sins, *Christs Teares over Ierusalem*, was dedicated to Lady Elizabeth Carey, wife of Sir George Carey, a wife both learned and devout. An 'intensely rhetorical work of spirituality and satire against urban vices', it earned Nashe a twofold reward. The payment from the Careys who evidently knew him was welcome. Most unwelcome was the prison sentence he picked up from the Lord Mayor and aldermen for calling London 'the seeded Garden of sin' as well as 'the Sea that sucks in all the scummy channels of the Realm'. Nashe fetched up in Newgate during a major plague epidemic, 'possible shackled, certainly in poverty and near-starvation'.[2] Nashe was a literary terrier – 'London, what are thy suburbs but licensed stews'; as for the prostitutes, they were syphilitic in his estimate at twenty, and before they reached forty they were skeletally thin. This physical and spiritual withering is the fault of the city and by implication the city fathers – 'justice somewhere is corrupted'. Nashe's sour view of London and its assorted excesses was occasioned by, no doubt, *terror mortis*, but some of the things he railed against were bound to happen as the city grew unevenly and at a spectacular rate. In 1598 John Stow in his *Survey* noted the manner of the first suburban sprawl, and expansion effected by migration to the city which made up for the tragic losses due to sickness. By 1600, it is reckoned that the population was some two hundred thousand people, all hankering for housing, daily bread and ale, and better health. So there were real problems in control; growth each year was by a number larger than the population of most provincial towns. Stow described the Tower Liberty, which surrounded the great river fortress-prison, as 'greatly straitened by encroachments (unlawfully made and suffered) for gardens and houses'; in the 1580s a Mr Heming had seized an opportunity to put up 'alehouses and houses of suspicious resort' by Tower Hill.

Gaming in a brothel was perhaps the second favourite way of throwing good money after bad in such an establishment.

In 1603, with playing in the theatres banned from 8 May to Christmas because of a particularly fierce outbreak of bubonic plague, the authorities fixed upon slum clearance as the crucial way to prevent further infection. A royal proclamation from the new monarch James I proposed the demolition of the worst slum quarters where gathered 'excessive numbers of idle, indigent, dissolute and dangerous persons'. In *Measure for Measure* there is a brief passage about this proposal and its consequences, although notionally the Vienna of Pompey and the bawd Mistress Overdone is the site. All the suburban brothels are to be pulled down to the consternation of the old woman, although Pompey seeks to console her with the thought that changing her dwelling need not lead to a change of trade: 'you that have worn your eyes almost out* in the service, you will be considered' (I.ii.102–3). The efforts of city aldermen and privy councillors to arrest development, suppress begging, curtail ale houses and shackle prostitution were commonly futile, because the surplus of rural population had to end somewhere and London snared most.

Unfortunately for 'cockatrice' (prostitute) and client, sixpence for sex very often meant, as the royal physician William Clowes noted, 'that among every twenty diseased persons that are taken in [at St Bartholomew's] fifteen of them have the pox'. His data for the prevalence of syphilis in the later part of Elizabeth's reign may be suspect,

---

* Primary optic atrophy; a classic venereal symptom.

because as a surgeon he sought to enhance the significance of his work, but his exasperated emphasis on prostitution is understandable. Nor was this confined to the medical profession. The more godly justices of the peace gave law enforcement an additional edge under the sincere belief that if the sinful nature of the English were not curbed, then national survival might be severely threatened. Many protestants surveying the ways of the world and the contamination, as they saw it, of so many aspects of the nation's life and culture, believed that they were living in the final phase of human history, the infamous 'last days' with the emphasis on depravity or evil rather than good. The Augustinian emphasis on the former and on humanity's dependence on the grace of God were key elements in English protestant thinking. There was a strong vein of this in Clowes, whose intention was to heal the deserving sick; the element of punishment from God in venereal sickness has to be acknowledged. If Clowes was alive today to specialize in sexually transmitted diseases he would doubtless be as judgemental; he might rewrite his references to 'ungodly life' and 'odious sin', but he would probably cling to his view that promiscuity threatened the whole land with poisoning.

William Clowes (the elder) was born in Warwickshire in about 1540, learned surgery as an apprentice to George Keble in London, and became a member of the Barber-Surgeons' Company. He had surgical experience treating the wounds of fighting men on land and at sea before becoming a surgeon at St Bartholomew's and later Christ's Hospital, so he 'represents an entire body of upwardly mobile yet marginal professionals who achieve increasing recognition in the 16th and 17th centuries'.[3] Publication of his pamphlet on venereal treatment in 1579, *A Short and profitable Treatise Touching the Cure of the Disease Called (Morbus Gallicus)*, was evidence of his position, because senior members of the Royal College of Physicians rarely if ever published. Indeed, many of them rose to their positions of eminence without any effort at original research. To publish in English without bumping up the text with details from medieval scholastic medicine was new and innovative, as was the topic. Syphilis was an ideal subject for investigation as far as Clowes was concerned because it was new and controversial still, and because it required practical solutions if such could be mustered. Not that he intended to provide a cure for everyone infected, because he had an inextinguishable sense that syphilis came from God and that there was a class of undeserving sick people who, being lewd and idle men and women, were ill through their own dispositions. Clowes wanted his countrymen and women to eschew opportunistic fornication, but he also advocated severe punishment for traders in flesh, and he wanted all magistrates 'the second surgeons appointed by god' to be as rigorous in sentencing as possible to frighten people out of their wickedness. So how many found his recommendation of stewed prunes useful as a preventative of sexually transmitted disease?

Clowes also gave a shadowy outline to the crude method of some despotic governments today in dealing with people with AIDS. He thought to contain the spread of syphilis by isolating infected persons, and his treatment then of his preferred patients (male and monied) offered dietary and clinical intervention. He discouraged pork, salted meat, fish, cheese, raw fruit and sweet wine, all of which would have figured in a quotidian diet over a week or so. He endorsed instead mutton, lamb, veal, hares and rabbit and game birds. Ducks and geese were anathematized while arbitrarily he favoured chickens and capons, as well as birds of the woods and mountains. After eating and evacuating, the principle element in the treatment was the use of mercury ointment. Almost as soon as syphilis became the disease of the incontinent, physicians like Torella and de Vigo began using mercury as a fumigatory, inunction, or by mouth. Their knowledge of it stemmed from its use by the Arabs for skin disorders and leprosy, and initially it was used in a solution strength of one part to forty. When the strength was upped in ointment to one part in eight by unscrupulous practitioners then the consequences were alarming indeed. The ointment was daubed on various places on the body and the patient, wrapped in a sheet and with his head covered, then went to bed with as many coverings as could be borne to induce sweating. Winter warmers like hot bricks and hot water-bottles could be stacked around the patient for a maximum of three hours, and this was repeated over several days. To relieve the disagreeable oral symptoms Clowes recommended a mouth wash and gargle of milk infused with violet leaves, syrup of violets and columbine leaves.

The mercury cure has been assessed in the light of modern medical practice. It was apparently efficacious in dealing with the primary symptoms, but it failed to cure the infections of secondary syphilis. At the tertiary stage it was again useful in dealing with cutaneous lesions, but there was always the unpredictable aspect of the patients' response to a toxic substance and the risk that the purposed cure might in fact kill. This was true in the case of a little-known surgeon, Tristram Lyde, who ended up in Rochester Assizes for administering the mercury cure to a clutch of women who subsequently died. His defence was that their sickness being so acute they required this treatment and that by failing to follow his prescriptive advice, by going out too soon, they had tragically wrecked his ministrations. The judge took this view as expert and accepted the plea. Lyde might have chose an alternative 'wonder' drug derived from a tree found in the West Indies and the northern coast of Latin America. The native people of Hispaniola (now Haiti and the Dominican Republic) called the tree *guaiacum*, and once Spanish sailors established to their own grief that they were infected they sought out a native cure from this mystery tree.

The cure (so-called) was introduced to Europe by the infected poet humanist Ulrich von Hutten in 1519, although his assertion that he had cured himself does not hold because he died in 1523. His tribute to it, *De guaiaci medicine et morbo gallico,* describes the use of the wood for a decoction. The text was widely translated and the so-called 'cure' was widely taken up. The reason for this breezy, uncritical response is obvious – terror of the disease and acute anxiety about the side-effects of the mercury cure, all eloquently listed by von Hutten.[4] Guaiac wood was a mystery item to physicians and non-specialists alike, and there was a tendency to confuse it with ebony: 'the juice of cursed ebona' in *Hamlet* for example. By the time Shakespeare was writing that play in around 1601 the guaiac cure was well known and regarded in many quarters as both suspect and dangerous if the physician was not taking a holistic approach. In *Lenten Stuffe* (1599) Thomas Nashe is highly sceptical of this 'cure', very likely because he too was infected with venereal disease – hence his early death in 1601. The Swiss physician Paracelsus was shocked that what he considered a bogus treatment was proclaimed as a cure, for like so many boldly proclaimed exotic treatments it was useless.

This assessment meant that the search for a corrective or cure went on in the New World because that was where the first encounter with syphilis had taken place. So hitherto obscure or unknown plants, like sassafras, sarsaparilla and china root, were ground up and boiled. Even home-grown saffron was optimistically mentioned by Shakespeare in *Alls Well That Ends Well* (1603), a layman who showed a considerable knowledge of the disease. In *Measure for Measure* (1604) Lucio makes one of the earliest references in English literature to the transmission of the disease from a drinking vessel. One symptom of syphilis was alopecia and being bald himself Shakespeare alludes frequently to this marker, but in *Timon of Athens* he elaborates on the symptoms of severe secondary and late syphilis. The play is dated to 1608, only a year after the marriage of Susanna Shakespeare to Dr John Hall, a Cambridge man with a large practice in Stratford and the surrounding area. If the playwright needed any instruction he could consult his own son-in-law. What was missing from Timon's speech to the two prostitutes is any reference to blindness which among others afflicted William Jaggard, publisher in 1599 of a Shakespeare scoop, two of the sonnets (138 and 144) which appeared with others in *The Passionate Pilgrim*.[5] When Doll Tearsheet is dying of syphilis in *Henry V*, Pistol refers to her treatment, the mercury fumigation whereby 'the patient was exposed to the fumes of cinnabar (mercuric sulphide, vermilion, and mercury ore)' which would be heated to smoking on a hot plate or chafing dish and the remnant powder used to dust the body. Doll has this done at an old house once used by lepers, the hospital of St Mary in Spitalfields.

William Clowes, who advanced socially through his practice, made a later revision, slightly downward, of the number attending his hospital who were syphilitic. Even so, the general picture of a shockingly prevalent disease remains for scrutiny, and for Clowes there was the vexatious certainty that it could be routed if only sin ceased. Conscious of the inevitability of sin it was therefore rather smart of

Holland's Leaguer was a famous and superior early seventeenth-century brothel on the notorious Bankside – though when Mrs Holland took control of it is uncertain.

him to specialize in a social disease, and logical that his attention would be focused on those who could afford to pay. According to Robert Greene, 'goodman Surgeon laughs in his purse'. For a writer like Nashe the vending of sex was a particularly meaningful metaphor embodying the submerged sickness of a great city. Middleton's later play *A Chaste Maid in Cheapside* presented such things as the logical culmination of the mercantile skills developed in London over many years. Evidently he liked to believe (against much evidence it has to be said) that fear of contracting the 'foul disease' even from prostitutes of the better sort (i.e. not sixpenny 'drabs') had the effect of causing a sexually active gentleman to pause thoughtfully:

When I behold a glorious dangerous strumpet,
Sparkling in beauty and destruction too,
Both at a twinkling, I do liken straight
Her beautified body to a goodly temple
That's built on vaults where carcasses lie rotting;
And so, by little and little, I shrink back again,
And quench desire with a cool meditation.

So says Leantio in Middleton's *Women Beware Women*. For the puritan Thomas Dekker the prostitute was the representative figure of the underworld, her commerce perfunctory and with no satisfactory product at the end of it other than an ephemeral instant of gratification. In his bourgeois imagination the 'creature of sale' was a conduit for filth and rot in the greater body of the nation. The pox, a lengthy process of bodily decay, was as catching as the plague, even though the former generally excluded the very young and the very old. Even the most cautious sexually active people outside a marriage of two virgins risked venereal infections including genital herpes, because the only defence was washing the genitals in white wine or vinegar. There was also the specious notion that post-coital 'hard pissing' might remedy the threat of infection, an idea presumably based on the sterility of urine. In superior brothels it was usual to have two chamberpots to each room of assignation, and the 'hard' surely refers to the extreme pressure on the bladder maintained while using the chamberpot. Dekker did not just point to brothels as abundant in towns and cities, multiplying the points of infection. He and others pointed to the dramatic increase in the number of places selling strong drinks, like ale (waning in popularity) and beer (increasing in popularity). A rackety alehouse with a few benches, mugs, candles and beer would lure in the impoverished people of a location as well as itinerants, people too far from or too impoverished to frequent inns and taverns. Dekker even deployed the image, unsavoury as it is, of alehouses erupting over the suburbs like the rash of a secondary syphilitic eruption. In one of his pamphlets he envisages the suburbs spewing out monsters that will destroy the city and this idea was picked up and reworked in Beaumont's comic parody *The Knight of the Burning Pestle*, written for the Blackfriars boy company in 1607. Syphilis is envisioned 'in the mythological shape of a giant monster devouring townspeople and storing them in its cave'. Barbaroso, as the monster is called, is actually a barber-surgeon and in his premises (cave) customers with the dreaded disease are variously treated. This topic played by boys makes laughter possible, though doubtless some in the audience twisted uncomfortably.

The phrase 'burning in hell' often had a double meaning in Renaissance England. The verse writer Samuel Rowlands has a gentleman who has been soldiering abroad for years return 'filthy full of French' after single combat with a wench. She sets his flask and touch-box on fire and the burning cannot be put out. The reader is asked to judge the man's valour in fighting with 'a spit-fire Serpent'. Distinguishing between the burning of gonorrhoea and other venereal infections taxed the clinical powers of barber-surgeons, often figuring the former as a precursor of the latter. So in 1594 John Hester, a Paracelsian nudged to the margins of clinical practice, could write that a man infected by gonorrhoea 'caused of the superfluous use of women, that are infected therewith' would suffer great pain when urinating and throughout an erection. According to his diagnosis this was the 'beginning of the French pox', and the error was repeated by the securely mainstream Scottish surgeon Peter Lowe two years later.[6] Urethral stricture and severe prostatitis caused excruciating pain and were not uncommon ways of killing an infected man. The great Danish astronomer Tycho Brahe (who had a silver nose to replace the one which had rotted) died of a strangury (urethral stricture causing acute retention). So too did Francis Tresham (d. 1605), one of the Gunpowder plotters. Moreover, the phrase 'The strangury hath undone me' appears as an example in the Latin–English dictionary compiled by William Horman, a book often used in grammar schools of the time. Relief of the obstruction was by a catheter and medical practitioners lived tolerably well from this item alone. One smart revision of the practice, substituting a fine, flexible plant stalk of mallow or parsley for the metal syringe used by John Arderne, was made by John Read in Armada year.

EPILOGUE

Ralph Waldo Emerson once noted that there is properly no history, only biography. With this slant in mind, historians may be inclined to think that the past will reveal everything if the ghost armies can be hauled from oblivion and interrogated. Alas, for every fact there is a counter-fact, and for all the myriad details exposed to scrutiny, there are tenebrous places littered with unrevealing shards of information, aspects of unremembered lives and the puzzle of curious passions. For example, women, it is certain, would have loved other women in Elizabethan England, and yet historians have so far failed to find more than one or two pointers towards lesbian relationships. For the moment, it is the invisible passion, but perhaps the evidence for it does indeed exist, and has so far been overlooked and misinterpreted. Or perhaps, like Queen Victoria, Elizabethans lacked the sexual imagination to construct such a possible relationship – which seems odd given the capacity of playwrights in the late 1590s and early years of the new century to recognize deviant sexuality in many other forms. The impediment to our knowledge of Elizabethan lesbianism may just be our current inability 'to crack the code organizing the conceptual categories of an earlier culture'. After all, we know at some unspoken level that human sexuality is one of the quirkiest things we encounter in our lives. Unlike the Dugum Dani people of New Guinea (cited by Greer), who have sex once a year and then give it little or no heed until twelve months later, the Elizabethans, beset by preachy moralists, repeated legislation, and the hideous threat of uncontrollable diseases, had little inclination to shackle their libidos strictly to the calendar. Sexual gratification was all too short-lived.

Despite the individual men and women who have appeared in this book, from courtiers and maids of honour to citizens and their wives, to drabs and pimps, we will never know the deeper aspects of our ancestors' sexual lives, for it must be acknowledged that the evidence is patchy (though necessarily fascinating), and it is thanks to poets and playwrights that some of the most vexing gaps can surely be filled – all the while bearing in mind the male bias of their texts and the slant due to dominating male fancies and private capriciousness. It was once argued that in a traditional society sexual relations were tainted with brutish appetites and lack of tenderness; it is a view that germinates in the evidence of widespread urban and suburban whoring. Then came a modifier, the late John Boswell, who thought (very probably erroneously) that he could properly advance the notion of a golden age of sexual toleration in the early Middle Ages – a time before councillors and law courts became more prescriptive and repressive.

In some respects the Elizabethans were rather modern; sex then could be as it is today, on a scale from ignorantly meagre to passionately spontaneous. There were those for whom it was sanctified by marriage, and hence desirable; those for whom sex meant procreation and drudgery, numerous children born only to die; and those for whom sex was simply part of the tense engagement of men and women, hence riddled with chicanery, gender misapprehensions and sometimes (as now) distrust akin to hatred. The seeming prominence of women in the literature of the Elizabethans is less of a surprise given the monarch's gender, yet it 'may be a metaphor for, or a symptom of, other cultural anxieties'. The seeping spread of a vast print culture steeped in humanistic thought brought about a crisis in male friendship 'as bonds of allegiance were increasingly based on the uncertain ground of verbal persuasion and promise'. Likely unnoticed at the time, this coincided with the endless acrimonious mess created by the procreative imperatives of Henry VIII. Just as the queens found their place at his court to be largely based on their womb, the men about a Henrician queen could soon be in trouble in her wake. Verbally based allegiance was undermined and they soon found that a swamp could tug down to extinction all manner of victims; the good, the bad, the dull and daring alike. And what troubled men most, what took them hither and thither in confusion was usually female chastity, that unseen trophy and emblem. Above all there was the question – was what this child of Eve said to be accepted as truth, or scorned as lies?

In their world bristling with binary oppositions the Elizabethans found creative tension; enough to reduce the decay of the spirit called boredom. Under the last of the strikingly dwindled Tudors, England abandoned breezy insularity to embark on global exploration and then colonization. This larger effort would then impinge at home. The manor-house at Downton, which was gifted to Ralegh and repaired by him in time for a royal visit in 1586, benefited from his exploratory spirit, for he seems to have torn apart a small sailing ship in order to modernize the manor, and the salted timbers remain there today. Yet he hardly lived in the house at all and instead it was occupied by his older brother and mother. To win the approval and gracious patronage of Elizabeth, Ralegh had to woo the queen ostentatiously and cannily; as a poet he had to be prepared for many privations in order to secure her attention and esteem. Literature was not enough and so English seamen and explorers sailed in wretched conditions to various isolated areas of the globe to challenge the unknown and to annex whatever seemed appropriate and promising. As men they hoped for a productive fecundity in their queen, and gradually time required them to shift this to their tribute discoveries. These were then celebrated in chorography – a descriptive survey of a region or land, usually accompanied by maps. There was rhapsodizing over new territory, and when his contemporaries satirized Ralegh's expedition to South America in the 1590s and his abortive attempt to locate the fabled city of El Dorado, Ralegh replied to them with a brilliantly detailed rebuttal: *The Discoverie of the large, rich and bewtiful Empyre of Guiana*.

Much to the south of that, the Indians of the Xingu region of Brazil believed a particular species of tree harboured an enticing female spirit, and by touching this tree the men of the tribe became aroused. Ralegh and his men had not penetrated that far, but note how vocabulary almost betrays him when he observed that 'Guiana is a country that yet hath her maidenhead'. As leader of an expedition that was away from England for months, Ralegh had to deal with the sexual urges of his men while they were among the cordial, relaxed Orinoco Indians, who feared the enslaving Spanish. The native women were truly a revelation; fragrant, gracefully proportioned, tanned and above all, virtually naked. While the female body in England sanctioned parts for scrutiny, there it was unselfconsciously shown as whole and comely. The shock of the nude and the sweetness of the women as they served food and drink to the travellers made continence the most exasperating export to this continent. Anticipating a bacchanal – his soldiers and sailors had quickly adjusted their palates to the local alcoholic drink of palm toddy – Ralegh made the strict rule that everything consumed or received had to be paid for and that no female should be sexually molested. His injunction on the lyphthoric must have been couched in bristling terms for when in England again he declared that none of his men had behaved improperly. It was the triumph of the dark ladies.

To tease his readers further, Ralegh's narrative made a digression to deal with the legendary Amazons – the nation of women living as he claimed on the borders of Guiana. Despite his apparent realism Ralegh allowed himself the luxury of sliding into his text certain exotic elements that undermined even in his day the larger credibility of his record. He claimed that in the remote interior lived headless giants, a story that had done the rounds in Europe, along with that of the battle-hardened female tribe, since antiquity. Quite brazenly he eroticized the mythic story, and for this licentious accent he had it that every April in a surge of vernal energy (by the European calendar), Amazons held a loose festival to which they invited men from the neighbouring tribes. The queens in this gynaecocracy selected the most apparently virile men for sexual partners, while the lesser specimens became the prizes assigned to the lesser women. The following month was an erotic carnival (vying with that of Rio de Janeiro today) and then the men departed. An Amazon delivered of a son made nothing of him and handed him over to his father, while all daughters were esteemed and their fathers rewarded. No doubt there is a compliment buried here to Elizabeth, although there was no guarantee she would take it as such. Incidentally, men who did not time their arrival in Amazon territory correctly were subjected to female retribution – a period of unremitting sexual labour followed by execution.

This was, of course, the fate of that Lord of Misrule the Earl of Essex, subject to the retribution of an Amazonian queen. Even in old age Elizabeth was likely to appear in her court in a diaphanous gown, and an unimpressed French ambassador described how she kept the front of her dress gaping, exposing a lot of wrinkled flesh. In this

This fine portrait of Robert Devereux, 2nd Earl of Essex, shows him in Garter robes and with the baton of Earl Marshal. He held that office after the failure in 1597 of the Islands Voyage, which should have mopped up Spanish bullion flooding from South America.

rather grotesque manner she continued the charade of being nurturing mother to the nation, and the image of her as a wet nurse was still used. If this seems bizarre to us, it did also strike some at the time as fanciful and hence liable in the 1590s to satire. A Catholic poet might be especially lured by this slant and John Donne's *Elegie: Going to Bed* was not written of the girl who became his wife, or of an unknown sexual partner, but of Elizabeth herself.[1] Still, if challenged for his insolence Donne had a defence that there is no direct allusion to Elizabeth, although the breastplate reference is a strong hint, and in any case the whole is couched in such fulsome language that it could do little harm. It would be privately read by a clique of like-minded young men, and the subversive pinching of the cult of Elizabeth in this piece on the 'dynamics of amatory relations' is not so strong that Donne was himself at risk. What the poem does is lightly call into question the temporary placing of a woman ruler beyond male domination, since patriarchy had God's hand in it. Gender in Tudor England was still a cosmological principle, shaping sex, rather than the other way around.

The dream of Simon Forman in midwinter 1597 which has become so famous, underlines this view. It is a dream of old Elizabeth herself, combining sober incident with quaint reflection. Instead of her court gown stiff with embroidery and armoured with jewels, she wears a 'coarse white petticoat' and is 'all unready' (for man and for God?), having it seems just quit her bed. The noctivagant little Forman and the unpredictable old shrew walk together in the dream, talking and arguing amicably

This was Elizabeth's favoured pattern of oak leaves and acorns which appeared as embroidery on her smock.

enough. Then at a main thoroughfare they come upon a throng of people with two men in an argument. One is tall, red-bearded, identified as a weaver, whose wits have scattered, and it is to Essex (obviously it is he who is meant) that Elizabeth speaks before at length he kisses her. Attempting then to live up to his surname, Forman intervenes to ease her away, offering advice on the weaver's state of mind. Leading her boldly by the arm along a muddy lane (the state of England) he is very aware of her clean, white, long smock (a word then freighted with sexual meanings in compound derivatives like 'smock-sworn' – addicted to sex). Forman hoists the hem of the smock suggestively at the back but can do nothing about the front, where for it to raise naturally Elizabeth's belly would have to swell. His comment is bawdy: 'I mean to wait upon you and not under you.' So passive service shifts into the sexual mode, advancing the male fantasy that 'methought she began to love me'. When out of sight of all who might spy on them in an age obsessed with domestic and political espionage, they prepare to kiss – then the dreamer awakes. Did Elizabeth ever dream anything like this? Alone in her bed – as ever – in a sleep unsupervised by outside agencies such as her privy councillors and bishops, the ungoverned activity of the mind in dreaming might beget anything.

APPENDIX I

There were many rumours and whispers generated during the reign of Elizabeth, with sordid suggestions about her supposed whimsical and even wicked sexual appetites. Given her affection – early on a considerable passion – for Lord Robert Dudley (from 1564 Earl of Leicester), it is not surprising that he was put up as the putative father of her child (or children). One young man claiming this illustrious mingling of blood in his veins was the interestingly named Arthur Dudley – Arthur being a Tudor name and linked to the legends of King Arthur – who appeared in the higher reaches of Spanish society in 1587. Given his notable story of being the child of Elizabeth and Leicester, Philip II of Spain had him interviewed by his English Secretary, Sir Francis Englefield, who recorded not only a biography, but as it seems a teasing effort by someone who had coached the young man in the details.[1]

To be even near believable to sceptics the story had to be yoked to reality. It was, as Dudley claimed, true that he had been raised as a child by one Robert Southern, formerly a servant of the mistress of the maids, Katherine Astley. Already married, Southern was summoned one day in 1562 to Hampton Court where he met another lady close to the queen's person. She asked Southern to find a wet nurse for a newborn child of one who had been careless of her honour. He evidently agreed, and the next day, in a corridor leading to the queen's private chamber the baby Arthur was given to Southern, who had the infant nursed by the wife of a miller just along the river in Molesey (Surrey). After that, Southern took the child to an unnamed village and there Arthur remained until weaned, at which point he joined Southern's own children in the family home. When Arthur was aged about eight years (c. 1570), John Astley, Master of the Jewel House, made Southern keeper of a royal house a short distance from London. The boy lived in the house while being tutored in a manner different from that of the Southern children; Arthur's was a genteel curriculum of Latin, French, Italian, music, dancing and arms. The sense of personal difference was palpable in Arthur's behaviour at fifteen when he argued with his foster-father, stole money from him and fled to Milford Haven in search of a passage. However, the little adventure was soon to end, for it was known to well-placed people, and George Devereux, brother of the late Earl of Essex (d. 1576), came after him with a Privy Council letter requiring his presence in London.

This source alerted Arthur to the fascinating possibility that Southern was not his father. Escorted to London the youth was reproved by the Privy Council, and by John Astley, who said now that he had paid for Arthur's education. At length Astley was prevailed upon to allow Arthur to travel to France with a serving man drawn from Leicester's household. His time there was inconsequential and he returned to England for further funds; then it was back to France before the ailing Robert Southern summoned him. After selling the office of royal housekeeper, Southern's income came from farming in the Vale of Evesham (Worcs.), and an inn. Now suffering from a paralysis (perhaps the after-effect of a stroke), Southern at length elected to reveal to Arthur Dudley his true parentage (as he thought). Being so infirm this could only be told – he could not write the story down – although presumably he might have employed a scrivener and a lawyer. Dudley did not wait; he quit Evesham before Southern's death and put the story to Ashley. It seems that his demeanour and that of Sir Drew Drury was so stern that Dudley decided on exile to France. There followed further adventures and then the last journey into Spain.

Documents at the Spanish archives at Simancas note Dudley's arrival in Madrid late in 1586 at a time of tension between Spain and England. English nationals were suspected (often correctly) of being intelligencers (that is spies) for Sir Francis Walsingham, the most diligent of English spymasters. Arthur Dudley was seen frequently at the residence of the French ambassador, and with the news of the execution of Mary, Queen of Scots, in February 1587 he disappeared. Later he was picked up at a port rendezvous and consequent to his replies to the governor of Guizpuzcoa's questions he was sent to Madrid to write his memoir. This was translated by Englefield. For a time Arthur Dudley received six crowns a day, although Philip did not consider releasing him. Arthur Dudley's front-line career ends in Spanish custody. Fade into history.

APPENDIX II

The schoolmaster in Evesham, John Smyth, was responsible for writing the inventory and will of Robert Southern, on which probate was granted early in May 1585.[1] The inventory is particularly useful in giving considerable insight into the interior and furnishings of a small town inn. Apart from being a yeoman (small farmer) and owner of some other properties, Southern kept an inn. There were a number then in the town and his did not rival the George and the Goat. It may have been in his tenement in Cole Street that he brewed beer and sold it, with customers sitting in the hall at two long trestle tables, with a spence or cupboard for food. The walls were hung with painted cloths as cheap substitutes for tapestries, and there was a small side table.

In the 'parlour next the street' which became a bedroom, there was one bedstead, a featherbed, a covering, a bolster, pillow and red blanket: value £4. There was also a truckle-bed with bedding: value 30s. In addition to the beds there were eight cushions, two carpets used then to cover tables, and curtains: value £3 13s 4d. Southern in his last sickness may have lived in the room for the inventory notes 'his apparel': value £4, and a 10s Bible.

Next to the parlour was another 'chamber' with a substantial wooden bed, a pair of simpler bedsteads and a truckle-bed. All had bedding and the room had too a square table, three stools, a chest and a casket. The painted cloths for the walls were included in the valuation: £4 3s 4d.

The remaining ground-floor room was the kitchen and among the listed contents were two cauldrons, a brass pot and brewing ladle, twelve platters, eight pottingers (or porringers for broth), sixteen saucers and six 'counterfeit dishes', three kettles, two dabnets, a chafing dish, six brass candlesticks, three pewter pots and a mortar and pestle. In the fireplace were andirons, an iron grate, a fire shovel, tongs, links and hooks: value 10s.

Over the parlour was the single upstairs room with a special joined bedstead with bedding and cushions: value £6. Again the room was hung with painted cloths, and there was another bed with bedding, two tables and three forms (sic).

Brewing items:

10 ways (one way equals forty-eight bushels) of malt worth £35
2 ways of barley £9
4 strikes of wheat (a strike equals a bushel or four pecks) 8s

4 vats; a hand malt-mill; 16 tubs and kimnels (any kind of domestic tub); plaster; hay; a square table; two forms; two ladders; wood and furses; plus one sow and three flitches of bacon – £1 13s 4d.

Tavern and Buttery items:

Nine silver spoons; two silver cups; nine barrels; a sieve; a kneading trough; a hogshead.

Apery (or Apiary)

Five pairs of flaxen sheets; six pairs of hempen sheets; two dozen table napkins; eight table-cloths and thirty-two 'stolles' of bees. (Bee-keeping was very popular in sixteenth-century Evesham and Bengeworth.)

With some miscellaneous items included, the value of Southern's Evesham articles was about £120, although the exact amount is now illegible.

ABBREVIATIONS

BL	British Library
BM	*Burlington Magazine*
CA	*Cultural Anthropology*
C&C	*Change and Continuity*
CM	*Cornhill Magazine*
EA	*Études Anglaises*
ELH	*English Literary History*
ELR	*English Literary Renaissance*
EM	*Early Music*
ERC	*Explorations in Renaissance Culture*
FMJ	*Folk Music Journal*
HJ	*Historical Journal*
HLB/Q	*Huntington Library Bulletin/Quarterly*
HT	*History Today*
HWJ	*History Workshop Journal*
JEGP	*Journal of English and Germanic Philology*
JHS	*Journal of the History of Sexuality*
JMEMS	*Journal of Medieval and Early Modern Studies*
JPC	*Journal of Popular Culture*
MLQ	*Modern Language Quarterly*
MLR	*Modern Language Review*
MP	*Modern Philology*
N&Q	*Notes and Queries*
ns	new series
PMLA	*Publications of the Modern Language Association of America*
RES	*Review of English Studies*
RQ	*Renaissance Quarterly*
SAQ	*South Atlantic Quarterly*
SEL	*Studies in English Literature, 1500–1900*
ShQ	*Shakespeare Quarterly*
ShSt	*Shakespeare Studies*
ShS	*Shakespeare Survey*
SR	*Southwest Review*
SP	*Studies in Philology*

TLS	*Times Literary Supplement*
TP	*Textual Practice*
TRHS	*Transactions of the Royal Historical Society*
TRSL	*Transactions of the Royal Society of Literature*
TSLL	*Texas Studies in Literature and Language*
WSIF	*Women's Studies International Forum*
WVMJ	*West Virginia Medical Journal*

SELECT BIBLIOGRAPHY

MANUSCRIPTS

BL Additional Ms. 25348

BL Additional Ms. 34063

BL Additional Ms. 38061, f. 314

BL Additional Ms. 5751, f. 38

BL Harley Ms. 295, f. 190

BL Harley Ms. 6286, ff. 1–119

   (Hertford – Grey Marriage Trial and Examination)

BL Lansdowne Ms. 27, n. 38, f. 78

BL Sloane Ms. 1683, f. 176

BOOKS

Agnew, J.C. *Worlds Apart: The Market and the Theatre in Anglo-American Thought, 1550–1750*, 1986

Amussen, S.D. *An Ordered Society: Gender and Class in Early Modern England*, 1988

Andreski, S. *Syphilis, Puritanism and Witch Hunt*, 1990

Anselment, R.A. *The Realms of Apollo: Literature and Healing in Seventeenth-century England*, 1996

Apperson, G.L. *Gleanings after Time*, 1907

Archer, I. *The Pursuit of Stability: Social Relations in Elizabethan London*, 1991

Axton, M. *The Queen's Two Bodies: Drama and the Elizabethan Succession*, RHS, 1977

Barish, J. *The Anti-theatrical Prejudice*, 1981

Barkan, L. *Transuming Passion: Ganymede and the Erotics of Humanism*, 1981

Barnard, E., *Evesham and a Reputed Son of Queen Elizabeth*, 1926

Bate, J. *Shakespeare and Ovid*, 1993

Ben-Amos, I.K. *Adolescence and Youth in Early Modern England*, 1994

Benson, P.J. *The Invention of the Renaissance Woman: The Challenge of Female Independence in the Literature and Thought of Italy and England*, 1992

Bentley, G.W. *Shakespeare and the New Disease: The Dramatic Function of Syphilis in Troilus and Cressida, Measure for Measure, and Timon of Athens*, 1989

Berg, van den, K.T. *Playhouse and Cosmos: Shakespearean Theatre as Metaphor*, 1985

Berlin, N. *The Base String*, 1968

Bradbrook, M.C. *John Webster, Citizen and Dramatist*, 1980

——. *Shakespeare and Elizabethan Poetry*, 1951

Bradford, C.A. *Blanche Parry*, 1935

Bray, A. *Homosexuality in Renaissance England*, 1982

Brézol, G. *Henri III et Ses Mignons*, 1912

Brinkworth, E.R.C. *Shakespeare and the Bawdy Court of Stratford*, 1972

Bristol, M. *Carnival and Theatre: Plebeian Culture and the Structure of Authority in Renaissance England*, 1985

Bruster, D. *Drama and the Market in the Age of Shakespeare*, 1992

Burford, E.J. *The Orrible Synne*, 1972

——. *London, the Synfull Citie*, 1990

Burt, R., and Archer, J.M. (eds). *Enclosure Acts, Sexuality, Property and Culture in Early Modern England*, 1994

Bush, D. *Mythology and the Renaissance Tradition in English Poetry*, 1963

Callaghan, D. *Women and Gender in Renaissance Tragedy*, 1989

Camden, C. *The Elizabethan Woman*, 1952

Caputi, A. *John Marston, Satirist*, 1961

Carroll, W.C. *The Great Feast of Language*, 1976

Clark, P. *The English Alehouse*, 1983

Clark, S. *Amorous Rites: Elizabethan Erotic Verse*, 1994

Coleman, E.A. *The Dramatic Use of Bawdy in Shakespeare*, 1974

Cook, A.J. *The Privileged Playgoers of Shakespeare's London, 1576–1642*, 1981

Cooper, S.M. *The Sonnets of* Astrophel and Stella: *A Stylistic Study*, 1968

Darmon, P. *Trial by Impotence: Virility and Marriage in Pre-Revolutionary France*, 1985

Davies, W.R. *Shakespeare's Boy Actors*, 1939

Debus, A.G. *The English Paracelsians*, 1965

Dibden, Sir L., and Healey, Sir C. *English Church Law and Divorce*, 1912

Donoghue, E.G. *Bridewell*, 1923

Durant, D. *Arabella Stuart*, 1978

Dutton, K. *The Perfectible Body: The Western Ideal of Physical Development*, 1995

Edmond, M. *Hilliard and Oliver: The Lives and Works of Two Great Miniaturists*, 1983

Ellis, H.A. *Shakespeare's Lusty Punning*, 1973

Emmison, F.G. *Elizabethan Life: Morals and the Church Courts*, 1973

Fabricius, J. *Syphilis in Shakespeare's England*, 1994

Falls, C. *Mountjoy, Elizabethan General*, 1955

Ferguson, M.W., Quilligan, M., and Vickers, N.J. (eds). *Rewriting the Renaissance: The Discourses of Sexual Difference in Early Modern Europe*, 1986

Finkelpearl, P. *John Marston of the Middle Temple*, 1969

Fletcher, A. *Gender, Sex and Subordination in England, 1500–1800*, 1995

Flynn, D. *John Donne and the Ancient Catholic Nobility*, 1995

Ford, B. (ed.). *The New Pelican Guide to English Literature, Vol. 2: The Age of Shakespeare*, 1982

Forker, C. *Fancy's Image*, 1990

Foucault, M. *The History of Sexuality, Vol. I: An Introduction*, 1978

Frantz, D.O. *Festum Voluptatis: A Study of Renaissance Erotica*, 1989

French, P. *John Dee: The World of an Elizabethan Magus*, 1972

Giddens, A. *The Transformation of Intimacy, Sexuality, Love and Eroticism in Modern Societies*, 1992

Goldberg, J. *Sodometries*, 1992

—— (ed.). *Queering the Renaissance*, 1994

Green, M. *Wriothesley's Roses*, 1993

Greenblatt, S. *Shakespearean Negotiations: The Circulation of Social Energy in Renaissance England*, 1988

Gurr, A. *Playgoing in Shakespeare's London*, 1987

Hackett, H. *Virgin Mother, Maiden Queen: Elizabeth I and the Cult of the Virgin Mary*, 1995

Hanna, J.L. *Dance, Sex and Gender: Signs of Identity, Dominance, Defiance and Desire*, 1988

Haselkorn, A.M. *Prostitution in Elizabethan and Jacobean Comedy*, 1993

Hay, M.V. *The Life of Robert Sidney, Earl of Leicester*, 1984

Haynes, A. *The White Bear: Robert Dudley, Elizabethan Earl of Leicester*, 1987

——. *Robert Cecil, 1st Earl of Salisbury: Servant of Two Sovereigns*, 1989

——. *Invisible Power: The Elizabethan Secret Services, 1570–1603*, 1992

——. *The Gunpowder Plot: Faith in Rebellion*, 1994

Henke, J.T. *Renaissance Dramatic Bawdy*, 1974

Honigmann, E.A. *John Weever: A Biography of a Literary Associate of Jonson and Shakespeare*, 1987

Hosking, G.L. *The Life and Times of Edward Alleyn*, 1952

Hotson, L. *The First Night of* Twelfth Night, 1954

Ingram, M. *Church Courts, Sex and Marriage in England, 1570–1640*, 1987

Jardine, L. *Still Harping On Daughters: Women and Drama in the Age of Shakespeare*, 1983

John, L.C. *The Elizabethan Sonnet Sequence*, 1938

Johnson, D.L. *Southwark and the City*, 1969

Judges, A.V. *The Elizabethan Underworld*, 1930

Kahn, C. *Man's Estate: Masculine Identity in Shakespeare*, 1981

Keach, W. *Elizabethan Erotic Narratives: Irony and Pathos in the Ovidian Poetry of Shakespeare, Marlowe and their Contemporaries*, 1977

Kernan, A. *The Cankered Muse: Satire of the English Renaissance*, 1959

—— (ed.). *Two Renaissance Mythmakers: Christopher Marlowe and Ben Jonson, Selected Papers from the English Institute*, 1975–6

Kimbrough, R. *Shakespeare and the Art of Human Kindness: The Essay toward Androgyny*, 1990

Koeld, S., and Noakes, S. (eds). *The Comparative Perspective in Literature: Approaches to Theory and Practice*, nd

Krueger, R. (ed.). *The Poems of Sir John Davies*, 1975

Lamb, M.E. *Gender and Authorship in the Sidney Circle*, 1990

Laquer, T. *Making Sex: Body and Gender from the Greeks to Freud*, 1990

Laurence, A. *Women in England, 1500–1760*, 1994

Lawner, L. *I Modi – The Sixteen Pleasures: An Erotic Album of the Sixteenth Century*, 1988

Lee, A.G. *The Son of Leicester*, 1964

Lever, T. *The Herberts of Wilton*, 1967

Levin, C. *The Heart and Stomach of a King: Elizabeth I and the Politics of Sex and Power*, 1994

Levine, L. *Men in Women's Clothing: Anti-theatricality and Effeminization, 1579–1642*, 1994

Lindley, D. *The Trials of Frances Howard: Fact and Fiction at the Court of King James*, 1993

Luna, de, B. *Jonson's Romish Plot: A Study of* Catiline *and its Historical Context*, 1967

Macfarlane, A. *Marriage and Love in England: Modes of Reproduction, 1300–1840*, 1986

Manley, L. (ed.). *London in the Age of Shakespeare*, 1986

Maurier, du, D. *Golden Lads: Anthony Bacon, Francis and their Friends*, 1975

Maus, K.E. *Inwardness and Theater in the English Renaissance*, 1995

McClure, N.E. (ed.). *Letters and Epigrams of Sir John Harington*, 1930

McLuskie, K. *Renaissance Dramatists*, 1989

Miyake, S. *Kabuki Drama*, 1963

Morris, H.C. *Richard Barnfield*, 1963

Mullaney, S. *The Place of the Stage: License, Play and Power in Renaissance England*, 1988

Nicholl, C. *The Reckoning: The Murder of Christopher Marlowe*, 1992

Novy, M. *Love's Argument: Gender Relations in Shakespeare*, 1984

Orgel, S. *Impersonations: The Performance of Gender in Shakespeare's England*, 1996

Outhwaite, R. *Clandestine Marriages in England*, 1995

Partridge, E. *Shakespeare's Bawdy*, 1968

Pequigney, J. *Such is My Love: A Study of Shakespeare's Sonnets*, 1985

Peter, J. *Complaint and Satire in Early English Literature*, 1956

Porter, R., and Hall, L. *The Facts of Life: The Creation of Sexual Knowledge in Britain*, 1995

Quaife, G.R. *Wanton Wenches and Wayward Wives*, 1979

Rawson, M.R. *Bess of Hardwick and her Circle*, 1910

Reay, B. (ed.). *Popular Culture in Seventeenth-Century England*, 1985

Ricks, C. (ed.). *English Poetry and Prose, 1540–1674, Sphere History of Literature in the English Language, Vol. 2*, 1970

Rose, M.B. *The Expense of Spirit, Love and Sexuality in English Renaissance Drama*, 1988

Rowse, A.L. *Shakespeare the Man*, 1973

———. *The Case Books of Simon Forman: Sex and Society in Shakespeare's Age*, 1974

———. *Discoveries and Reviews: From Renaissance to Restoration*, 1975

Salgādo, G. *The Elizabethan Underworld*, 1977 (rev. edn 1994)

Sedgwick, E.K. *Between Men: English Literature and Male Homosocial Desire*, 1985

Sharpe, J. *Defamation and Sexual Slander in Early Modern England: The Church Courts at York*, Borthwick Papers 58, 1981

Shell, M. *Elizabeth's Glass*, 1993

Shepherd, A. *Gender and Authority in Sixteenth-Century England*, 1994

Shepherd, S. *Marlowe and the Politics of Elizabethan Theatre*, 1986

Smith, B. *Homosexual Desire in Shakespeare's England*, 1994

Stallybrass, P., and White. A. *The Politics and Poetics of Transgression*, 1986

Stone, L. *The Crisis of the Aristocracy*, 1965

———. *Family and Fortunes: Studies in Aristocratic Finance in the Sixteenth and Seventeenth Centuries*, 1973

Traub, V. *Desire and Anxiety: Circulations of Sexuality in Shakespearean Drama*, 1992

Turner, B.S. *The Body and Society*, 1984

Williams, N. *All the Queen's Men: Elizabeth I and her Courtiers*, 1974

Williams, P. *The Tudor Regime*, 1979

Wilson, V. *Society Women in Shakespeare's Time*, 1924

Woodbridge, L. *Women and the English Renaissance: Literature and the Nature of Womankind, 1540–1620*, 1984

Zimmerman, S. (ed.). *Erotic Politics: Desire on the Renaissance Stage*, 1992

ARTICLES

Angell, P. 'Light on the Dark Lady: A Study of Some Elizabethan Libels', *PMLA*, LII, XLIII, 1937

Austern, L. ' "Sing Againe Syren": Female Musicians and Sexual Enchantment in Elizabethan Life and Literature', *RQ*, 42, 1989

Banner, L. 'The Fashionable Sex', *HT*, 41, 1992

Belsey, C. 'Disrupting Sexual Differences: Meaning and Gender in the Comedies' in J. Drakakis (ed.), *Alternative Shakespeare*, 1985

Boehrer, B.T. 'Early Modern Syphilis', *JHS*, 1, 2, 1990

Boose, L. 'The 1599 Bishops' Ban, Elizabethan Pornography, and the Sexualisation of the Jacobean Stage' in R. Burt and J.M. Archer (eds), *Enclosure Acts, Sexuality, Property and Culture in Early Modern England*, 1994

Bradbrook, M.C. 'Hero and Leander', *Scrutiny*, II, 1933

Bray, A. 'Homosexuality and the Signs of Male Friendship in Elizabethan England', *HWJ*, 29, 1990

Burnett, M.T. 'The "Trusty Servant"; A Sixteenth-century English Emblem', *Emblematica*, 6, 2, 1992

Callaghan, D. 'Female Impersonation on the Stage', *JMEMS*, 26, 2, 1996

Clark, S. '*Hic Mulier, Haec Vir*, and the Controversy over Masculine Women', SP, LXXXII, 1985

Colthorpe, M. 'The Marriage Dates of Lady Catherine Grey and Lady Mary Grey', *N&Q*, ns 33, September 1986

Cook, A.J. '"Bargaines of Incontinencie", Bawdy Behaviour in the Playhouse', *ShSt*, 10, 1977

Crossman, R. 'Making Love Out of Nothing at All; The Issue of Story in Shakespeare's Procreation Sonnets', *ShQ*, 41, 1990

Cross, G. 'Marston's *Metamorphosis of Pigmalion's Image*', *EA*, t. XIII, 3, 1960

DiGangi, M. 'Asses and Wits: The Homoerotics of Mastery in Satiric Comedy', *ELR*, 25, 1995

Duncan-Jones, K. 'Was the 1609 *Sonnets* Really Unauthorized?', *RES*, XXXIV, 1983

——. 'Much Ado with Red and White: The Earliest Readers of Shakespeare's *Venus and Adonis*', *RES*, XLIV, 1993

——. 'Nashe in Newgate', *TLS*, 22 March 1996

Eccles, M. 'Mary Frith, The Roaring Girl', *N&Q*, ns 32, March 1985

Falls, C. 'Penelope Rich and the Poets: Essays by Divers Hands', *TRSL*, XXVIII, 3rd ser., 1956

Ferguson, M.W. 'A Room Not Their Own: Renaissance Women as Readers and Writers' in S. Koeld and S. Noakes (eds), *The Comparative Perspective in Literature: Approaches to Theory and Practice*, nd

Fletcher, A. 'Men's Dilemma: The Future of Patriarchy in England', *TRHS*, IV, 1994

Foster, D.W. 'Mister W.H. R.I.P.', *PMLA*, 102, 1987

——. '"Against the Perjured Falsehood of your Tongues"; Frances Howard on the Course of Love', *ELR*, 24, 1, 1994

Frantz, D.O. '"Leud Priapians" and Renaissance Pornography', *SEL*, 12, 1972

Gammon, V. 'Song, Sex and Society in England, 1600–1850', *FMJ*, 4, 3, 1982

Goldberg, J. 'Sodomy and Society: The Case of Christopher Marlowe', *SR*, 69, 1984

Gove, M. 'New Community is Merely Old Coercion', *The Times*, 18 May 1996

Griffiths, P. 'The Structure of Prostitution in Elizabethan London', *C&C*, 8, 1, 1993

Haller, W. and M. 'The Puritan Art of Love', *HLQ*, 5, 1941–2

Holmes, M. 'Shakespeare's London', *HT*, 14, 1964

Howard, J.E. 'Cross-dressing, The Theatre, and Gender Struggle in Early Modern England', *ShQ*, 39, 4, 1988

——. 'Sex and Social Conflict: The Erotics of the Roaring Girl' in S. Zimmerman (ed.), *Erotic Politics: Desire on the Renaissance Stage*, 1992

Hudson, H.H. 'Penelope Devereux as Sidney's Stella', *HLB*, 7, 1935

Huebert, R. 'Tobacco & Boys & Marlowe', *SR*, XCII, 2, 1984

Hulse, C. 'Stella's Wit: Penelope Rich as Reader of Sidney's Sonnets' in M.W. Ferguson *et al.* (eds), *Rewriting the Renaissance*, 1986

Ingram, M. 'The Reform of Popular Culture? Sex and Marriage in Early Modern England' in B. Reay (ed.), *Popular Culture in Seventeenth-century England*, 1985

Jardine, L. 'Twins and Travesties: Gender, Dependency and Sexual Availability in *Twelfth Night*' in S. Zimmerman (ed.), *Erotic Politics: Desire on the Renaissance Stage*, 1992

Jones, D. 'Sidney's Eroticism', *JEGP*, 73, 1974

Kirsch, A. 'The Polarization of Erotic Love in *Othello*', *MLR*, 73, 1978

Laquer, T. 'Orgasm, Generation and the Politics of Reproductive Biology', *Representations*, 14, 1986

Lee, J. 'Who is Cecilia, What was she? Cecilia Bulstrode and Jonson's Epideictics', *JEGP*, 85, 1, 1986

Leininger, L.J. 'Exploring the Myth of the Lustful Murderess', *Topic*, 36, 1982

Leinwand, T. 'Redeeming Beggary/Buggary in *Michaelmas Term*', *ELH*, 61, 1994

Margetts, M. 'Lady Penelope Rich: Hilliard's Lost Miniatures and a Surviving Portrait', *BM*, 130, 1988

McPherson, D. 'Aretino and the Harvey-Nashe Quarrel', *PMLA*, 84, 1969

Merrix, R.P. 'The Vale of Lillies and the Bower of Bliss: Soft-core Pornography in Elizabethan Poetry', *JPC*, 19, 4, 1986

Montrose, L.A. '"Shaping Fantasies", Figurations of Gender and Power in Elizabethan Culture', *Representations*, 44, 2, 1983

Neill, M. 'Unproper Beds: Race, Adultery, and the Hideous in *Othello*', *ShQ*, 40, 4, 1989

Newman, K. 'Portia's Ring; Unruly Women and Structures of Exchange in *The Merchant of Venice*', *ShQ*, 38, 1, 1987

Ongaro, G. 'New Documents on the Bassano Family', *EM*, 8, 1992

Orgel, S. 'Nobody's Perfect, or Why did the English Stage take Boys for Women? *SAQ*, 88, 1, 1989

Porter, J. 'Marlowe, Shakespeare and the Canonization of Heterosexuality', *SAQ*, 88, 1, 1989

Rackin, P. 'Androgyny, Mimesis, and the Marriage of the Boy Heroine on the English Renaissance Stage', *PMLA*, 102, 1989

Roche, T. 'Shakespeare and the Sonnet Sequence' in C. Ricks (ed.), *English Poetry and Prose, 1540–1674, Sphere History of Literature in the English Language, Vol. 2*, 1970

Rowe, K. 'Elizabethan Morality and the Folio Revisions of Sidney's *Arcadia*', *MP*, 37, 1939–40

Salingar, L.G. 'The Elizabethan Literary Renaissance' in B. Ford (ed.), *The New Penguin Guide to English Literature, Vol. 2: The Age of Shakespeare*, 1982

Seigel, C. 'Hands off the Hothouses: Shakespeare's Advice to the King', *JPC*, 20, 1, 1986

Sharpe, J.A. 'Plebeian Marriage in Stuart England: Some Evidence from Popular Literature', *TRHS*, 36, 1986

Shepherd, S. 'What's So Funny about Ladies' Tailors? A Survey of Some Male (Homo)sexual Types in the Renaissance', *TP*, 6, 1, 1992

Shugg, W. 'Prostitution in Shakespeare's London', *ShSt*, 10, 1977

Sinfield, A. 'Sexual Puns in *Astrophel and Stella*', *Essays in criticism*, 24, 1974

Sorenson, F. 'Sir Walter Ralegh's Marriage', *SP*, XXXIII, 1, 1936

Stallybrass, P. 'Patriarchal Territories: The Body Enclosed' in Ferguson, M.W. *et al.* (eds), *Rewriting the Renaissance*, 1986

Steen, S.J. 'Fashioning an Acceptable Self: Arabella Stuart', *ELR*, 18, 1988

Thompson, A. 'Death by Water: The Originality of *Salmacis and Hermaphroditus*', *MLQ*, 40, 2, 1979

Traut, V. 'The (In)significance of "Lesbian" Desire in Early Modern England' in S. Zimmerman (ed.), *Erotic Politics: Desire on the Renaissance Stage*, 1992

Turner, M. 'Pastoral and Hermaphrodite: A Study in the Naturalism of Marlowe's *Hero and Leander*', *TSLL*, 17, 1975

Turner, R.K. 'Dekker's "Back-door'd Italian"', *N&Q*, January 1960

Vaughan, V.M. 'Daughters of the Game: *Troilus and Cressida* and the Sexual Discourse of 16th-century England', *WSIF*, 13, 3, 1990

Vest, W.E. 'William Shakespeare, Syphilographer', *WVMJ*, 34, 1, 1938

Vicary, G.Q. 'Visual Art as Social Data: The Renaissance Codpiece', *CA*, 4, 1989

Wall, A. 'For Love, Money or Politics? A Clandestine Marriage and the Elizabethan Court of Arches', *HJ*, 38, 3, 1995

Walsh, W.P. 'Sexual Discovery and Renaissance Morality in Marlowe's *Hero and Leander*', *SEL*, 12, 1972

Watson, D.G. 'The Contrarieties of *Venus and Adonis*', *SP*, 75, 1978

Williams, G. 'An Elizabethan Disease', *Trivium*, VI, 1971

Woods, P.M. 'Greene's Conny-Catching Courtesans: The Moral Ambiguity of Prostitution', *ERC*, XVIII, 1992

Wright, U.K. 'Shakespeare and Nicholas Breton', *CM*, 6, 1939

Zitner, S.P. 'Gosson, Ovid and the Elizabethan Audience', *ShQ*, 9, 1958

UNPUBLISHED THESIS

Merton, C., 'The women who served Queen Mary and Queen Elizabeth; ladies, gentlewomen and maids of the privy chamber 1553–1603', Ph.D., Cambridge University, 1992

NOTES

PREFACE

1. BL Add. Ms. 5751, f. 38

CHAPTER ONE

1. M.B. Rose, *The Expense of Spirit, Love and Sexuality in English Renaissance Drama* (1988), pp. 15–17
2. S.D. Amussen, *An Ordered Society: Gender and Class in Early Modern England* (1988), p. 111
3. L. Stone, *The Crisis of the Aristocracy* (1965), pp. 661–2
4. Amussen, op. cit., p. 106
5. S. Orgel, *Impersonations: The Performance of Gender in Shakespeare's England* (1996), p. 17
6. A. Nixon, *The Dignitie of Man* (1612), pp. 112–13
7. A. Wall, 'For Love, Money or Politics? A Clandestine Marriage and the Elizabethan Court of Arches', *HJ*, 38, 3 (1995), p. 528
8. Ibid., p. 513
9. Amussen, op. cit., p. 111
10. D. Bruster, *Drama and the Market in the Age of Shakespeare* (1992), p. 41
11. Amussen, op. cit., p. 114
12. Sir L. Dibden and Sir C. Healey, *English Church Law and Divorce* (1912)

CHAPTER TWO

1. S. Doran, *Monarchy and Matrimony: The Courtships of Elizabeth I* (1996), p. 8
2. Ibid., p. 9
3. BL Add. Ms. 38061, f. 314
4. BL Lans. Ms. 27, n. 38, f. 78
5. P. French, *John Dee: The World of an Elizabethan Magus* (1972), p. 194
6. M. Shell, *Elizabeth's Glass* (1993), p. 13
7. Ibid., p. 14
8. H. Hackett, *Virgin Mother, Maiden Queen: Elizabeth I and the Cult of the Virgin Mary* (1995), p. 142

9. Shell, op. cit., pp. 19–20
10. Ibid., p. 22
11. A. Haynes, *The White Bear: Robert Dudley, Elizabethan Earl of Leicester* (1987)

CHAPTER THREE

1. C. Merton, 'The women who served Queen Mary and Queen Elizabeth: ladies, gentlewomen and maids of the privy chamber 1553–1603', unpublished Ph.D., Cambridge University, 1992
2. M. Colthorpe, 'The Marriage Dates of Lady Catherine Grey and Lady Mary Grey', *N&Q*, ns 33, September 1986, p. 319
3. A. Haynes, *Robert Cecil, 1st Earl of Salisbury: Servant of Two Sovereigns* (1989)
4. D.W. Foster, 'Against the Perjured Falsehood of your Tongues', *ELR*, 24, 1 (1994), pp. 84–5
5. W. Camden, *Annales* (1625), p. 28
6. M. Axton, 'The Queen's Two Bodies: Drama and the Elizabethan Succession', RHS, 1977, pp. 50–1

CHAPTER FOUR

1. C. Merton, op. cit., p. 10
2. Ibid., p. 139
3. N. Williams, *All the Queen's Men: Elizabeth I and her Courtiers* (1974) p. 104
4. L. Stone, *Family and Fortune: Studies in Aristocratic Finance in the Sixteenth and Seventeenth Centuries* (1973) pp. 178–9
5. A.G. Lee, *The Son of Leicester* (1964), pp. 53–5
6. A.L. Rowse, *The Case Books of Simon Forman: Sex and Society in Shakespeare's Age* (1974), pp. 201–2
7. L. Hotson, *The First Night of Twelfth Night* (1954) p. 107
8. A. Fletcher, *Gender, Sex and Subordination in England 1500–1800* (1995), pp. 66–7
9. Ibid., p. 68
10. Stone, *Family and Fortune*, p. 258
11. T. Lever, *The Herberts of Wilton* (1967), p. 61
12. A.L. Rowse, *Discoveries and Reviews: From Renaissance to Restoration* (1975), pp. 69–70

CHAPTER FIVE

1. M.E. Lamb, *Gender and Authorship in the Sidney Circle* (1990), p. 31
2. Ibid., pp. 52–8
3. M. Edmond, *Hilliard & Oliver: The Lives and Works of Two Great Miniaturists* (1983), p. 84

CHAPTER SIX

1. G. Ongaro, 'New Documents on the Bassano Family', *EM*, 8 (1992) p. 409

2. M.W. Ferguson, 'A Room Not Their Own: Renaissance Women as Readers and Writers' in S. Koeld and S. Noakes (eds), *The Comparative Perspective in Literature: Approaches to Theory and Practice*

3. L. Manley (ed.), *London in the Age of Shakespeare* (1986), pp. 273–4

4. P.M. Woods, 'Greene's Conny-Catching Courtesans: The Moral Ambiguity of Prostitution', *ERC*, XVIII (1992), p. 111

5. Ibid.

6. M. Gove, 'New Community is Merely Old Coercion, *The Times*, Saturday 18 May 1996, p. 20

7. P. Griffiths, 'The Structure of Prostitution in Elizabethan London', *C&C*, 8, (i) (1993), p. 44

8. Ibid., p. 45

9. Ibid., p. 48

10. I. Archer, *The Pursuit of Stability: Social Relations in Elizabethan London* (1991), p. 3

11. A. Haynes, *Invisible Power: The Elizabethan Secret Services, 1570–1603* (1992), p. 157

12. Archer, op. cit., p. 232

13. Ibid., p. 233

14. C. Seigel, 'Hands off the Hothouses: Shakespeare's Advice to the King', *JPC*, 20, 1 (1986), p. 84

15. Ibid., p. 85

CHAPTER SEVEN

1. Hackett, op. cit., p. 54

2. Rowse, *Simon Forman*, p. 45

3. B. Smith, *Homosexual Desire in Shakespeare's England: A Cultural Poetics* (1994), pp. 83–4

4. V. Traub, 'The (In)significance of "Lesbian" Desire in Early Modern England' in S. Zimmerman (ed.), *Erotic Politics: Desire on the Renaissance Stage*, p. 157

5. Quoted in J.A. Sharpe, 'Plebeian Marriage in Stuart England: Some Evidence from Popular Literature', *TRHS*, 36 (1986), p. 81

CHAPTER EIGHT

1. R. Merrix, 'The Vale of Lillies and the Bower of Bliss: Soft-core Pornography in Elizabethan Poetry', *JPC*, 19, 4 (1986), p. 5

2. C. Nicholl, *The Reckoning: The Murder of Christopher Marlowe* (1992), p. 53

3. K. Duncan-Jones, 'Much Ado with Red and White: The Earliest Readers of Shakespeare's *Venus and Adonis*', *RES*, ns, XLIV (1993), p. 495
4. S. Clark, *Amorous Rites: Elizabethan Erotic Verse* (1994), p. xxxvi
5. Duncan-Jones, op. cit., p. 490
6. K.R. Dutton, *The Perfectible Body: The Western Ideal of Physical Development* (1995), p. 59
7. D. Bush, *Mythology and the Renaissance Tradition in English Poetry* (1932; rev. edn. 1963), p. 184
8. A. Thompson, 'Death by Water: The Originality of *Salmacis and Hermaphroditus*', *MLQ*, 40, 2 (1979), p. 104

CHAPTER NINE

1. Lamb, op. cit., p. 3
2. L.G. Salingar, 'The Elizabethan Literary Renaissance' in B. Ford (ed.), *The New Pelican Guide to English Literature, Vol. 2: The Age of Shakespeare* (1982), p. 93
3. L. Lawner, *I Modi – The Sixteen Pleasures: An Erotic Album of the Sixteenth Century* (1988), pp. 30–1
4. Ibid., pp. 32–3
5. C. Hulse, 'Stella's Wit: Penelope Rich as Reader of Sidney's Sonnets' in M.W. Ferguson, M. Quilligan and N.J. Vickers (eds), *Rewriting the Renaissance: The Discourses of Sexual Difference in Early Modern Europe* (1986), p. 273
6. A. Sinfield, 'Sexual Puns in *Astrophel and Stella*', *Essays in Criticism*, 24 (1974), pp. 343–4
7. T. Roche, 'Shakespeare and the Sonnet Sequence' in C. Ricks (ed.), *English Poetry and Prose, 1540–1674, Sphere History of Literature in the English Language, Vol. 2* (1970), p. 104
8. R. Crossman, 'Making Love Out of Nothing at All: The Issue of Story in Shakespeare's Procreation Sonnets', *ShQ*, 41 (1990), p. 471
9. Ibid., p. 485
10. K. Duncan-Jones, 'Was the 1609 *Sonnets* Really Unauthorized?', *RES*, XXXIV, (1983), pp. 154–5
11. D.W. Foster, 'Mister W.H. R.I.P.', *PMLA*, 102, (1987)

CHAPTER TEN

1. Crossman, op. cit., p. 474
2. S. Shepherd, 'What's So Funny about Ladies' Tailors? A Survey of Some Male (Homo)sexual Types in the Renaissance', *TP*, 6 (1992), p. 19
3. Ibid., p. 25

4. M. DiGangi, 'Asses and Wits: The Homoerotics of Mastery in Satiric Comedy', *ELR*, 25 (1995), p. 183

5. G. Brézol, *Henri III et Ses Mignons* (1912)

6. D. du Maurier, *Golden Lads: Anthony Bacon, Francis and their Friends* (1975), p. 67

7. Shepherd, op. cit., p. 25

8. Smith, op. cit., p. 49

9. Orgel, op. cit., p. 5

10. S. Miyake, *Kabuki Drama* (1963), p. 16

CHAPTER ELEVEN

1. J.E. Howard, 'Cross-dressing, The Theatre and Gender Struggle in Early Modern England', *ShQ*, 39, 4 (1988), pp. 418–40

2. Ibid., p. 422

3. Research by Professor R.M. Benbow. Cited by Howard, 'Cross-dressing', p. 420

4. M. Eccles, 'Mary Frith, The Roaring Girl' *N&Q*, ns 32, March 1985, p. 66

5. J.E. Howard, 'Sex and Social Conflict: The Erotics of the Roaring Girl' in Zimmerman, op. cit., p. 175

6. S. Clark, '*Hic Mulier, Haec Vir*, and the Controversy over Masculine Women', *SP*, LXXXII, (1985)

7. Howard, 'Sex and Social Conflict', p. 187

CHAPTER TWELVE

1. K.E. Maus, *Inwardness and Theater in the English Renaissance* (1995), p. 119

2. P. Darmon, *Trial by Impotence: Virility and Marriage in Pre-Revolutionary France* (1985)

3. BL Ms. Sloane 1683, f. 176. First noted by Edmond, op. cit., p. 204

4. Edmond, op. cit., p. 176

5. Maus, op. cit., p. 133

6. D. Lindley, *The Trials of Frances Howard: Fact and Fiction at the Court of King James* (1993), p. 96

7. Ibid., pp. 145–6

8. *CSPS*, III, 475

9. Maus, op. cit., p. 129

10. A. Haynes, *The Gunpowder Plot: Faith in Rebellion* (1994), p. 86

11. B. de Luna, *Jonson's Romish Plot: A Study of 'Catiline' and its Historical Context* (1967), pp. 156–69

12. DiGangi, op.cit., pp. 184–5

13. Ibid.

CHAPTER THIRTEEN

1. L.E. Boose, 'The 1599 Bishops' Ban, Elizabethan Pornography, and the Sexualisation of the Jacobean Stage' in R. Burt and J.M. Archer (eds), *Enclosure Acts, Sexuality, Property and Culture in Early Modern England* (1994), p. 190
2. D.O. Frantz, *Festum Voluptatis: A Study of Renaissance Erotica* (1989), p. 143
3. Lawner, op. cit., p. 9
4. D. McPherson, 'Aretino and the Harvey-Nashe Quarrel', *PMLA*, 84, (1969) p. 1551
5. W. Keach, *Elizabethan Erotic Narratives: Irony and Pathos in the Ovidian Poetry of Shakespeare, Marlowe and their Contemporaries* (1977), p. 158
6. N.E. McClure (ed.), *Letters and Epigrams of Sir John Harington* (1930), p. 151
7. Ibid., p. 280
8. D. Flynn, *John Donne and the Ancient Catholic Nobility* (1995), p. 25
9. Boose, op. cit., p. 186
10. Lawner, op. cit., p. 55
11. R. Krueger (ed.), *The Poems of Sir John Davies* (1975), p. 143
12. R.K. Turner, 'Dekker's "Back-door'd Italian" ', *N&Q*, January 1960, p. 25
13. E.A. Honigmann, *John Weever: A Biography of a Literary Associate of Jonson and Shakespeare* (1987), p. 24

CHAPTER FOURTEEN

1. J. Fabricius, *Syphilis in Shakespeare's England* (1994), pp. 57–83
2. K. Duncan-Jones, 'Nashe in Newgate', *TLS*, 22 March 1996, p. 15
3. B.T. Boehrer, 'Early Modern Syphilis', *JHS*, 1, 2 (1990)
4. Fabricius, op. cit., p. 38
5. W. Shugg, 'Prostitution in Shakespeare's London', *ShSt*, 10 (1977), p. 302
6. Fabricius, op. cit., p. 56

EPILOGUE

1. A.C. Labriola, 'Painting and Poetry of the Cult of Elizabeth I: The Ditchley Portrait and Donne's *Elegie: Going to Bed*, SP, XCIII (1996), pp. 49–50.

APPENDIX I

1. BL Harl. Ms. 295, f. 190

APPENDIX II

1. Worcester Probate Registry, File AD. 1585, 11

INDEX